The Definitive Guide to PC-BSD

Dru Lavigne

Apress®

The Definitive Guide to PC-BSD

Copyright © 2010 by Dru Lavigne

All rights reserved. No part of this work may be reproduced or transmitted in any form or by any means, electronic or mechanical, including photocopying, recording, or by any information storage or retrieval system, without the prior written permission of the copyright owner and the publisher.

ISBN-13 (pbk): 978-1-4302-2641-3

ISBN-13 (electronic): 978-1-4302-2642-0

Printed and bound in the United States of America 9 8 7 6 5 4 3 2 1

Trademarked names may appear in this book. Rather than use a trademark symbol with every occurrence of a trademarked name, we use the names only in an editorial fashion and to the benefit of the trademark owner, with no intention of infringement of the trademark.

PC-BSD and the PC-BSD logo are registered trademarks of iXsystems Inc.™ and are used with permission.

The mark FreeBSD is a registered trademark of The FreeBSD Foundation and is used by Dru Lavigne with the permission of The FreeBSD Foundation.

NetBSD® is a registered trademark of The NetBSD Foundation, Inc. and is used with permission of the NetBSD Foundation.

Linux is a registered trademark of Linus Torvalds.

President and Publisher: Paul Manning
Lead Editor: Frank Pohlmann
Technical Reviewers: Sevan Janiyan, Soeren Straraap and Alexander Erenkov
Editorial Board: Clay Andres, Steve Anglin, Mark Beckner, Ewan Buckingham, Gary Cornell, Jonathan Gennick, Jonathan Hassell, Michelle Lowman, Matthew Moodie, Duncan Parkes, Jeffrey Pepper, Frank Pohlmann, Douglas Pundick, Ben Renow-Clarke, Dominic Shakeshaft, Matt Wade, Tom Welsh
Coordinating Editor: Fran Parnell
Copy Editors: Mary Ann Fugate, Ginny Munroe, Nancy Sixsmith, and Sharon Wilkey
Production Support: Patrick Cunningham
Indexer: Toma Mulligan
Artist: April Milne
Cover Designer: Anna Ishchenko

Distributed to the book trade worldwide by Springer-Verlag New York, Inc., 233 Spring Street, 6th Floor, New York, NY 10013. Phone 1-800-SPRINGER, fax 201-348-4505, e-mail orders-ny@springer-sbm.com, or visit www.springeronline.com.

For information on translations, please e-mail rights@apress.com, or visit www.apress.com.

Apress and friends of ED books may be purchased in bulk for academic, corporate, or promotional use. eBook versions and licenses are also available for most titles. For more information, reference our Special Bulk Sales–eBook Licensing web page at www.apress.com/info/bulksales.

The information in this book is distributed on an "as is" basis, without warranty. Although every precaution has been taken in the preparation of this work, neither the author(s) nor Apress shall have any liability to any person or entity with respect to any loss or damage caused or alleged to be caused directly or indirectly by the information contained in this work.

The source code for this book is available to readers at www.apress.com. You will need to answer questions pertaining to this book in order to successfully download the code.

Dedicated to BSD users everywhere

Contents at a Glance

Contents

Foreword

PC-BSD first began back in early 2005 with a simple beta release, which only provided a basic graphical installer to get a system loaded with FreeBSD 6 and KDE 3. This release was simply to test out the functionality of our installer and to begin laying the groundwork for a new method of package management for the open source desktop. However, the biggest drive for creating PC-BSD actually began in the years prior to the first release, as I had begun to dabble in open source desktops on our family computers.

Our first experience with open source on the desktop was very mixed. Naturally, not all hardware would work properly, and after some initial struggles we ended up with some fairly stable systems. However, as we began using the systems on a daily basis, we quickly ran into other problems in the area of package management that could not be easily solved. By design, the various open source systems would simply treat every software package as a part of the core desktop. Thus, when we wished to perform updates to a particular application, the software manager would determine which other packages on the system needed to be updated to complete the task. While this would usually work without a hitch, too often for our comfort something would end up getting changed or broken in a (seemingly) unrelated piece of software just from doing something simple such as trying to update a small desktop application.

Because of this experience, I began delving into these problems and eventually came to the conclusion that the package managers themselves were not necessarily at fault, but rather the underlying designs were the cause of the trouble. I wanted instead to see a system in which applications were kept separate from the base operating system, and as a result have far fewer potential points of failure. I had been a fan of FreeBSD in the past, and appreciated their clear distinction between their base system and the tree of applications (ports). This got me thinking. Why can't the same idea be implemented around a desktop version of BSD? Thus PC-BSD was born.

At the beginning work was slow, but after the first few beta releases, we began to attract further developers who greatly expanded our efforts. The PBI format went through several evolutions in order to improve its "self-contained" nature and improve application stability. The latest revisions to the PBI format make it possible to offer more complex applications in a self-contained format, including complete window managers such as Gnome or XFCE, which was unthinkable at the creation of the standard.

Now, five years later, PC-BSD has continued to mature and expand its desktop accessibility for novices and experts alike. The PBI tool-chain has grown and improved, as have the numbers of applications available in the format. New graphical configuration tools have been created to manage networking, firewall, users, services, system updating and more. More advanced applications have also been offered, such as a Jail Management suite and a Thin-Client Server module. The upcoming release of version 8.0 is the culmination of a lot of work by a small but committed team of developers, and ups the ante in desktop usability. We are looking forward to continuing work on PC-BSD by making it easier, faster, and more stable than ever, and hope you will come along for the ride.

Kris Moore
Founder and Lead Developer of the PC-BSD project

About the Author

■**Dru Lavigne** is a network and systems administrator, IT instructor, curriculum developer, and author of *BSD Hacks* and *The Best of FreeBSD Basics*. She is currently the Editor-in-Chief of the Open Source Business Resource, a free monthly publication covering open source and the commercialization of open source assets. She is founder and current Chair of the BSD Certification Group Inc., a nonprofit organization with a mission to create the standard for certifying BSD system administrators. She is on the Board of the FreeBSD Foundation.

About the Technical Reviewers

■**Sevan Janiyan** is based in Brighton, Sussex, in England. He looks after SMEs in the south east of England, consulting on Microsoft Windows Server, Microsoft Exchange, OS X Server, OpenBSD and FreeBSD at Venture 37 (`www.venture37.com`).

Sevan holds the following certifications: MCSA, MCSE 2000 & 2003, ACSA 10.4, CCENT. He started with the BSDs back when FreeBSD 5.0 was released in January 2003 and has since branched out to OpenBSD and NetBSD, using the BSDs for much of the infrastructure. He contributes patches to Free/Open/NetBSD and he maintains several ports in the FreeBSD tree.

In his spare time, Sevan likes to DJ and listen to comedy. He keeps a blog at `www.geeklan.co.uk`.

■**Søren "Xride" Straarup** was born in 1978, and hamradio licensed in 1992. He has been using FreeBSD since 1998, and has used FreeBSD at work since 2000, both as sysadmin and developer. Søren became a FreeBSD ports committer in 2006.

■**Alexander Erenkov** was born in Pripyat, near Kiev (Ukraine). At an early age he was evacuated because of the Chernobyl disaster to the city of Kiev, where he resides to this day. He graduated in physics and mathematics from the Lyceum, going on to attend Kiev Polytechnic Institute, which he soon abandoned due to the inconsistency of the training material and modern technology at that time. In 2002 Alexander discovered the world of open source software, including FreeBSD, as both a user and administrator. He used his favorite programming language, Java, to develop web games focused on high throughput from 2005 to 2008. After that era ended, Alexander began to write and maintain the CRM system for a company that sells contextual advertising, devoting his free time to improving the PC-BSD operating system. In September 2009, with the help of foreign sponsors, he organized and conducted the first FreeBSD/PC-BSD conference in Kiev, Ukraine.

In 2010, Alexander began providing consulting services on free software and related technologies, and is optimistic about the future.

Acknowledgments

I would like to thank the many BSD users that I have met and worked with over the years. Your enthusiasm and willingness to share your experiences constantly remind me that BSD is more than an operating system; it is a community.

Special thanks to Frank Pohlmann and Fran Parnell from Apress. Their hard work and dedication are the reason that this book has gone from a good idea to the resource you now hold in your hands.

Introduction

For years, the BSD family of operating systems has been a popular choice for developers and system administrators. The BSDs provide well-engineered development processes, secure and stable operating systems, well-written documentation, and a license that allows users to freely modify the system to meet their needs. However, it was traditionally difficult for a casual computer user to get started using a BSD system due to an initially steep learning curve. What was needed was a desktop BSD that allowed users to start using the operating system immediately and still allowed them to "peek under the hood" as they wanted to increase their knowledge of how things work.

The PC-BSD project was started in 2005 to address this need and has since matured into a stable, feature-rich, and easy-to-use operating system. Its userbase and popularity continue to grow among existing BSD users and users who are looking for alternatives to Windows, Mac, or Linux. Just as Ubuntu has revolutionized the Linux desktop, PC-BSD has revolutionized the BSD desktop.

PC-BSD has been designed to appeal to everyone, from casual computer user to the most advanced computer hacker. Things "just work," meaning you don't have to know how things work just to get them to work. Things are also infinitely customizable, where the only limit is literally how much you are willing to learn. PC-BSD is also suited to users with special needs—it can be easily customized for users with disabilities or users who read languages other than English.

PC-BSD also provides a vibrant community of end users, translators, writers, and developers. If joining an open source community interests you, you'll enjoy the friendliness, enthusiasm, and helpfulness of other PC-BSD users.

It is our hope that you enjoy the information in this book and learn all kinds of interesting things as you read through it. This book is meant to be "done" as much as "read," and every page contains something you'll want to try out on a system. So, grab a computer, the latest version of PC-BSD, and prepare to explore the PC-BSD operating system!

What You'll Find in This Book

The Definitive Guide to PC-BSD is divided into five parts that move the reader from basic to advanced tasks. Novice users will benefit from reading the book from the beginning while more advanced users can start at the sections that catch their interest. If you come across a technical term you don't understand and it is not explained in that section, it was introduced earlier on in the book.

Part 1 is meant to get you started with PC-BSD. It provides an introduction to free and open source software, the BSD family of operating systems, and how PC-BSD fits into the picture. It then gets you started with PC-BSD by showing you how to run a live DVD or install PC-BSD into a virtual environment or directly onto your computer, either to run the DVD as a live operating system or to install PC-BSD on your system.

Part 2 allows you to get comfortable with using PC-BSD. Its beginning chapters introduce you to the KDE4 desktop, showing you how to customize your desktop and to find the things you need. It also shows you how to perform common computing tasks using PC-BSD. Later chapters show you how to change and configure every aspect of your operating system. If you're looking for a reference on "how do I?", this is the section of the book to zero in on.

Part 3 teaches you how to find, install, and manage software on your PC-BSD system. The initial chapters introduce you to PC-BSD's push button installer system that allows even brand-new users to safely manage their software. Later chapters introduce more advanced software management systems such as the FreeBSD packages system and the FreeBSD ports system.

Part 4 introduces you to the PC-BSD community and the resources that are available when you need help using your PC-BSD system. Users new to the open source way of doing things can learn about netiquette and how to effectively use forums, wikis, IRC, and mailing lists. This section of the book initially shows you how to get help and its later chapters provide suggestions on how more advanced users can give back to the PC-BSD community.

Part 5 is the most advanced section of the book. Its first chapter shows you how to perform advanced tasks such as creating customized installations, setting up a thin client network, and managing FreeBSD jails. The last chapter introduces you to the PC-BSD system and PBI development processes and shows how developers can assist the PC-BSD community.

## PART 1

Getting Started
with PC-BSD

CHAPTER 1

■ ■ ■

Introducing PC-BSD

Did you ever wish that you could just use your computer without becoming frustrated by the experience? How many times have you found yourself asking: why can't I browse the Internet or use email without worrying about viruses? Why can't I find software that doesn't crash or freeze my computer? Why do I have to rely on a technical friend or family member to keep my system up-to-date? Why does software cost so much? Why do I have to become a computer expert just to use a computer?!!

The good news is: you don't have to become a computer expert just to use a computer. In fact, you don't even have to spend money on computer software. You can browse the web, use email and social networks, create documents and presentations for work or school, play games, watch videos, and listen to music using high quality software at no cost.

Sound too good to be true? The idea takes some getting used to, but by the end of this book you'll wonder why you ever paid for software in the first place. This introductory chapter will very briefly describe the origins of free software and introduce you to the PC-BSD operating system.

A Little History

Computers and software have been around for over 60 years, so it can be useful to have some historical context on why things are the way they are. In the beginning, computers were huge, taking up entire floors worth of space, and cost hundreds of thousands of dollars. Computer manufacturers made their money selling hardware and computer users were expected to create their own software. It quickly became apparent to users that sharing the software they created with each other provided many benefits. It saved everyone from reinventing the same wheel and freed up their time to actually use the computer hardware they had invested so much money in. This software sharing evolved into associations of users that still exist to this day. Examples include SHARE, created by IBM users in 1955, and DECUS (now called the HP User Society), which was created by Digital Equipment users in 1961. In the beginning, software was created by users and didn't cost any money, and sharing communities were created by and for people using the same software.

Things began to change in the 1970s as lower-cost personal computers were introduced and software began to be sold as a product.[1] Over time, users purchasing software became the norm and the members of software communities became limited to computer scientists and programmers.

Free and Open Source Software

In 1985, a computer scientist at MIT named Richard Stallman became frustrated that software he had created through academic research was being sold for profit by companies. In response, he wrote the GNU Manifesto[2] and launched the Free Software movement. According to Stallman, software is "free" not when it is obtained at no cost, but when it gives the user the following freedoms:

> *Free software is a matter of the users' freedom to run, copy, distribute, study, change and improve the software. More precisely, it means that the program's users have the four essential freedoms:*

> - *The freedom to run the program, for any purpose (freedom 0).*

> - *The freedom to study how the program works, and change it to make it do what you wish (freedom 1). Access to the source code is a precondition for this.*

> - *The freedom to redistribute copies so you can help your neighbor (freedom 2).*

> - *The freedom to improve the program, and release your improvements (and modified versions in general) to the public, so that the whole community benefits (freedom 3). Access to the source code is a precondition for this.*

> *A program is free software if users have all of these freedoms. Thus, you should be free to redistribute copies, either with or without modifications, either gratis or charging a fee for distribution, to anyone anywhere. Being free to do these things means (among other things) that you do not have to ask or pay for permission.*

The Free Software Definition[3]

---

[1] See "Elements of Operating System and Internet History: A BSD Perspective" for a complete history. This book is available from its author at http://users.soe.ucsc.edu/~brucem/.

[2] http://www.gnu.org/gnu/manifesto.html

[3] http://www.gnu.org/philosophy/free-sw.html

Whenever the term "free" is used in this book, it is referring to the above definition of free, not to the cost of the software.

Free software does not include shareware that can only be used at no cost for a limited amount of time. Free software does not include demo software that only provides some features and nags you to buy the full product in order to access all of the features. Free software does not include spyware or trojans, which are meant to harm your computer.

You are not engaging in software piracy if you download or use free software. Free software has already given you the freedom to use and share it with your friends without having to first pay a cost or ask for permission. Think of free software as a return to the original days of computers, when users shared their programs to help each other use their computers effectively.

In 1998, a group of free software users decided to create a new term to describe free software. They felt a new term was needed so users wouldn't confuse "freedom" with "no cost." They coined the term "open source" and started the Open Source Initiative[4] to promote its use. While technical users may debate the nuances of each term, from a user perspective it is safe to assume that any software that calls itself "free/libre" or "open source" allows you to legally download, use, and share it at no cost.

BSD Software

Nearly a decade before Richard Stallman wrote his GNU Manifesto, computer scientists at the University of California at Berkeley were sharing the changes they were making to the Unix operating system with users at other universities. These changes were known as the Berkeley Software Distribution or BSD Unix.[5] The changes included a working implementation of TCP/IP, the software that computers still use today to access the Internet and files on other computers.

BSD also pioneered the concept of creating and sharing software over a network. In this way, a community of software users could help each other out, even though they all lived in different parts of the world. When the users at Berkeley stopped contributing changes to BSD in the early 1990s, the global community of users took over and continued development of the operating system.

One group of users decided to concentrate on making BSD work on many different types of computers (the technical term is porting to other computer architectures). They formed the NetBSD project in March 1993. NetBSD currently supports 57 architectures,[6] making it the most ported operating system in the world and earning it the motto "of course it runs NetBSD!"

Another group of users decided to concentrate on personal computers and getting as many applications as possible to work with the operating system. They formed the FreeBSD project in November 1993. As of December 2009, FreeBSD supports over 21,000 applications, all of which are free to use.

A group of NetBSD users decided to concentrate on operating system security and started the OpenBSD project in December 1994. OpenBSD includes a number of security features absent or optional in other operating systems, and its motto is "Only two remote holes in the default install, in a heck of a long time!"

---

[4] http://www.opensource.org/

[5] See "Twenty Years of Berkeley Unix: From AT&T-Owned to Freely Redistributable" for a more complete history (http://oreilly.com/catalog/opensources/book/kirkmck.html).

[6] http://netbsd.org/ports/

Despite their original focus goals, all of the BSD communities support multiple architectures, provide thousands of free applications, and have a reputation for being secure. The BSD communities also work closely with each other, and new features created by one project tend to find their way into the other projects over time.

PC-BSD

In 2005, a FreeBSD user started experimenting with some scripts to make installing and using FreeBSD easy for the casual computer user. His goal was to create a no-cost operating system that is so intuitive and easy to use, you shouldn't have to constantly bug your technical friends in order to figure out how to do things. The result was PC-BSD, the focus of this book.

PC-BSD is open source software, meaning that you have been given permission to install, use, and share it. PC-BSD has a vibrant community of other PC-BSD users with whom you can share your PC-BSD experiences, tips, questions and answers. Experienced PC-BSD users can also share their programs and add-ons. This book will introduce you to that community and give you the confidence and tools you'll need to help others as you move along the path from casual to experienced PC-BSD user.

PC-BSD is still FreeBSD under the hood, meaning that existing FreeBSD users have access to all of the FreeBSD features they expect. As new versions of FreeBSD are released, so are versions of PC-BSD. This means that PC-BSD users benefit from all of FreeBSD's features as they are introduced.

Why PC-BSD Instead of FreeBSD?

PC-BSD is based on FreeBSD, so a natural question arises: "Why use PC-BSD instead of FreeBSD?"

FreeBSD is a popular open source operating system. It does have a reputation for being better suited to technical users than to casual computer users. For example, after installing FreeBSD, the user is left with a command prompt and is expected to know how to configure the graphical environment, networking and sound, and how to install additional applications. While these tasks are very well documented and easy to do (once you know what you're doing), it does assume that you either know what you are doing or have the time to learn. While the learning experience can be very satisfying, it can also be frustrating to new users or users who need their computer to "just work" right now.

No Previous Knowledge Required

PC-BSD doesn't require any previous knowledge since the operating system is pre-configured for you. It provides an easy-to-navigate desktop, a browser that is connected to the Internet, working sound, dozens of installed applications, and an easy way to browse for and install additional software. The first time you boot into PC-BSD, you can just start using it.

Stability and Security

FreeBSD has a reputation for being a very stable and secure operating system. PC-BSD builds on this base by adding several features that make it easy for you to keep your system secure. The installation pre-configures the built-in firewall to allow access to the Internet but to prevent other systems from damaging your computer. A firewall utility is included should you wish to adjust your firewall settings.

PC-BSD includes a utility that automatically checks for security updates and newer versions of software. This application will pop-up when an update is available, describe the update, and provide a button for you to install the update.

Viruses on BSD systems are extremely rare (I have been using BSD daily for over ten years without running antivirus software and have never been infected by a virus). PC-BSD does support easy-to-install antivirus software should you wish to use it.

Friendly and Helpful Community

It may seem strange to include community as a feature of an operating system, but once you learn how to tap into a community's resources you'll realize why community is so important. No operating system is perfect. Sometimes an "intuitive" feature doesn't make sense to you and sometimes things don't work like they should. What do you do if your technical friends aren't available or don't know the answer?

Access to other PC-BSD users from around the world is a valuable resource. Someone else will have experienced the same problem and can tell you what they did to fix it. And if the problem turns out to be a bug in the software, others in the community can fix the software so it doesn't happen again. The community is also a great place to learn about applications you haven't tried before and to hang out with other PC-BSD users—this can be especially helpful if none of your friends has tried PC-BSD yet.

The PC-BSD community has a reputation for being friendly and helpful. We'll offer tips in this book on how to introduce yourself to the community and access its resources.

Best of Both Worlds

PC-BSD isn't just for the casual computer user; it is also well suited to existing FreeBSD users. I started using PC-BSD after nearly a decade of using FreeBSD as my desktop. I already knew how to configure a FreeBSD desktop, but wanted to try PC-BSD's pre-configured install. I stayed with PC-BSD because I liked its additional features.

For users already familiar with FreeBSD, PC-BSD provides the best of both worlds: a pre-configured desktop and FreeBSD. You can still install software using the FreeBSD ports and packages collections,[7][8][9] and you can try PC-BSD's software installer. You can still keep your software up-to-date using traditional tools, and you can try PC-BSD's update utility. You can still manually configure networking and the firewall, and you can try PC-BSD's graphical utilities. Heck, you can change the desktop and still access the PC-BSD graphical utilities through the command line. If you're a curious power-user like myself, you can even turn your PC-BSD installation into a FrankenBSD as you discover all kinds of novel ways to integrate FreeBSD with PC-BSD's features. This book will cover all of these user possibilities, allowing the reader to decide whether to use PC-BSD as-is or delve into further experimentation.

---

[7] http://www.freebsd.org/doc/en_US.ISO8859-1/books/handbook/ports.html

[8] http://www.freshports.org

[9] http://www.freebsd.org/ports/index.html

Why Not Linux?

If you're familiar with free software, you have probably heard of or used Linux before. You may even be wondering if PC-BSD is a Linux distro (it is not). PC-BSD aims to allow any user to use FreeBSD on his or her computer, much like Ubuntu[10] aims to allow any user to use Linux on his or her computer. Both are examples of easy-to-use open source operating systems.

The answer to the question "why use PC-BSD over a Linux distribution such as Ubuntu?" depends upon whom you ask. Some PC-BSD users experience fewer problems using PC-BSD's software installer and update utilities. Some find PC-BSD to be better documented or find the PC-BSD community to be more helpful. Some like the PC-BSD desktop better than the Ubuntu desktop. Some like that it is based on FreeBSD. So, really, it depends upon whom you ask.

The real answer may be to try both and to experience each operating system for yourself. Both will allow you to use your computer effectively, at no cost. If you've used Ubuntu before, keep an open mind as you go through this book. PC-BSD will accomplish the same tasks as Ubuntu, but it will do some things differently. We're confident that by the end of this book, you will be among the growing number of happy PC-BSD users.

Summary

This chapter has introduced you to the concept of free software and the importance of community. It has briefly described PC-BSD and the benefits it can provide to the casual computer user as well as more experienced FreeBSD and Linux users.

In the next chapter we will dive right in and demonstrate how to install PC-BSD onto your computer.

---

[10] http://www.ubuntu.com

CHAPTER 2

■ ■ ■

Installing PC-BSD

PC-BSD was designed to be easy to install. Even if you've never installed an operating system before, the default settings provided by the installer will allow for a quick and successful PC-BSD installation. If you have a spare computer and a PC-BSD DVD, you can install and start using PC-BSD in under 30 minutes.

This chapter is designed for both novice and advanced users. If you don't know what you're doing and are afraid of losing the data on your computer, start with the section "Using the Live DVD" later in this chapter. This will enable you to try out PC-BSD without destroying the data on your computer. You can then read through the rest of the chapter as you become more comfortable with the idea of performing an installation that will replace the current operating system on your computer with PC-BSD.

This chapter discusses all of the possibilities that can occur during an installation. By understanding what each setting does, you can decide whether you want to change it or accept the default setting. I will let you know if a setting is meant for advanced users or requires additional understanding of how computers work.

This chapter also discusses settings of interest to advanced users who would like to perform an installation that doesn't overwrite the existing operating system. I will show you how to create free space for the PC-BSD installation and how to configure a boot manager so multiple operating systems can exist on one computer.

What's New in PC-BSD 8

This book was written to PC-BSD version 8.0, which was released in February 2010. Some of the notable features of this release include the following:

> **New system installer:** The system installer was completely rewritten. It now enables users to test their keyboard layout and to install FreeBSD or PC-BSD, and provides a summary of the installation settings. The back end of the installer is scriptable, allowing advanced users to fully customize their installations.

> **Software Manager:** This now includes a software browser, enabling users to easily find and install software in the same utility that is used to remove and update installed software.

> **Life Preserver:** PC-BSD now includes an easy-to-use backup utility.

Nvidia for AMD64: Nvidia GeForce[1] video cards are now fully supported on both the 32- and 64-bit versions of PC-BSD.

Adobe Flash Player 10: As of this writing, 10 is the latest version of Flash, meaning you can view any flash content in PC-BSD.

KDE 4.3.4: As of this writing, this is the latest version of KDE. Chapter 3 introduces you to the KDE desktop.

New USB system: The entire USB system was rewritten for FreeBSD 8,[2] making it easier to work with USB devices.

Filesystem support: PC-BSD now supports encrypted filesystems and the ZFS filesystem. See the "Disk Setup" section in this chapter for more information about selecting a filesystem during installation.

System Requirements

To install PC-BSD, you must first determine whether the hardware on your computer meets the minimum requirements. If your computer is fairly new (less than 5 years old), it should be fine. If your computer is older, double-check that it meets the minimum requirements. I'll first list the requirements and then show you how to find out what hardware is installed on your computer.

Minimum for PC-BSD Installation

At a bare minimum, your computer needs to meet the following hardware requirements:

CPU: Pentium 2 (introduced in 1997)

Disk space: 10GB of free space

Memory: 256MB of RAM

Minimum for FreeBSD Installation

The FreeBSD installation is meant for advanced users. Existing FreeBSD users should be aware that the PC-BSD installer does not allow you to select which FreeBSD distributions to install—for example, User, Developer, or Minimal. The minimum requirements listed next are based on the requirements of the installer. If you're looking for a FreeBSD minimal installation on a low-end computer, you should install from FreeBSD media instead of the PC-BSD installer.

Available disk space: 4GB of free space

Memory: 256MB of RAM

---

[1] www.nvidia.com/object/geforce_family.html

[2] Advanced users can read the technical details here: http://svn.freebsd.org/viewvc/base?view=revision&revision=184610.

Recommended

Although the minimum requirements will allow you to install PC-BSD, you can never have too much CPU, disk space, or RAM. In fact, the more you have, the better your computing experience. The PC-BSD project recommends the following minimum hardware in order to get the most out of PC-BSD:

> **CPU:** Pentium 4 or higher (introduced in 2000)
>
> Available disk space: 30GB of free space
>
> **Memory:** 512MB of RAM
>
> **Video:** Some advanced features such as desktop effects and 3D games require a 3D video card. PC-BSD supports 3D acceleration on most Nvidia cards and some Intel integrated cards.

Determining Hardware Settings

There are many utilities available for determining what hardware is installed on a computer. I will demonstrate how to use Parted Magic because this open source program can also be used to create free space on your computer. How to create free space is discussed in the "Creating Partitions" section at the end of this chapter.

Instructions for downloading and burning Parted Magic to a CD are available from http://partedmagic.com/download.html. After you have the CD, insert it into your CD drive, boot the computer, and press the spacebar when you see the menu shown in Figure 2-1.

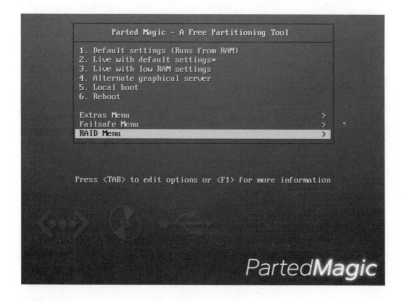

Figure 2-1. *Main menu for the Parted Magic CD*

■ **Tip** If you don't see this menu, your computer is not set to boot from its CD drive. You will need to access your BIOS[3] and change the boot order[4] so your computer boots from CD first.

To determine the hardware on your system, press the spacebar when you see the Parted Magic menu to stop it from loading. Use your up arrow to highlight the Extras menu and press Enter. Press Enter again to start the Hardware Detection Tool (HDT).

■ **Tip** Parted Magic also provides a graphical interface to show you your hardware, but that tool may not give you all of the information you'll need about your video card.

You can now use your up and down arrow keys to highlight entries, and your left and right arrow keys to move between menus. Use the right arrow key to expand a menu and the left arrow key to go back.

You should write down the following information:

Disks ➤ Disk 1: Make note of the size of the disk. If you are planning on installing PC-BSD without losing the current operating system(s) on the computer, carefully record the Size and Type for each partition.

Memory ➤ Bank 0: Note the Size. Repeat for each of the listed Banks (the number of banks will depend on your hardware). Adding up all of the listed sizes will show the total amount of RAM on the computer.

Processor: If the FSB setting is higher than 66, your CPU meets the minimum installation requirements. Also check the X86_64 setting. If it is set to No, you must install the 32-bit version of PC-BSD. If it is set to Yes, you must install the 64-bit version of PC-BSD.

VESA ➤ VESA Bios: The Vendor and Product will be needed when you select your optimal video settings, as seen in the "Post Installation" section at the end of this chapter.

When finished, arrow down to Reboot and remove the CD.

---

[3] See http://michaelstevenstech.com/bios_manufacturer.htm for instructions on how to access your BIOS.

[4] This how-to demonstrates how to change boot order: www.hiren.info/pages/bios-boot-cdrom.

Obtaining PC-BSD

If you don't have a copy of PC-BSD, you can download and burn your own DVD for free or you can purchase a DVD at a nominal cost. This section will demonstrate the available methods for obtaining PC-BSD. If you already have a PC-BSD DVD, you can skip ahead to the next section.

Downloading and Burning a .iso File

If you want to download and burn your own DVD, the PC-BSD web site (`http://www.pcbsd.org`) contains everything you need to get started. The main page of the web site always indicates which version is the "Current Release", and that is the one that you want to download. Occasionally, the front page will also describe a future release that is in its testing phase (we will show you how to participate in testing releases in Chapter 12). Unless you are helping the community test a release, you don't want to download a testing release; you can spot these as the version name will include the word "beta" or "RC", which stands for release candidate. It will also have a different version number than the one indicated by "Current Release". As of this writing, the current release of PC-BSD is 8.0—the number after the 8 may be higher when you go to download the current release.

To download PC-BSD, click on the Download link at the top of the pcbsd.org web site. You will see information similar to that seen in Figure 2-2.

PC-BSD is released under the BSD license

Before downloading PC-BSD, you may want to have a look at the quick guide. You can report issues on the bug tracker or on the mailing list. If you like PC-BSD, please consider making a donation! If you would like to help mirror these files, you may get the rsync information here.

Can't download huge files or want to support us by buying a boxed edition? DVDs and CDs are available for purchase at the PC-BSD Store!

Get PBI files:
www.pbidir.com

Provider of enterprise servers for open source and corporate sponsor of PC-BSD

Upcoming Events

SCaLE Expo
Feb 19-21 2010

AsiaBSDCon
March 11-14 2010

BSDCan
May 11-14 2010

PC-BSD 32Bit (i386) Downloads

- PC-BSD CD #1 32bit (i386) - System install CD1
- PC-BSD CD #2 32bit (i386) - System Install CD2
- PC-BSD CD #3 32bit (i386) - Optional Components
- PC-BSD DVD 32bit (i386) - Complete install + Optional Components
- PC-BSD USB 32bit (i386) - Complete install + Optional Components
- PC-BSD Boot-Only CD 32bit (i386) - Boot only CD for network & internet installs
- PC-BSD Boot-Only USB 32bit (i386) - Boot only USB for network & internet installs

PC-BSD 64Bit (amd64) Downloads

- PC-BSD DVD 64bit (amd64) - Complete install + Optional Components
- PC-BSD USB 64bit (amd64) - Complete install + Optional Components
- PC-BSD Boot-Only CD 64bit (amd64) - Boot only CD for network & internet installs
- PC-BSD Boot-Only USB 64bit (amd64) - Boot only USB for network & internet installs

Other Downloads and Docs

Figure 2-2. Download page of pcbsd.org web site

Notice that there are several hyperlinks to choose from. Before downloading anything, determine if your computer is 32 or 64 bit, as described in the previous section on "Determining Hardware Settings". You can then choose which file(s) to download.

If you have a fast Internet connection, download the DVD version that matches your hardware (32 or 64 bit). The DVD version contains everything you need, but it is a large download—about 4GB. If you have a slow Internet connection or a limit on how much you can download, consider downloading the CD files instead. These files are a smaller download (about 700MB each), but you will need to download both CD #1 and CD #2 to complete the installation, plus CD #3 if you want to install additional software during the installation. Advanced users also have the option to download USB and boot-only images.

■ **Note** This book will refer to the "PC-BSD DVD". If you are using CDs instead, you can use them to do everything in this chapter except the section on "Using the Live DVD" as the CD version does not contain the live version of PC-BSD.

If you click a hyperlink to start a download, it will indicate the name of the file that will be downloaded, its size, and the MD5 sum of the file. The filename will end in .iso, indicating that it is an image that is meant to be burned to a CD or DVD media. This means that the CD/DVD drive in your computer needs to be writable—it will be marked as CD-RW or DVD-RW, where the W means that it is capable of writing. You will also need an application that is designed to write .iso files to media. If you have never burned a CD or DVD before, click on the "quick guide" link seen in Figure 2-2 and read the section on "Burning the installation CD-ROM/DVD" first. It contains step-by-step instructions for burning on Windows, Linux/BSD (Unix), and Mac OSX.

■ **Tip** If this seems too complicated, click on the Store link to purchase a DVD, or get a friend to help you burn your own.

If you decide to download a file, click the arrow next to its Download button. This will allow you to choose a download site—pick the one that is closest to your geographic region. Once the download is finished, you should check that the MD5 sum on the file you downloaded is the same as the MD5 sum next to the download link. This will ensure that the file you downloaded is correct. The section entitled "Data Integrity Check" in the user guide shows you how to do this for Windows and Linux/BSD. Mac OSX users can use the following command at a command prompt:

```
openssl md5 name_of.iso
```

Replace "name_of.iso" with the name of the file that you downloaded.

In the rare event that the md5 is not the same value, this indicates that there was a problem with the download. You will need to download the file again, preferably from a different mirror. If you are an advanced user, you should email the PC-BSD testing mailing list (described in Chapter 11) so the developers can check to see if there is a problem with the file on the download mirror.

Once you have verified the file's checksum, you can burn the DVD or CD using your favorite burning application or the instructions in the user guide.

■ **Tip** The PC-BSD project also gives away thousands of DVDs each year at free software conferences. The main page of the pcbsd.org web site lists the location of these conferences in the Upcoming Events section. If a conference is near you, drop by the PC-BSD booth to pick up a DVD and talk with people from the PC-BSD project.

Purchasing PC-BSD

While PC-BSD is freely available, it does require a bit of work on your part to download and burn a PC-BSD .iso file. If you don't want to be bothered with burning your own DVD, have limited Internet connectivity, or want to show your support for PC-BSD, consider purchasing a copy.

If you click the Store link on the pcbsd.org web site, you will see options to Purchase Retail CD Package or Other Items. Both options are discussed below.

> **Retail CD Package:** This option will take you to the PC-BSD page at FreeBSD Mall (http://www.freebsdmall.com) where you can purchase the latest DVD of PC-BSD, a subscription which will automatically send you a DVD whenever a new version of PC-BSD is released, a copy of this book containing the latest DVD, or a copy of this book containing the latest DVD in a deluxe boxed set.

> **Other Items:** This option will take you to the PC-BSD page at Cafepress.com where you can purchase items such as t-shirts, stickers, hats, mugs, and mousepads.

Using the Live DVD

A live DVD[5] enables you to take an operating system for a "test drive" to see whether you like it before committing to an installation of the operating system on your computer. It is also an excellent way to check whether the operating system understands all of your computer hardware. If it works on the live DVD, it will also work when you install the operating system.

To use the PC-BSD live DVD, insert your PC-BSD DVD into your computer's DVD tray and boot your system. When you see the Welcome to PC-BSD menu shown in Figure 2-3, press your spacebar to pause the menu. You can then press the number 3 key to boot PC-BSD in Live mode.

---

[5] http://en.wikipedia.org/wiki/Live_CD

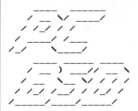

```
        Welcome to PC-BSD!

1. Boot Installer [default]
2. Boot Installer with ACPI disabled
3. Boot in Live Mode
4. Boot in Safe Mode
5. Boot with verbose logging
6. Boot to emergency console
7. Run X in VESA mode
8. Escape to loader prompt



Select option, [Enter] for default
or [Space] to pause timer   10
```

Figure 2-3. PC-BSD boot menu

You will see a series of text messages on your screen as PC-BSD boots.

That's it! After the computer finishes booting, you can use the live environment and skip ahead to Chapter 3 to learn more about getting comfortable with using PC-BSD.

Here are some things to be aware of when using the live DVD:

- Bootup is slower because everything needs to be copied from the DVD to the live filesystem.

- Everything mentioned in this book should work from the live DVD. However, any changes you make are copied to the live filesystem and will disappear when you reboot.

- If you create any files, save them to a USB drive or floppy before rebooting. Otherwise, they will disappear.

- The live filesystem is small (about 30MB), so you will need to download or create large files on a USB drive.

- If your computer does not have much RAM, you will find the live DVD slower than the installed version of PC-BSD.

- Remember: A live DVD is a tool to try out an operating system. If you want to use the operating system on a regular basis, you should install it instead.

Using a Virtual Environment

A virtual environment allows you to perform an installation into a "virtual" computer. From a practical point of view, this means that you can install and use PC-BSD within a window on your existing operating system. This installation is *virtual* because it does not overwrite any of the data on your computer and you can continue to use your existing operating system as usual. However, the installation is *real* in that it allows you to fully use the operating system that was installed into that window, just as if it were the only operating system on your computer.

To perform this bit of magic, you need to first install a virtual computing application. We recommend the VirtualBox application because it is free, easy to use, and available for Windows, Mac OS X, Linux, and BSD. You can download the Windows, Mac, and Linux versions of VirtualBox from `www.virtualbox.org/wiki/Downloads`. Existing FreeBSD users can install the VirtualBox package or port. Existing PC-BSD users can install the VirtualBox PBI by using Software Manager.

■ **Tip** In this book, you will learn how to install packages, ports, and PBIs. For now, install the version of VirtualBox for your existing operating system.

After the VirtualBox program has been installed and started, you will need to create a virtual machine. This machine contains the settings for the window where you will install PC-BSD. Figure 2-4 shows the initial VirtualBox screen.

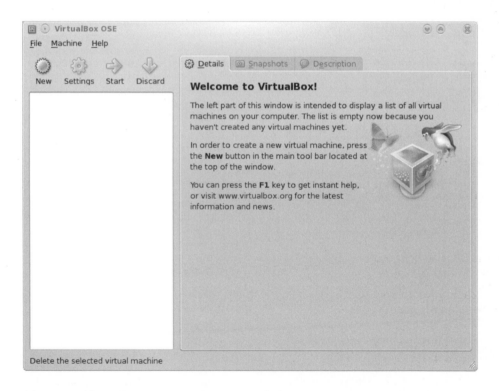

Figure 2-4 *The Welcome to VirtualBox screen, before creating any virtual machines*

Click the New icon to start the New Virtual Machine Wizard. Your machine will need the following settings to successfully install PC-BSD into it:

Name: Choose a name that makes sense to you.

OS Type: Select BSD from the drop-down Operating System menu and keep FreeBSD as the version.

Base Memory Size: Change this number to 256.

Virtual Hard Disk: Keep the default settings of the boot hard disk and create a new hard disk.

Storage Type: Keep the default of Dynamically Expanding Storage.

Location: Give the folder a name that makes sense to you and double-check that its location is in an area with enough disk space to hold the size of the virtual machine.

Size: This needs to be changed to at least 10GB.

After you are finished, your new virtual machine will appear, as seen in Figure 2-5.

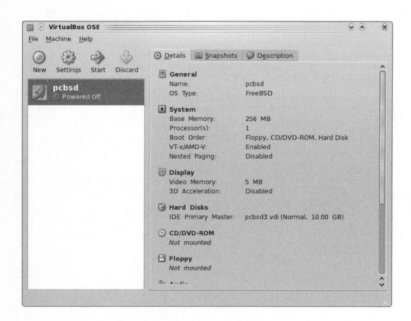

Figure 2-5. *Settings for the virtual machine named pcbsd*

Before installing PC-BSD, there is one more setting that you need to configure. Click the Settings icon and highlight the CD/DVD-ROM setting, as seen in Figure 2-6.

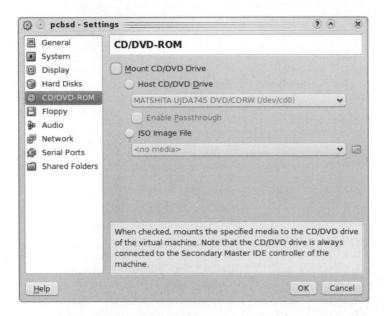

Figure 2-6. Choosing the installation media for a virtual machine

Select the Mount CD/DVD Drive check box, which should select the make and model of your drive. If you have multiple DVD drives or you have plugged in an external USB DVD drive, use the drop-down menu to select the DVD drive you wish to install from.

If you have downloaded PC-BSD, you can mount the .iso file directly without having to first burn it to a DVD. Select the ISO Image File radio button and use the Browse Folders icon to browse to the location where you saved the ISO. When you are finished, click OK to save your changes.

You are now ready to install PC-BSD into your virtual machine. If you are installing from a DVD, insert the DVD disk into the drive you specified earlier. Click the Start button, which will start the virtual machine in its own window, as seen in Figure 2-7

Figure 2-7. Installing PC-BSD within a virtual machine by using VirtualBox

You can then perform the installation as described in the next section.

■ **Tip** Don't worry, installing into a virtual machine will not affect your current operating system. The installation only "exists" within the window of the virtual machine.

There are a few things you need to be aware of when using PC-BSD in a virtual environment:

- You need to press the Ctrl key on the right side of your keyboard to switch back and forth between the virtual machine and the applications running on your operating system. For example, if you try to click your mouse or type something and nothing happens, press your right Ctrl key to activate your mouse/keyboard in that area.

- A virtual environment uses a lot of memory. If your computer does not have much RAM, you will need to be patient because everything will be slower. Closing unused programs may speed things up for you a bit.

- After you've installed an operating system into the machine, you will need to tell your virtual machine that you want to boot the operating system, not install it all over again. Highlight the virtual machine entry and click Settings ➤ System to access the menu seen in Figure 2-8. Highlight the Hard Disk entry in the Boot Order section and use the up arrow to move it to the top of the list.

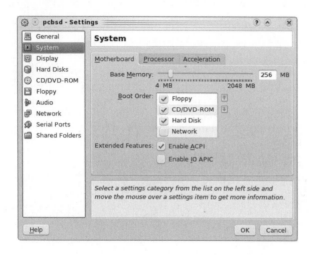

Figure 2-8. Selecting which virtual machine device to boot from

Once installed, PC-BSD can be used as if it were installed on the computer, because the virtual machine will save all of your changes. If you plan to download large files, make sure the size of your virtual machine is large enough to hold those files. PC-BSD will boot whenever you start the virtual machine and will shut down whenever you close the virtual machine.

Installation

If you have a spare computer, the best way to use PC-BSD is to install it onto the computer. It will be much faster than using the live DVD or a virtual environment. If you don't care about what is on the computer now, you can just install PC-BSD and it will erase everything on the computer so it can use all the disk space that came with the computer.

However, if you need to keep the operating system that is currently on the computer, things get more complicated. One solution to make things less complicated is to install PC-BSD onto an external USB drive. If the USB drive is plugged in when you run the Parted Magic CD, it will tell you the size of the drive. Be sure to select the correct drive from the drop-down menu when you reach the "Disk Setup" section of the installation.

The most complicated way is to install PC-BSD onto the same hard drive as your current operating system. If you plan to do this, carefully read the "Advanced Installation" section of this chapter before starting the installation, and triple-check that you are installing into the correct partition in the "Disk Setup" portion of the installation.

■ **Caution** It is important to realize that the default installation assumes that you want to overwrite everything on your computer, or that you have an existing partition that contains no data. If you want to keep your existing operating system, carefully read the "Advanced Installation" section at the end of this chapter before starting the install.

To start the PC-BSD installation, insert your PC-BSD DVD. This time, don't press anything when you see the Welcome to PC-BSD menu (Figure 2-2), because the default option is to start the installer. If you wish to save some time, watch the text messages after the menu and type **n** when the installer asks whether you want to check the integrity of the installer archive. The installer will automatically detect your video card and mouse/pointer device. After the installer is loaded, you will see the Welcome & Language Selection screen seen in Figure 2-9.

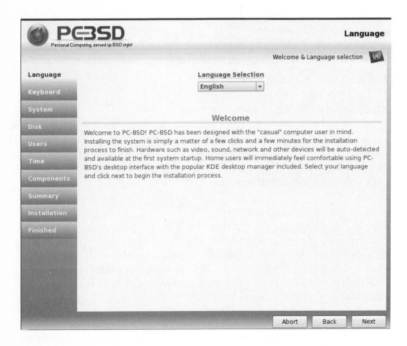

Figure 2-9. PC-BSD installer Welcome & Language Selection screen

The drop-down Language Selection menu enables you to select your language.

Each menu in the installer provides three options: Abort (stop the installation and reboot the computer), Back (return to the previous screen), and Next (move on to the next screen). When finished with this screen, click Next to continue.

Keyboard Setup

The next installation screen, seen in Figure 2-10, enables you to select your keyboard model, layout, and variant. If you are unsure, just leave the settings as is, because the default settings will work. If you know that you want to customize these settings, deselect the Use Default check box. If you have a nonstandard keyboard, you can then select your keyboard from the Keyboard Model drop-down menu. If your keyboard contains non-English characters, highlight your language in the Preferred Layout menu. If you have a Dvorak keyboard, highlight your variant in the Preferred Variant menu. If you modify any of these settings, you can test that your settings are correct by typing into the test settings box. If you decide you want to go back to the default settings, select the Use Default check box.

Figure 2-10. PC-BSD Keyboard Setup screen

Installation Type

The next screen, seen in Figure 2-11, enables you to choose what type of installation to perform. In this example, the user has selected Network/Internet as the Installation Source.

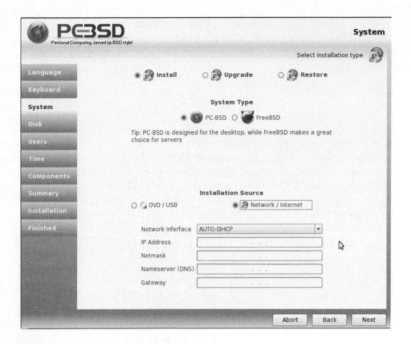

Figure 2-11. *Select Installation Type screen*

To install PC-BSD, you can just accept the default installation type settings and click Next. Here are all the possible options:

Install: This option will format (erase all data) on the disk partition specified in the next menu.

Upgrade: Select this option when a newer version of PC-BSD becomes available. Chapter 13 shows you how to upgrade your existing PC-BSD system to a newer version.

Restore: Advanced users can select this option to repair a PC-BSD system by returning it to its original settings. This option does not keep your data, meaning you have to back it up first. See Chapter 13 for instructions on how to restore your system.

PC-BSD: This option installs PC-BSD.

FreeBSD: This option can be used by advanced users to install the FreeBSD operating system. This installation does not install the X window system, meaning there is no graphical user interface. This option assumes that you already know (or are willing to learn) how to configure a FreeBSD system.

DVD/USB: This option uses the inserted DVD to install PC-BSD.

Network/Internet: This enables advanced users to install over an Ethernet network card, as described in the next paragraph. Note that it is quicker to install from the DVD.

If your computer is attached to the Internet via an Ethernet network card, you can install the system from a server on the Internet or from a specified server (for example, a server at work or school that has been set up for this purpose). If your Internet provider provides your computer with a network address automatically (most do), keep the default setting of AUTO-DHCP and click Next. The installer will attempt to connect to the Internet and, if successful, will fill in the Select Installation Source screen, seen in Figure 2-12, for you.

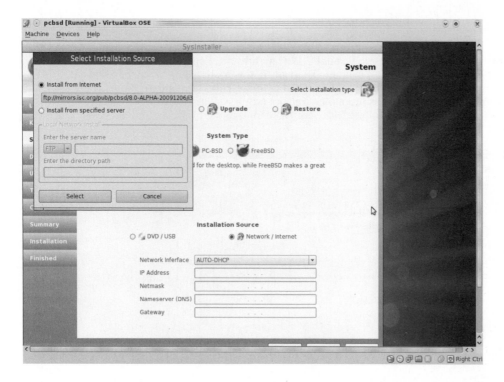

Figure 2-12. The installer has successfully connected to the Internet and selected an installation server.

The default selection will work. However, if you are connecting to a custom installation server (for example, at work), select the Install from Specified Server radio button and enter the settings provided by your system administrator.

Disk Setup

This screen is meant for advanced users to customize their disk partition layout. If you don't consider yourself to be an advanced user, you should either leave this screen as is, perform the installation on a test computer or virtual environment, or get an advanced user to double-check your changes.

■ **Caution** The installer assumes that you want to install PC-BSD on your computer and to erase its current contents. If this is not your intent, you should do one of the following instead: use the live DVD until you are ready to install, find an extra computer to install on, or carefully create and choose a free partition on your hard drive to install into. If you decide to go ahead with the installation, make sure you first back up the data on your computer that you consider important.

I recommend that the first time you install PC-BSD (or any other operating system, for that matter), you use a computer on which you don't want to keep any of the existing data. If you become an advanced user and want to try out new things, you can try more-complex configurations where you dual-boot, meaning the computer has more than one operating system installed.

Figure 2-13 shows a screenshot of the Disk Setup screen.

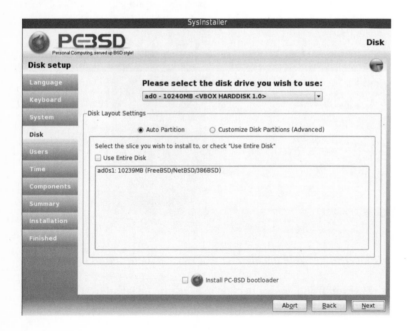

Figure 2-13. Disk Setup screen

The easiest disk layout assumes that you want PC-BSD to take up your computer's entire hard drive. Simply select the Use Entire Disk check box, and the installer will set up everything for you (auto-partition). Remember, this will remove all data that is currently on that hard drive.

■ **Tip** If you forget to select the Use Entire Disk box, you will see this error when you click Next: "The install requires a disk/slice with at least 10000MB of disk space."

If you are installing PC-BSD onto an external USB drive, select it from the drop-down menu at the top of the screen. After a drive is selected, any existing partitions will show in the box under the Use Entire Disk check box. Advanced users can select which partition to install into. If you want to keep an operating system on one of the partitions, it is important that you select the correct partition to erase and install PC-BSD into. Use the partition information you recorded in the "Determining Hardware Settings" section to check that you have selected the correct partition.

■ **Caution** If you want to install into a specific partition, *do not* select the Use Entire Disk check box! Instead, highlight the desired partition and click Next.

Advanced users can customize their disk layout by selecting the Customize Disk Setup (Advanced) radio button. This will change the screen to the one seen in Figure 2-14. In this screenshot, the user has clicked the + button to add a new partition, which is known as a *slice*.

■ **Tip** If you don't know what a disk partition is, you should stick with the default of Auto Partition.

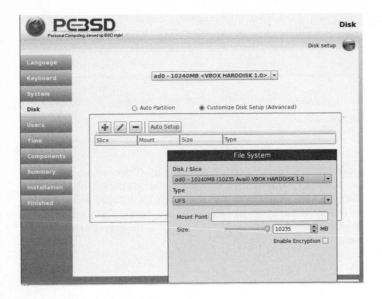

Figure 2-14. Creating a slice in the customized Disk Setup screen

When adding a slice (disk partition), you can customize the following:

Disk/Slice: The names of the entries that appear in this menu depend on whether the disk has any existing partitions. If you select the name that does not include the letter *s* followed by a number (ad0 in this example), you are configuring the entire disk. If you select a name that includes the letter *s* followed by a number, you are configuring an existing partition. The installer will show you the size of the partition and the type of filesystem (for example, NTFS, Linux, FreeBSD), which should give you a hint about what is already installed on that partition.

Type: PC-BSD is able to install several types of filesystems. Table 2-1 provides a description of each filesystem type available in the Type drop-down menu. If you're not familiar with filesystems, the default value of UFS is fine.

Mount Point: This indicates the names of the filesystems. Table 2-2 shows the most commonly used mount points.

Size: The size will depend on your needs and the amount of disk space you have to work with. Table 2-2 provides some suggestions to get you started.

Enable Encryption: PC-BSD uses geli[6] to provide encryption on any filesystem and mount point, including SWAP, ZFS, and /.

---

[6] http://en.wikipedia.org/wiki/Geli_%28software%29

Table 2-1. *Filesystem Types Supported by the PC-BSD Installer*

Filesystem Type	Description
UFS	The Unix File System, which is the default used by PC-BSD.
UFS+S	Adds soft updates.[7]
UFS+J	Adds journaling.[8]
ZFS	Filesystem developed by Sun Microsystems that adds a lot of features.[9]
SWAP	Used on only swap[10] partitions. You need to create one swap partition that is at least two times the size of the computer's RAM.

Table 2-2. *Typical Mount Points and Their Sizes*

Mount Point	Description
/	This mount point, pronounced *root*, is mandatory as it holds the administrator's home directory as well as the operating system. It should be at least 1024MB (or 1GB). Because it can be the only mount point, it can be as large as the entire disk or partition (minus space for the swap partition). Most advanced users allocate 1GB to a few GBs for root and divide up the disk/partition with other mount points. This enables them to separate their data and to make backups and system restores easier.
/usr	This is typically where the user home directories and user data are stored and will typically take up most of the disk/partition. Some advanced users like to make multiple /usr mount points (for example, /usr1, /usr2) to logically divide their data (for example, music, video, other data).
/var	This is typically where *variable* data (data that changes often) is stored. Examples include log files, print jobs, and unread e-mail. The size of the partition will be larger if the system is a logging, print, or mail server. Otherwise, a few GBs is usually sufficient.
SWAP	This will be set up for you if you select the SWAP filesystem.

---

[7] http://en.wikipedia.org/wiki/Soft_updates

8 http://en.wikipedia.org/wiki/Journaling_file_system

[9] See the FreeBSD Handbook for an overview of using ZFS: www.freebsd.org/doc/en_US.ISO8859-1/books/handbook/filesystems-zfs.html

[10] http://en.wikipedia.org/wiki/Swap_space

Figure 2-15 shows an example created by clicking the Auto Setup button. By default, the installer will create 2GB for /, 1GB for /var, RAM times 2 for SWAP, and the rest of the available space to /usr. The same sizes are used if you click the Auto Partition button.

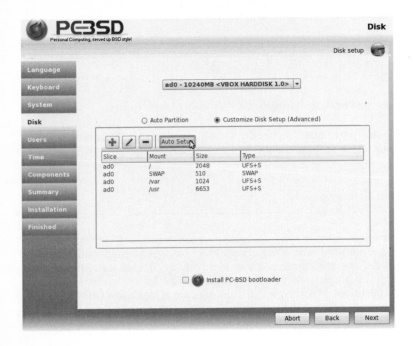

Figure 2-15. Default partition sizes created by the installer if you select Auto Setup or Auto Partition

The final option on this screen is the Install PC-BSD Bootloader check box. Whether you select this check box depends on whether PC-BSD will be the only operating system on the computer:

- If PC-BSD will be the only operating system on the computer, leave this check box deselected.

- If you will be dual-booting PC-BSD with another operating system, *you must* select this check box so the boot code will be written to disk—this will be needed, even if you decide to use another boot manager.

- If you plan to add another operating system later, select this option so the PC-BSD boot code is written to disk.

See the "Booting Multiple Operating Systems" section at the end of this chapter to learn how to successfully boot all of your installed operating systems.

User Creation

The next screen, seen in Figure 2-16, is used to set the administrative password, set up the primary user account, and create any additional user accounts for the system.

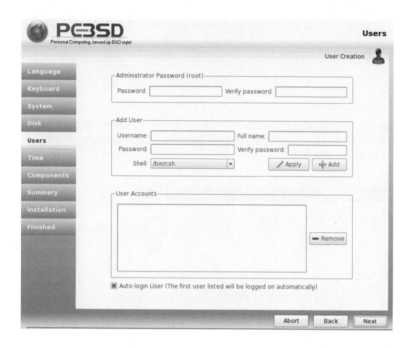

Figure 2-16. User Creation screen

The administrator password is also known as the *root password* or the *superuser password*. You will need to use this password whenever you make a change to the operating system. Throughout this book, I will let you know whenever a task requires this password. This screen asks you to input the password twice and will tell you if the passwords do not match. It will also force you to create the root password, meaning that this text box can't be left empty.

The Add User section is for the user who uses the computer most often (probably you). You will need to remember the username and password; again, the installer will ask you to type the password in twice and will tell you if the values do not match. Advanced users can select their favorite shell from the drop-down menu. If you don't have a favorite shell or don't know what a shell is, the default value is fine. After you have input the user values, click the +Add button to create the user. If the +Add button doesn't work, you have forgotten to fill in one of the fields in the Add User section.

You can create as many user accounts as you need and should create a separate account for every user who will use the computer. If you create multiple accounts, the user who uses the computer most often should be created first so that user is first in the list. If you mess up an account, simply highlight it in the list, click – Remove, and try again.

The Auto-Login User check box indicates whether the first user in the list has to type in their password when the computer boots up. The default setting allows that user to be logged in automatically. This is convenient if you are the only user on the computer and you are not worried about anyone else starting your computer and seeing your stuff. If you do not like this default, deselect this check box so that every time the computer boots up, it will present a login screen that will require you to type in your username and password.

■ **Tip** The "Login Manager" section in Chapter 7 shows you how to change the auto-login feature if you change your mind after the system is installed.

Date and Time Zone

This screen, seen in Figure 2-17, enables you to select your time zone from the drop-down menu. Pick the city that is closest to your geographic area. This will allow your computer to automatically adjust its time whenever daylight savings time starts or stops.

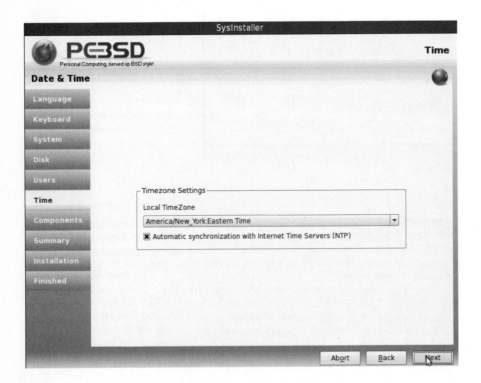

Figure 2-17. Date & Time selection screen

By default, the Automatic Synchronization with Internet Time Servers (NTP) check box is selected. NTP[11] is an abbreviation for the Network Time Protocol, which allows a computer to receive its time from a time server on the Internet. Accurate time is needed for some applications (especially those that share data over a network) to work properly. You can deselect this check box if you don't want your computer to connect to a time server.

Optional Components

The Optional Components screen, seen in Figure 2-18, enables you to select additional software to install with the operating system.

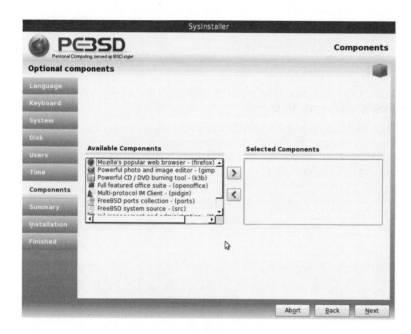

Figure 2-18. *Optional Components screen*

Here is a brief description of each available component:

> **Firefox:** Fast, customizable, and secure web browser that supports tabbed browsing and hundreds of plug-ins. See `www.mozilla.com/en-US/firefox/personal.html` for more details.
>
> **GIMP:** Image manipulation and creation utility, similar to Photoshop. Screenshots are available at `www.gimp.org/screenshots/`.

---

[11] `http://en.wikipedia.org/wiki/Network_Time_Protocol`

K3B: Easy-to-use CD/DVD burner. Screenshots are available at
`http://k3b.plainblack.com/screenshots`.

OpenOffice: Complete office suite, similar to and compatible with Microsoft
Office. See `www.openoffice.org` for more information.

Pidgin: Instant messaging client that supports AOL Instant Messenger (AIM),
MSN, Yahoo!, Google Talk, and many more chat networks. See `www.pidgin.im`
for more information.

FreeBSD ports collection: Allows advanced users to install additional software.
Chapter 10 demonstrates how to use the ports collection.

FreeBSD system source: Allows advanced users to view and use the source for
the underlying FreeBSD operating system. Some of the tasks described in
Chapter 14 require a system source.

The Warden: Allows advanced users to easily manage and administer FreeBSD
jails. The Warden is discussed in Chapter 13.

VLC: Media player for DVDs, CDs, and streaming video. Screenshots are
available at `www.videolan.org/vlc/screenshots.html`.

To install an optional component, highlight it in the Available Components list and click the right
arrow to move it to Selected Components. You can use your Ctrl key to select multiple components. If
you change your mind, you can use the left arrow to move a component back. The components that
show in the Selected Components list will be installed for you.

■ **Note** If you are installing from CD instead of DVD, you will be prompted to insert CD #3 if you select to install
any additional components.

Installation Summary

The Pre-Install Summary screen, seen in Figure 2-19, provides a summary of your selections.

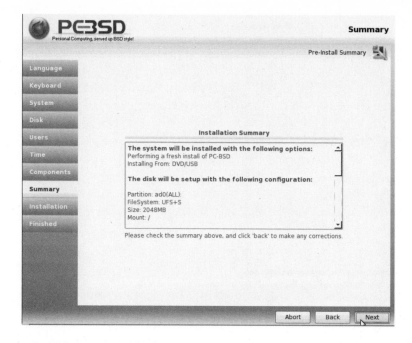

Figure 2-19. *Pre-Install Summary screen*

The summary indicates the following:

- Whether this is a fresh install, upgrade, or system restore.

- Whether you are installing from a DVD or from a specified network location.

- How the disk will be formatted. You will want to verify that you've selected the correct hard drive or installation partition and review the size of the partitions that will be created.

- Which additional software components will be installed.

- Which user account(s) will be created.

This screen provides your last chance to go back and change your selections or to Abort the install. After you click Next and answer Yes to the "Start the installation now?" message, the specified hard drive/partition will be erased and the installation of PC-BSD will begin. During the installation, a progress bar, seen in Figure 2-20, will show the progress of the installation.

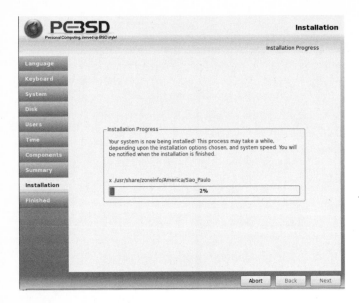

Figure 2-20. Installation Progress screen

When the installation is finished, you'll receive the message seen in Figure 2-21. Click the Finish button and remove the installation DVD so the computer can boot into the installed version of PC-BSD.

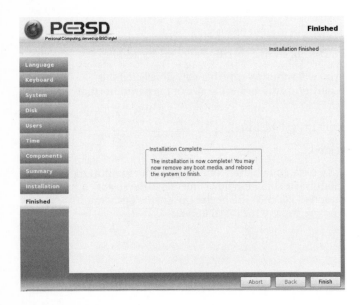

Figure 2-21. Installation Complete message

If Something Goes Wrong

PC-BSD could fail to install on your computer, although that possibility is rare.

After the installation has started, its progress is written to various logs. The installer also sets up several virtual terminals where you can input commands and review the logs. You can access the first terminal by pressing Ctrl+Alt+F2. Type **root** at the login prompt to log in to the terminal, and then **cd /tmp** to access the location where the logs are located.

■ **Tip** Use Alt+F7 to return to the installation screen. Alt+F3 through Alt+F6 represent the remaining virtual terminals.

The following logs are created in /tmp:

> **.pc-sysinstall/pc-sysinstall.log:** Everything the installer does gets copied here. The error will be at the bottom of this log, and everything that succeeded will be before the error. If the install is successful, a copy of this log can be found at **/pc-sysinstall.log** on the newly installed system.

> **sys-install.cfg:** All of the settings you selected in the installation menus are stored here.

> **xstartup.log:** X is the software that is used to load up the graphical interface. If the installer has problems with your video hardware, the error will be in this log.

Advanced users can review the logs to see what went wrong. If the problem is not clear after reading the log, skim through Chapter 11, which shows you how to get help. You will want to make a copy of the log files so you can include the information other users will need to help you. One method is to e-mail a copy of the log to yourself by using the following command, which will send an e-mail with a subject of "installation log":

```
# cat xstartup.log | /usr/bin/mail -s "installation log" myname@mycompany.com
```

Replace **xstartup.log** with the name of the log file you would like to e-mail to yourself and replace **myname@mycompany.com** with your own e-mail address.

You can also save the log file to a USB thumb drive. After inserting the drive, you can mount it, copy the log file, and umount the drive with the following commands. Don't forget to type in that **umount** command *before* you remove the thumb drive so PC-BSD knows that you are finished using it.

```
# mount -t msdos /dev/da0s1 /mnt
# cp /tmp/xstartup.log  /mnt
# umount /mnt
```

Post Installation

The first time you boot into PC-BSD, the Display Settings screen, seen in Figure 2-22, will prompt you to confirm your display settings. Select the name in the drop-down Video Card menu that most closely matches the Vendor and Model settings you wrote down for your video card.

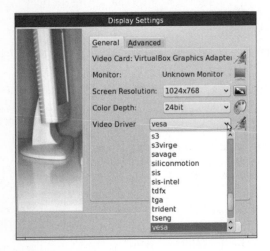

Figure 2-22. Selecting the video driver and resolution for the newly installed PC-BSD system

---

■ **Tip** The "Determining Hardware Settings" section at the beginning of this chapter describes how to find out your video hardware settings if you do not know what video card is installed on the computer.

You can also change your screen resolution at this time. The resolutions that are available will depend on what settings are supported by your video hardware. When finished, click Apply and then OK so your settings can be tested. If you like the resolution, click Yes when you see the Confirm Resolution screen. If you don't like the resolution, click No so you can try another resolution.

■ **Tip** If you have problems configuring your display settings, use the default Video Electronics Standards Association (VESA) settings, which will work but may not provide your favorite resolution. See Chapter 11 to learn how to get help for the best settings supported by your video hardware.

After your resolution has been set, the system will finish booting into PC-BSD.

■ **Tip** If you are installing PC-BSD into VirtualBox and have problems setting the resolution, use System Settings as described in the "Display" section of Chapter 6.

Congratulations! You have successfully installed your PC-BSD system! You are ready to move on to Chapter 3 to learn how to get comfortable with your new operating system.

■ **Tip** If you are connected to the Internet and there are software updates available for your system, you'll receive an informational message on your screen. If you want, skip ahead to the "Software Manager" section of Chapter 8 to learn more about system updates.

Advanced Installation

Creating Partitions

By default, the PC-BSD installer assumes that you want to either replace the existing operating system on the computer or that you have an extra partition that you can install into. If you want to keep your existing operating system and it is currently installed into the only partition on your computer, you will need to shrink that partition to create some free space that can be used to install PC-BSD. The PC-BSD installer will not do this for you, meaning that you will have to use another application for this purpose.

■ **Caution** *Always* back up your data *before* resizing a partition, just in case!

What utility you use depends on your current operating system:

Vista: Use the Disk Management utility and the instructions from
`http://windows.microsoft.com/en-US/windows-vista/Can-I-repartition-my-hard-disk`.

Mac OS X: Use the Disk Utility and the instructions at
`www.makemacwork.com/resize-disk-partitions.htm`.

Ubuntu: You can install and use[12] gparted with the following commands:

```
# sudo apt-get install gparted
# sudo gparted
```

You can also use the Parted Magic CD, introduced in the "Determining Hardware Settings" section, to create free space. This time, boot with the Parted Magic CD and wait for it to load its graphical environment. You can then click the Partition Editor icon on the desktop to display your current partition information, as seen in Figure 2-23.

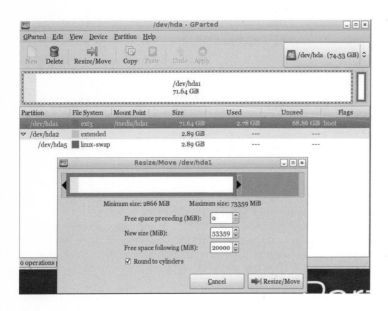

Figure 2-23. *Resizing a partition by using Parted Magic*

We will use the same example for the rest of this chapter. The computer in this example is currently running Ubuntu 8, which has been installed onto the entire hard drive. Ubuntu has created one large partition (71.64GB), plus a small extended partition (2.89GB), plus a small swap partition (2GB).

Right-click the partition you want to resize and select Resize/Move from the menu. Input the amount of free space you want to create at the end of the existing partition. Remember, this must be at least 10GB (10000MiB) and should be larger if you will be saving a lot of large files in PC-BSD.

In this example, free space of 20GB was created by inputting **20000** and then clicking in the New Size input box. The new partition will show as unallocated after you click the Resize/Move button. To save your changes, click the Apply button. A message will ask, "Are you are sure you want to apply the pending operations?" Click Apply and wait for the application to indicate that all operations were successful. Depending on the size of the drive, this will take a few minutes.

---

[12] Usage instructions are available at `http://gparted.sourceforge.net/docs/help-manual/C/gparted_manual.html`.

After the free space is available, it needs to be turned into a partition. To do so, click Partition ➤ New, as seen in Figure 2-24.

Figure 2-24. Creating a new partition in Parted Magic

The default settings are fine, because they will use all of the free space and create a primary partition (which is necessary for an installation). The filesystem is only temporary because it will be overwritten by the PC-BSD installer. If you want, add a descriptive label. Click Add and then Apply.

Once finished, you can close Partition Editor and click the icon in the lower-left corner to log out. Don't forget to remove the CD after the system starts to reboot. Remember the size of the partition you created so you can find it easily in the Disk Setup screen (Figure 2-14) during the PC-BSD installation. In this example, it will be displayed as ad0s3:20002MB (Linux native). The number was slightly lower than what showed in Parted Magic because of the Round to Cylinders option.

Booting Multiple Operating Systems

If you selected to install the PC-BSD boot loader, it will provide a simple menu at boot time that probes the type of filesystems (hence, operating systems) installed on the computer. To continue the example seen in the previous section, the PC-BSD boot loader menu looks like this:

```
F1  Linux
F2 ?
F3 FreeBSD

F6 PXE
Boot: F1
```

F1 is the first partition containing Ubuntu. F2 was the small partition created by Ubuntu. F3 is the PC-BSD installation. F6 indicates that this computer's network card supports booting over a network.[13] The value after Boot indicates which operating system will boot if you don't make a selection. To make a selection, use the key on your keyboard that matches the menu selection; for example, to boot PC-BSD, use the F3 key.

Although PC-BSD will properly probe the partitions, it may or may not be able to load each of the listed operating systems. Whether an operating system boots depends on which bootloaders those operating systems expect to be loaded from and where their boot info has been written to disk.

In this example, Ubuntu should boot by typing F1, but it does not because of the way its boot code is currently installed. The next section will show how to fix this.

You should test each operating system in your PC-BSD boot menu to see whether it boots. You will need to read the rest of the chapter if an operating system does not boot. You may find that each operating system boots, but you would like to try an alternate (different-looking) boot manager. If this is the case, see the upcoming "Using the GAG Boot Loader" section.

If You Prefer GRUB

Many Linux operating systems, including Ubuntu, use the GNU Grand Unified Bootloader (GRUB)[14] boot loader. If you prefer the GRUB boot loader to the PC-BSD boot loader, or if the PC-BSD boot loader won't boot your Linux operating system, you will need to run the GRUB utility. Insert your Linux DVD and select to boot into its live DVD. If your Linux DVD does not have a live DVD option, you can still use a live CD such as Knoppix.[15]

We will continue with our Ubuntu example. To boot into the live version of Ubuntu, insert the Ubuntu DVD and select Try Ubuntu Without Any Change to Your Computer from the menu. After the live DVD has loaded, click Applications ➤ Accessories ➤ Terminal and type the following commands:

```
# sudo grub
[sudo password for dru:
Probing devices to guess BIOS drives. This may take a long time.
      [ Minimal BASH-like line editing is supported.  For
         the first word, TAB lists possible command
        completions. Anywhere else TAB lists the possible
        completions of a device/filename. ]

grub> root (hd0,     (press tab to see menu)
 Possible partitions are:
      Partition num: 0,  filesystem type is ext2fs, partition type 0x83
```

---

[13] The "Thin Client Server" section in Chapter 13 shows you how to boot over a network.

[14] www.gnu.org/software/grub/

[15] www.knoppix.org

```
Partition num: 2,  [BSD sub-partitions immediately follow]
       BSD Partition num: 'a',  Filesystem type unknown, partition type 0xa5
       BSD Partition num: 'b',  Filesystem type unknown, partition type 0xa5
       BSD Partition num: 'd',  Filesystem type unknown, partition type 0xa5
       BSD Partition num: 'e',  Filesystem type unknown, partition type 0xa5
Partition num: 4,  filesystem type unknown, partition type 0x82
```

In our example, Ubuntu is in partition 0, PC-BSD is in partition 2, and partition 4 is the SWAP filesystem. Because we want Ubuntu to boot from GRUB, we want to select and set up the 0 partition, which contains Ubuntu:

```
grub> root (hd0,0)
```

```
grub> setup (hd0)
 Checking if "/boot/grub/stage1" exists... yes
 Checking if "/boot/grub/stage2" exists... yes
 Checking if "/boot/grub/e2fs_stage1_5" exists... yes
 Running "embed /boot/grub/e2fs_stage1_5 (hd0)"... 16 sectors are embedded.
Succeeded
 Running "install /boot/grub/stage1 (hd0) (hd0)1+16 p (hd0,0)/boot/grub/stage2
/boot/grub/menu.1st"... succeeded
Done.
```

```
grub> quit
```

GRUB is now configured to replace the PC-BSD boot loader menu and properly load Ubuntu. However, don't reboot yet, because you still have to tell GRUB about PC-BSD. Continue on to the next section to add PC-BSD to the GRUB boot menu.

If You Need to Add PC-BSD to GRUB

In order to add PC-BSD to your current GRUB boot menu, you'll first need to determine what version of GRUB you are using:

```
# grub - -version
grub (GNU GRUB 0.97)
```

Next, add an entry for PC-BSD to the GRUB menu list. This command will open that file in a graphical editor:

```
# sudo gedit /boot/grub/menu.lst
```

You should see your existing Ubuntu entries toward the end of the file. If this file is empty, check for errors in the commands mentioned in the previous section.

If the operating system is using a version of GRUB less than 2, as seen in our example, add the following lines after the last menu entry:

```
title         PC-BSD 8
rootnoverify  (hd0,2)
chainloader   +1
boot
```

If the operating system is using a version of GRUB 2 or higher, add these lines instead:

```
title     PC-BSD 8
root      (hd0,2,a)
kernel    /boot/loader
boot
```

Reboot the computer and press Esc when you see the GRUB boot loader message. You should now be able to boot into either Ubuntu or PC-BSD.

If You Want to Replace GRUB

Before adding another boot loader, you need to make sure that a boot sector is written to the Linux partition. To do so, find the device name for your Linux partition by running this command while booted into Linux:

```
# sudo fdisk -lu | grep Linux
/dev/sda1          63    109274129    54637033+    83    Linux
/dev/sda5   150239943    156296384     3028221    82    Linux swap / Solaris
```

In our example, Ubuntu Linux is installed on /dev/sda1. To make sure boot code is written on that device, use the following:

```
# sudo grub-install /dev/sda1
Searching for GRUB installation directory ... found: /boot/grub
Installation finished. No error reported.
This is the contents of the device map /boot/grub/device.map.
Check if this is correct or not. If any of the lines is incorrect,
fix it and re-run the script 'grub-install'.

(hd0)  /dev/sda
```

■ **Caution** If you don't install boot code on the Linux partition *before* installing another boot loader, you may not be able to boot your Linux installation!

Using the GAG Boot Loader

There are other boot loaders available that are easier to configure than the PC-BSD or GRUB boot loaders. We recommend the Graphical Boot Manager (GAG), which can boot up to nine operating systems. It is easy to use, and screenshots are available at http://gag.sourceforge.net/pics.html.

■ **Caution** If you are replacing GRUB with GAG, make sure that you follow the instructions in the "If You Want to Replace GRUB" section *before* installing GAG!

Download GAG,[16] unzip the download, and burn the file named cdrom.iso to a CD. Boot from the CD, which will bring up a menu of the following options:

```
1: Read instructions
2: Read FAQ
3: Read license
4: Install GAG
5: Uninstall GAG (Restores MBR)
```

Press 4 to install GAG. Select your keyboard from the keyboard type screen and your language from the language screen. In the next screen, press S to set up GAG, and then press A to add your first operating system to the boot menu.

Continuing our example, GAG shows the following partitions:

```
Key     Partition type
 A      Boot from floppy
 B      83h Linux EXT2
 C      A5h FreeBSD
 D      82h
```

In this example, Ubuntu is probed as B, and PC-BSD as C. I'll press B and type in a description of **Ubuntu 8**. GAG will then give an option to enter a password. If a password is entered, it will be needed before GAG will boot Ubuntu. If I just press Enter, GAG won't require a password. GAG will then provide a menu of icons to go with the entry. I'll select D to choose the Tux penguin.

I'll then press A to add the second operating system, press C to select FreeBSD, type in **PC-BSD 8** for the description, add no password, and press F to select the Beastie icon.

When you have finished adding all of your operating systems, press H to save your changes to the hard disk. You should receive a GAG Installed Successfully message. Press R to return to the main menu, and your entries should now show in the boot menu. Remove the CD, and reboot the computer to test that you can boot into each of the operating systems.

---

[16] http://gag.sourceforge.net/download.html

Summary

This chapter has shown you how to "test drive" PC-BSD by using the live DVD or a virtual environment. It has also covered every aspect of installation, from a default installation to more-complex installation scenarios.

Using the
PC-BSD Desktop

CHAPTER 3

■ ■ ■

Customizing the Desktop

Now that you've successfully installed PC-BSD, you'll want to become familiar with your new system. Part 2 of this book will show you how to customize your PC-BSD environment, perform common computing tasks, and configure every aspect of your system. You'll discover a lot of cool features as you work your way through the chapters in Part 2. These chapters are also handy to refer to whenever you're wondering "How do I do this?"

KDE4

PC-BSD version 8.0, the focus of this book, uses the KDE4 (KDE version 4) desktop environment by default.

■ **Tip** In Windows, the desktop is part of the operating system. This means that you can customize your desktop, but you can't install a different desktop. In open source, the desktop is separate from the operating system, meaning you can choose which desktop environment to install and use. PC-BSD pre-installs the KDE desktop for you—later in this chapter we'll show you how to change desktop environments if you decide that you would like to try another desktop.

Like PC-BSD, KDE[1] is a free software project with its own large user community. The goal of KDE is to provide a desktop that includes commonly used applications that can be run on computers running Linux, BSD, Windows, or Mac OSX. This project wishes to make its software available to anyone, including the disabled and those who speak a language other than English.

---

[1] http://www.kde.org

■ **Note** The reader can find many more resources for using the KDE desktop at the KDE website. We recommend the KDE 4.0 Visual Guide.[2]

Because the desktop is separate from the operating system, you may find KDE on other free operating systems, such as some versions of Linux. Much of the information found in Part 2 of this book also applies to other operating systems running KDE4. However, PC-BSD adds some extra utilities that you will not find on other operating systems. As we come across these utilities, we will tell you so that you will know which features came with KDE and which are unique to PC-BSD.

Default Desktop Components

When you first log into your PC-BSD system, and before you start any of your own customizations, your desktop will look similar to Figure 3-1:

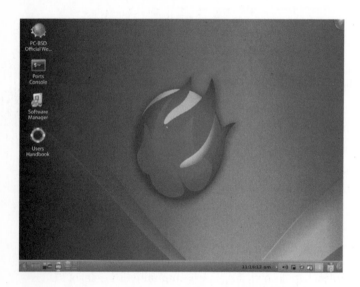

Figure 3-1. Default KDE desktop on a PC-BSD system

The KDE desktop has several components: the plasma panel, the plasma workspace, and the plasma dashboard. Each component is introduced below.

---

[2] http://www.kde.org/announcements/4.0/guide.php

Plasma Panel (Taskbar)

Along the length of the bottom of your desktop is a gray taskbar, which is known as the KDE4 plasma panel, but which is commonly referred to as the taskbar. As seen in Figure 3.1 the default plasma panel on a PC-BSD system contains several icons. If you hover your mouse over any icon in the taskbar, you will see some information about the application that icon represents. You can click on any icon to open its associated application, or right-click the icon to receive a menu of options.

Working from left to right, the default taskbar contains the following icons:

Kickoff: In most versions of KDE, this is a white letter K on a blue background. On PC-BSD systems, the PC-BSD logo (which looks like a flame) is used instead. Kickoff is the KDE application launcher and is discussed in detail in Chapter 4.

Show the Desktop: If you have several windows open, you can click this button to quickly minimize all windows. Click the icon again to return the windows to the desktop.

Show the Plasma Dashboard: Click to start the plasma dashboard. Using the plasma dashboard is explained in the next section.

Device Notifier: This icon will notify you when a new device or media, such as a USB thumb drive or DVD, is inserted.

Pager: This icon looks like four squares, where each square represents a virtual desktop. Think of a virtual desktop as an area where you can group the applications you have opened in a way that makes sense to you. For example, you could use one virtual desktop for gaming and another virtual desktop as your productivity area for doing work. Simply click on the squares to switch between virtual desktops.

Digital Clock: Click on the clock to access the multi-year calendar and click again to close the calendar. If you right-click the clock and select Digital Clock Settings, you can configure its appearance or change the time zone.

System Tray: This area of the panel is to the left of the digital clock and appears to be in its own rectangle. It is preceded by an arrow, which lets you expand the system tray to see all of its icons. By default, the system tray contains the following icons:

- **KMixer:** If you click on the speaker icon, you'll see a slider, which you can use to adjust sound volume. You can also hover over the icon and adjust the volume with the scroll wheel of your mouse. If you click on the Mixer button below the slider, you'll be presented with more sliders to fine-tune your sound settings.

■ **Tip** If you have problems with sound in an application, open Mixer ➤ Settings ➤ Configure Channels and check all the Show/Hide boxes. Uncheck the Mute boxes and adjust the sliders to see if that fixes the lack of sound.

- **Klipper:** This clipboard tool keeps a history of your copy operations so you can paste into other applications.

- **PC-BSD Update Manager:** This utility is found only on PC-BSD systems and is used to keep your operating system and installed applications up-to-date. It is discussed in detail in Chapter 8.

- **KOrganizer:** This is KDE's calendar and reminder utility. KOrganizer supports many other features, including integration with KDE's personal information management program (Kontact), journaling, and blogging. To learn more about KOrganizer, click on its icon, then press F1 to access the KOrganizer Handbook.

- **Notifications:** Click this icon to receive a list of currently running or recently completed jobs, such as file downloads.

■ **Tip** To access any application's Help or Handbook, press F1 from within that application's window.

Two icons appear after the system tray:

Trash: Click this icon to see which deleted files have been saved to the trash bin. Trash is discussed further in Chapter 4.

Plasma: This icon looks like a color palette. It is used to configure widgets, and to add additional panels. These are discussed in detail later in this chapter.

Plasma Workspace

The area above the plasma panel is known as the plasma workspace. This is the area that users typically associate with their desktop wallpaper. By default, the PC-BSD workspace contains four useful icons:

PC-BSD Official Website: This icon is a handy way to access the PC-BSD forums, online documentation, and other resources available from the PC-BSD website. We'll discuss these resources in Chapter 11.

Ports Console: This icon allows you to install FreeBSD ports and packages. Chapters 9 and 10 detail how to use Ports Console.

Software Manager: This utility allows you to easily install software and is unique to PC-BSD. Individual applications that can be installed using the PC-BSD's Software Manager are known as PBIs.[3] How to install PBIs is discussed in detail in Chapter 8.

Users Handbook: Click this link to read the online PC-BSD Users Handbook.

As you read through Part 2 of this book, you'll find that the plasma workspace is very customizable.

Plasma Dashboard

This component is invisible until you either click the Show the Plasma Dashboard icon in the taskbar or press Ctrl+F12. If you have any applications, they, along with the taskbar, will disappear from view and your screen will look similar to the one in Figure 3-2. Don't panic. You can either click anywhere within the plasma workspace or press Ctrl+F12 again to return to your previous view.

Figure 3-2. Plasma dashboard

___

■ **Tip** If you don't see the menu in the upper right-hand corner, click on the plasma icon (the one that looks like a color palette).

___

[3] PBI is short for Push Button Installer.

The Dashboard can be used to add widgets or change folder view settings, both of which are described in more detail in this chapter. While these settings can be configured elsewhere, using the Dashboard provides an uncluttered workspace for making your changes.

Customizing the Plasma Panel

Now that we know what the default desktop looks like, it is time to customize! Figure 3-3 shows a panel that has seen several changes. Kickoff has been moved closer to the system tray, 12 application shortcuts have been added to the left of Kickoff, and several applications have been opened and minimized—these show to the left of the K3B icon. A news reader has been added to the system tray (square orange icon next to Kickoff), most of the default system tray applications have been removed, and a calendar widget has been added, which shows that the date is currently the 6th.

Figure 3-3. *Customized plasma panel*

Removing Icons

To remove an icon, simply right-click it and select Remove this Icon from the pop-up menu. It will instantly be removed from the panel.

To remove an icon from the system tray, right-click it and select Quit. A pop-up message will ask if you want to start the application the next time you login. If you select Start, it will disappear now and reappear the next time you login. If you click Do Not Start, it will stay out of the system tray. If you click Cancel, it will cancel the quit operation and remain in the system tray.

Adding Icons

Kickoff can be used to add application icons to the plasma panel. Doing so allows you to quickly access your favorite applications. Simply click on the icon in the taskbar to start the application. If you know the name of the application you would like to add, type its name into Kickoff. In this example, we'll add the Yahtzee game.

Click on Kickoff and begin to type the word yahtzee into the Search box. Once Yahtzee appears in the menu, right-click its entry in the menu and select Add to Panel as seen in Figure 3-4. An icon will be added to your taskbar; click on the icon to start playing Yahtzee.

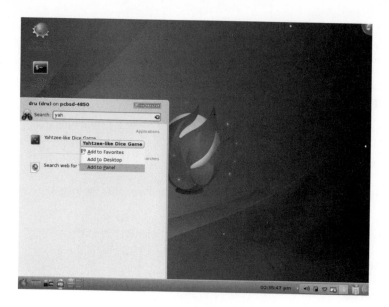

Figure 3-4. *Adding Yahtzee to the plasma panel*

Note that the pop-up menu provides two other options to quickly access the selected application. If you select Add to Favorites, Yahtzee will be added to a Favorites menu in Kickoff as seen in Figure 3.5:

Figure 3-5. *Yahtzee added to favorites*

If you select Add to Desktop, an icon will be added to your plasma workspace. This is similar to creating a desktop shortcut in Windows.

If you wish, you can add an application in all three places since you are not limited to just one choice.

If you don't know the name of the application you would like to add but know what type of application you want to use, try using Kickoff's search feature. For example, if you want to burn a CD but don't know which utility to use, type in the search term cd. If you hover over the results, you'll receive a description of the program. Figure 3-6 returns two search results. Hovering over K3b shows that it is used for CD and DVD burning. Hovering over KsCD shows that it is a CD player.

■ **Tip** Your search results may vary, depending upon which software you installed during or after the installation of PC-BSD.

Figure 3-6. Using Kickoff's search feature to find an application

If you still can't find a suitable application, click on Applications within Kickoff and browse through the various categories to see if any of the applications look interesting. We'll show you how to install additional applications in Chapter 8.

Changing Icon Graphic

To change an icon's graphic, right-click the icon and select either Icon Settings or Properties from the pop-up menu. On the General tab, you'll see a picture of the icon in the upper left-hand corner. Click on the picture to access the Icon Source screen shown in Figure 3-7. The default is to show the icons for

Applications. Click on Applications to access the menu to select a different type of icon. If you have a set of icons that you have downloaded from elsewhere, click the Other icons button to browse to the location where you saved your icons.

Figure 3-7. Selecting a different graphic for an icon

Adding Widgets

A KDE widget, also known as a plasmoid, is a small program that has only one purpose. There are widgets that show the time, monitor a laptop's battery status, or show the current temperature. There are several ways to add widgets in KDE:

- Press Ctrl+F12 to access the Dashboard. This will add the widget to the plasma workspace.

- Right-click the plasma workspace and select +Add Widgets from the pop-up menu. This will add the widget to the plasma workspace.

- Click or right-click the plasma icon in the upper right corner of your screen and select +Add Widgets from the pop-up menu. This will add the widget to the plasma workspace.

- Click the plasma icon in the plasma panel and select +Add Widgets from the menu. This will add the widget to the taskbar.

■ **Tip** Widgets can be unlocked (the default) or locked. If widgets are locked, you will see Unlock Widgets instead of Add Widgets. Once you click on Unlock Widgets, you can then add a widget using any of the above methods.

In this example, we'll add a widget to the taskbar. Figure 3-8 shows the Add Widgets screen with All Widgets selected to show additional choices. Note that you can browse through all widgets or select a category of widgets to browse. You can also see which widgets are currently running.

Figure 3-8. +Add Widget screen

If you highlight a widget and click Add Widget, its icon will be added to the plasma panel. You can then click on the icon in the panel to access the associated application.

Most widgets have their own configuration settings. Right-click a widget's icon to access its pop-up menu. If you decide that you no longer want the widget in your panel, select the Remove option in its right-click menu.

Installing New Widgets

Figure 3-8 indicates that is possible to Install New Widgets. If you click on that button, you can choose to Download New Plasma Widgets or Install Widget from Local File. If you click on the Download option, you'll see an installer menu similar to Figure 3-9:

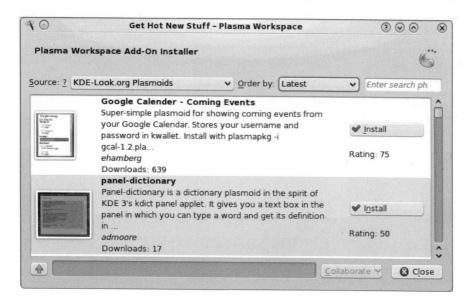

Figure 3-9. Install new widgets

This menu allows you to sort widgets by Latest, Most Downloads, or Highest Rated. You can also enter a search phrase.

If you prefer, you can use your web browser to search through the hundreds of widgets (plasmoids) available from kde-look.org. If you find a plasmoid you like, download it and use the Install Widget from Local File menu option to browse to the location where you saved the widget.

■ **Tip** Browsing through kde-look.org can become addictive and time consuming! It contains thousands of free plasmoids, themes, wallpapers and other eye-candy for your KDE desktop.

More Panel Settings

You may have noticed when you clicked on the plasma icon to add a widget that there were several other settings, as seen in Figure 3-10:

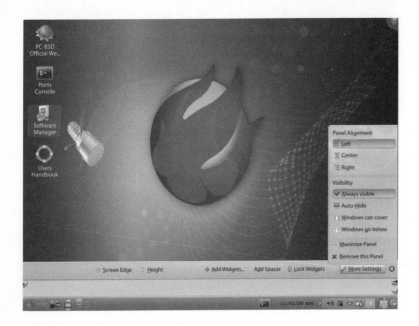

Figure 3-10. *Additional panel settings*

Moving from left to right then bottom to top, these settings allow you to do the following:

Screen Edge: Move the position and size of the taskbar. Click on Screen Edge and continue to hold down as you drag your mouse to a corner of your screen. If you don't like the new position of the taskbar, drag it to a different corner until you find a position you like. You can also use the three slider arrows in the bar between the taskbar and the settings to adjust the length of the taskbar.

Height: Adjust the height of the task bar. Click on Height and continue to hold down with your mouse as you increase or decrease the height of the taskbar. Increasing the height will also increase the size of any icons, making the taskbar easier to read. Adjust until you find a height that works for you.

+Add Widgets: Add single-use applications as described in the previous section.

Add Spacer: Separate areas of the taskbar. For example, you could separate your graphics utilities from your web browsers. Click on Add Spacer and a box with two gray lines will appear next to the plasma icon. Click on the box and four arrows will appear. Drag the box to the area of the task bar where you'd like the space to appear, then click elsewhere to let go of the box. The box will be replaced by a space on the taskbar. If you don't like its position, you can right-click the space to Remove it and try again.

Lock Widgets: Prevent taskbar icons from being added or removed. The plasma icon will also disappear, meaning panel settings cannot be modified. Simply right-click any icon and select Unlock Widgets when you need to make changes to the taskbar.

If you click on More Settings, you'll find the following:

Remove this Panel: If you select this option, you will be asked if you really want to remove this panel. If you do, you can add another panel by right-clicking the plasma icon in the upper right-hand corner of your screen and selecting +Add Panel. However, the new panel will be empty and you'll have to re-add all of your icons and widgets.

■ **Tip** If you accidently remove the original panel, you'll find several of the original icons in the +Add Widgets screen. Kickoff is listed as Application Launcher and the virtual desktop pager is listed as Pager.

Maximize Panel: If after adjusting your task bar it no longer extends to the edge of your screen, clicking this option will extend it for you.

Visibility: Select one of four choices: Windows go below, Windows can cover, Auto-hide, or Always visible. The currently selected option will be highlighted with a gray bar. For example, in Figure 3-10, Always visible is the current visibility option being used. If you select Auto-hide, the taskbar will disappear until you hover the mouse near its location. If you select Always visible, the section of an open window that is dragged near the panel will disappear.

■ **Note** You can configure a window to override the panel's Always visible setting by right-clicking the window's title bar ➤ Advanced ➤ Keep Above Others. This setting will also keep that window above other open windows.

Panel Alignment: Select one of three choices: Right, Center, or Left. Changing a setting changes the position of the slider arrows used to adjust the placement of the taskbar.

Folder Views

In KDE, a folder view provides convenient access to the contents of the directories that you use most often. A folder view can appear as a movable area that sits on top of your workspace; it is transparent, meaning you can still see your wallpaper and other icons underneath the folder view. This section will show you how to add folder views to your workspace or panel, configure folder views, add contents to a folder view, and customize your folder view settings.

Adding a Folder View

In KDE, folder views are widgets. To add a new folder view to your desktop, right-click the plasma workspace ➤ +Add Widgets ➤ Folder View ➤ Add Widget ➤ Close. By default, a folder view of your home directory will be created. If you wish the folder to display the contents of a different directory, follow the instructions in the section on Configuring Folder Views.

Adding a Folder View to the Panel

You can also add a folder view to the plasma panel by clicking on the taskbar's plasma icon ➤ +Add Widgets ➤ Folder View ➤ Add Widget ➤ Close. Again, the default folder view location will be your home directory. An icon of a blue folder will be added to your taskbar. To see the contents of the folder view, click on the icon. Figure 3-11 shows the contents of the Home folder view from both the plasma workspace and the plasma panel.

Figure 3-11. Folder view of Home from the plasma workspace and the plasma panel

Configuring Folder Views

If you hover your mouse anywhere in a plasma workspace folder view, a toolbar appears on the folder view's right edge.

■ **Tip** If the toolbar does not appear, widgets are locked. Unlock widgets to access the toolbar.

This toolbar contains four icons. Moving from the top down, these icons allow you to do the following:

Resize: This icon is a square with arrows. Move your mouse while holding down on this square until the folder view is the desired size.

Rotate: This icon looks like a circular arrow. Move your mouse while holding down on this icon and the folder view will rotate in either direction.

Configure: This icon looks like a wrench. Click on the icon to open the Folder View Settings seen in Figure 3-12. You can change the directory the folder view represents by selecting another directory in the Show a place drop-down menu or you can Specify a folder by using the browse for directory icon.

Remove: The letter X will immediately remove the folder view without asking you first. Don't worry—it is easy to create another folder view if you do this by mistake!

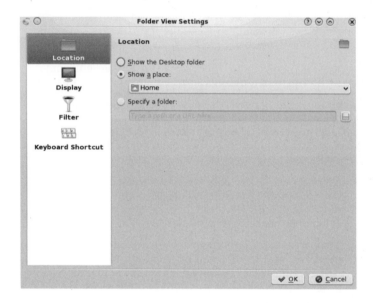

Figure 3-12. Folder view settings accessed from Configure icon of folder view toolbar

Adding Contents to a Folder View

To add an application to a folder view, highlight the application in Kickoff and use your mouse to drag it to the folder view. A pop-up menu will ask if you want to copy the application, link a shortcut, or cancel the operation.

If you have created multiple folder views, you can drag and drop any type of icon between folder views. Highlight the icon and drag it with your mouse to the other folder view. A pop-up menu will ask if you want to move, copy, link, or cancel the operation.

More Folder View Settings

Regardless of whether the folder view is on your workspace or panel, if you right-click the folder view you will access a menu of further options. These allow you to do the following:

Create New:

- **Folder:** Note that this is a subdirectory of the folder view, not another folder view.

- **Text file:** After giving the file a name, double-click on the new file's icon to add text to the file.

- **HTML file:** After giving the file a name, right-click the new file's icon to Open with Kwrite, if you want to edit HTML tags manually. Alternately, if you have an html editor, select Open With from the right-click menu and select the editor from your installed applications. If you double-click the icon, it will open the HTML file in your web browser.

- **Link to Location (URL):** type in the URL and give the link a useful name. Whenever you wish to go to that website, simply double-click the link icon.

- **Link to Application:** In the General tab, select an icon and give the link a useful name. Then click on the Application tab and use the browse button to find the application you wish to create a shortcut to. Once the link is created, you can start that application from your folder by double-clicking on its icon. This is similar to making a shortcut in Windows.

- **Link to Device:** This allows you to create a shortcut to the following devices: CD-ROM, CDWRITER, camera, DVD-ROM, floppy, hard drive, another file system (listed as MO Device in the right-click menu), a remote directory on another open source operating system (NFS), and ZIP device.

Undo: This option allows you to undo your last operation. Note that Ctrl+z appears next to this menu item. In KDE, keyboard shortcuts are listed next to their function in a menu. In other words, you can also press Ctrl+z to undo your last copy operation. In Chapter 7 we will show you how to create your own shortcuts.

Paste: Ctrl+v will also paste your last copy/cut operation from the clipboard into the currently selected file. If you press Ctrl+v multiple times, it will re-paste the text each time.

Icons: This option does not appear in the menu if the folder view is in the taskbar. If the folder view is on the plasma workspace, it allows you to

- **Sort Icons:** By name, size, type, or date. If you uncheck Folders First, subdirectories will be sorted with the other files; otherwise, they will be listed before files.

- **Align to Grid:** If this option is unchecked, you can drag your icons anywhere and they may become cluttered over time. Checking this box will keep the icons neatly aligned.

- **Lock in Place:** If this option is checked, the icon will always bounce back to its original position, even if you try to move it.

Refresh View: This option can be used to refresh the folder view if you make a change that doesn't immediately show in the view (e.g., add files to a subdirectory or edit a file).

Open with Dolphin: Dolphin is KDE's explorer utility, similar to Windows Explorer or Gnome Nautilus. Dolphin is discussed in detail in Chapter 4.

Folder View Settings: This is another way of accessing the settings available from the wrench icon of the folder toolbar.

Remove this Folder View: This option immediately removes the folder view.

Folder View or Panel Options: These allow you to do the following.

- **+Add Widgets**: Another way to add a widget.

- **+Add Panel**: Another way to add a panel.

- **Run Command**: Only available if the folder view is on the plasma workspace. It starts KRunner, which is discussed in detail in Chapter 4.

- **Lock Widgets**: Prevents changes to widgets and panels until Unlock Widgets is selected in Desktop Options.

- **Lock Screen**: Only available if the folder view is on the plasma workspace. It prevents access to the desktop unless you unlock the screen using your password. This is handy if you need to leave your desktop when other users are around.

- **Leave**: Only available if the folder view is on the plasma workspace. Logout of your desktop session.

- **Folder View Settings**: Only available if the folder view is on the plasma workspace. It allows you to set the desktop's appearance. This is discussed in more detail later on in this chapter.

- **Panel Settings**: Only available if the folder view is on the plasma panel.

- **Remove this Panel**: Only available if the folder view is on the plasma panel.

Configuring Windows

Every application you start in KDE opens in its own window. The top of the window is known as the title bar and will contain the name of the application. If you grab the title bar with your mouse, you can drag the window to any location in your workspace.

■ **Tip** You can also use a folder view's title bar to move the folder view.

If you double-click the title bar, the window will maximize, or take up your entire screen. If you double-click the title bar again, it will return to its original size. If you hover near a corner of the window, a double arrow will appear. You can then use your mouse to resize the window to the desired size.

By default, a window's title bar lists the name of the application as its title. To the left of the title is the On all desktops button; to the right of the title are the minimize, maximize/restore, and close buttons. Those buttons represent the following functions:

On all desktops: Allows you to access the window from any virtual desktop. The default is to only show the window on the current virtual desktop.

Minimize: Minimizes the window to the taskbar. Click on the minimized window to return it to your workspace.

Maximize/Restore: Makes the window fullscreen or restores a maximized window to its original size.

Close: Terminates the application. If the application has any unsaved changes, such as an editor, it should prompt you to save your changes.

Advanced Window Options

You can access many window settings by right-clicking a window's title bar. Figure 3-13 shows a listing of the Advanced settings.

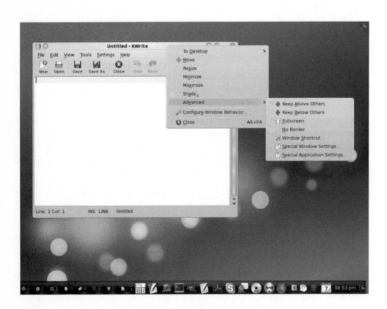

Figure 3-13. Advanced window settings

The settings found by right-clicking a window's title bar allow you to do the following:

To Desktop: Check which virtual desktops you would like the window to appear in.

Move: Allows you to easily move the window with the mouse. Click the window when you are finished to stop the move.

Resize: Allows you to change the size of the window with the mouse. Click when you are finished to stop the resizing.

Minimize/Maximize: Provides the same function as the minimize/maximize icons in the title bar.

Shade: Hides the window and just shows the title bar. Right-click the title bar and uncheck shade to see the window again.

Advanced: This option includes the following settings.

- **Keep Above Others:** The window will stay above other windows. This can be handy when you are working in one window and need to view information from another window. You may have to resize or move your windows since the other windows will stay below this window. If you set two windows to this setting, click on the window you want to see and it will become the top window; click on the other window for it to jump to the top.

- **Keep Below Others:** This window will always stay below other windows, meaning you may have to move or resize it to see its contents.

- **Fullscreen:** In fullscreen mode, the window's title bar, all other windows, and the panel disappear. A dialog message will remind you to press Alt+F3 to access the menu settings so you can toggle off fullscreen mode.

- **No Border:** This mode removes the title bar. Use Alt+F3 to access the title bar again.

- **Window Shortcut:** This allows you to create a shortcut for launching the window. If there is currently no shortcut, the shortcut dialog will say None. Click on the word None and it will change to the word Input. Type in your shortcut (e.g., Alt+d) and the word Input will change to your shortcut. If you don't like that shortcut, click it again and the word will change back to Input so you can try again. Be aware that window shortcuts are only for the lifetime of the window. When you close the window, the shortcut disappears.

- **Special Window/Application Settings:** These settings are discussed in the next section.

The remaining settings after Advanced include

Configure Window Behavior: These settings are detailed in a following section.

Close: Provides the same function as the X in the title bar.

Special Window Settings

Figure 3-14 shows the menu and informational message you receive when you select a window's Advanced ➤ Special Window Settings or Special Application Settings after right-clicking the window's title bar.

Figure 3-14. Special Window Settings or Special Application Settings configuration menu

You'll find that there are dozens of settings you can apply that affect only the window or application that you are configuring. If a setting looks interesting, check its box. This will activate its Do Not Affect drop-down menu of options. Most options deal with when to apply the change and if the change should be temporary or permanent. Some settings, such as Position and Desktop, will activate a third column where you can either type in a value or select from a list of options.

If you change a setting, press OK to see if you like the change. If not, simply go back into Special Window Settings and try again.

There are many reasons, besides curiosity, for wanting to change a window's special settings. As an example, have you ever opened a window and wished that it had opened in a different location in your workspace or opened at a different size? Special Window Settings allow you to specify exactly where and at what size that window will open, either now or permanently.

Configuring Window Behavior

Figure 3-15 shows the menu you receive when you right-click a window's title bar and select Configure Window Behavior.

Figure 3-15. Configure Window Behavior menu

This section discusses the configurations available for each option listed in the left frame of this menu.

Desktop Effects

KDE supports many effects that can transform your computer from merely useful to cool. Effects include animating a window when it is opened, minimized, maximized, or closed. Unlike Special Window Settings, effects apply to all windows, not just the window that opened the Configure Window Behavior menu. This video[4] contains a tour of some of the most popular desktop effects.

By default, effects are turned on, and if your video card supports it, compositing will be enabled. If so, spend some time in the All Effects tab to see which effects appeal to you. To try out an effect, check its box. Each effect includes

- a wrench icon, which lets you change its configuration or return it to its default configuration.

- an informational icon, which provides a brief description of the effect and contact information for the person who created the effect.

---

[4] http://video.google.com/videoplay?docid=344124698954082445#

■ **Note** Some video cards do not support desktop effects. If compositing is disabled and Resume Compositing fails, or if you receive an error message when you press Apply to try out an effect, you'll need to do some homework to see if your video card can be configured to work with desktop effects. See Chapter 11 to learn how to get help from the PC-BSD community.

If you know the name of the effect you would like to enable, type its name into the search bar on the All Effects tab to quickly find that effect. Some popular desktop effects include

Present Windows: Provides an overview of your open windows. Once you have enabled this effect, you can arrange all of your open windows side-by-side by pressing the top-left corner of the workspace with your mouse or by pressing Ctrl+F9. Ctrl+F10 will show the windows from all virtual desktops.

Desktop Cube Animation: Each virtual desktop is a side of a cube that can be rotated to select and switch to a virtual desktop.

Desktop Grid: Displays all of your virtual desktops or workspaces in a grid so you can easily drag windows between virtual desktops or select a virtual desktop. Once this effect is activated, Ctrl+F8 shows the grid. The desktop grid also supports animations.

Taskbar Thumbnails: Enables live previews of minimized windows when you move the mouse over an entry in the taskbar.

Translucency: Allows you to see the contents of a window even if another window is covering it. This effect supports several configuration settings, such as making drop-down menus translucent.

There are many ways to add animation to window events such as minimizing, closing, or moving. Try Explosion, Wobbly Windows, Fall Apart, and Magic Lamp.

Windows

This section allows you to configure the look and feel of window titles. It contains two tabs:

Window Decoration: The appearance of a window's title bar is controlled by a theme. The default theme is Nitrogen. If you click on this word, you'll see a list of other themes. If you select a theme, the bottom of the screen will show you a preview of what the title bar will look like. If you then click Apply, you'll notice that all of the title bars in any open windows will change to the new theme. Depending upon the theme, there will be several settings that you can change. These include the window title border size, where in the title the window's name appears, and whether you want stripes on either side of the window title.

Buttons: This tab allows you to customize the positions of the window title buttons. You can drag and drop to change the order of the buttons and press Apply to try out the new button positions.

Actions

This section contains two tabs:

> **Titlebar Actions:** This tab allows you to configure what happens when you double-click the title bar (the default is to maximize the window) or roll the mouse wheel over the title. You can also configure your mouse buttons to raise or lower active and inactive windows.
>
> **Window Actions:** This tab allows you to configure how you bring an inactive window into focus with your mouse buttons. You can also configure a modifier key, such as Alt or Ctrl, to work with your mouse buttons to configure an action such as raise or resize the window.

■ **Tip** While you can have many windows open on your workspace, only one window is considered active or "in focus," meaning it will accept input. When you click on an inactive window, it comes into focus and becomes the active window. Watch the title bar of your windows—depending upon your theme, the title bar of the active window will look slightly different from the inactive windows.

Focus

This section allows you to configure a delay when you activate a window and provides some controls for window switching on multiple virtual desktops.

Moving

This section provides the following options for when you move a window:

- Display content in moving windows.
- Display content in resizing windows.
- Display window geometry when moving or resizing.
- Allow moving and resizing of maximized windows.

It also allows you to set the size of the snap zone.

Advanced

This section allows you to do the following:

> **Enable hover:** When you shade a window (by choosing that option after right-clicking the title bar) the window disappears and you only see the title bar until you un-shade it. If you enable hover before shading a window, the window will reappear if you hover your mouse near the title bar.

Placement: Indicates where a window will be placed when it is started. The default Smart option will try to start the window in a section of the workspace not occupied by another window.

Window-Specific

This section allows you to access the configurations set in the Special Windows Settings, which were discussed earlier in this chapter. You can modify or delete the current configurations or add a new configuration.

Configuring Themes and Wallpapers

If you right-click your workspace and select Folder View Settings, you will see a menu similar to Figure 3-16.

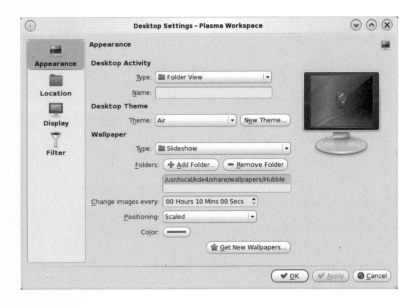

Figure 3-16. *Desktop Settings menu*

The Appearance portion of this menu allows you to set the following:

Desktop Type: The default type is Folder View, meaning that your desktop will look like a traditional desktop, with the contents of your Desktop directory showing as icons on your workspace. If you change to Desktop view, the icons will disappear. This setting will affect all of your virtual desktops.

Theme: Several themes are already installed for you. You can select a different theme from the drop-down menu. Desktop themes affect the look of panels and folders and provide a preview of their look. If you click on the New Theme button, it will open a window where you can browse and search through plasma themes at kde-look.org.

Wallpaper Type: KDE4 supports different types of wallpapers. Each option will show you a preview of the current selection. The configuration options that appear depend upon the type of wallpaper you select:

- **Color:** When selected, click on the Color bar that appears to select the color. To create a custom color, click on a colored area in the left-hand square and it will show up in the little square next to its HTML value. If you like that color, click on Add to Custom Colors. You can also click on the eyedropper icon, then click on a color from another window, and save that selection as a custom color.

- **Virus:** When selected, it will let you browse for an image and set an update interval and maximum number of viruses. Once you Apply, the wallpaper will change to your picture and the viruses will slowly eat it over time.

- **Mandelbrot:** Allows you to select three colors and the mandelbrot quality.

- **Weather:** This type of wallpaper gives you a view of the local weather anywhere in the US, UK, and Canada. Select the provider, type in a city, and click Search to receive a list of matching cities. Once you apply, your desktop should change to a picture representing the current weather conditions. If it doesn't, try another city.

- **Pattern:** Allows you to select from several patterns and to customize the foreground and background colors.

- **Image:** Allows you to browse for an image, and choose its position and a border color. Note that the border only shows in certain positions.

- **Slideshow:** Lets you select a directory of images and configure how often the images change.

- **Globe:** Lets you choose from several map themes, the type and quality of map, and the type of rotation.

Several of the wallpaper types provide a Get New Wallpapers button to allow you to browse through kde-look.org's wallpapers. If you install a wallpaper, it will be added to the drop-down selection menu for that type of wallpaper.

Switching Desktop Environments

As you have seen throughout this chapter, KDE is a highly customizable desktop environment with many features. While KDE is the default PC-BSD desktop, it is not the only desktop that was installed for you.

There are several reasons for switching desktop environments:

- KDE is resource-intensive and may run too slowly on older computer hardware.

- Some users don't like all of the bells and whistles provided by KDE and prefer a simpler desktop.

- Some users are curious or want to switch desktops "just because they can."

You will need to logout in order to switch your desktop. Click Kickoff ➤ Leave ➤ Logout. Once your session has ended you'll see a Welcome to pcbsd login box in the center of your screen. Before typing in your username and password, click on the button with three horizontal lines in the lower-left corner of the login box. A session type pop-up menu will show you which desktop environments are available to log into. The next two sections will demonstrate selecting Fluxbox and TWM from this menu.

Fluxbox

Fluxbox[5] is a light-weight desktop that is well suited to older hardware or users who prefer a desktop with less eye-candy than KDE. Select Fluxbox from the session type menu, then input your username and password to login. Figure 3-17 shows a default fluxbox session. Right-clicking the workspace produced the application launcher menu seen in the center of this figure.

Figure 3-17. Fluxbox running on PC-BSD

---

[5] http://www.fluxbox.org/

The fluxbox taskbar contains fewer icons than the KDE taskbar, but it still provides access to Kmixer, Klipper, and the PC-BSD system updater tool. Most of the applications available from a KDE session should also work in fluxbox, though you will have to manually start them from the command line if they are not listed in the application menu.

■ **Tip** If you need to switch your keyboard layout in fluxbox to support your alphabet, see `http://fluxbox-wiki.org/index.php?title=Switch_Keyboard_layout`.

TWM

If you'd like to try a desktop with absolutely no bells and whistles, select TWM[6] from the session type menu.

■ **Tip** Unless you select another option in the session type menu when you login, PC-BSD will automatically start your last desktop environment.

Figure 3-18 shows a TWM session.

---

[6] `http://xwinman.org/vtwm.php`

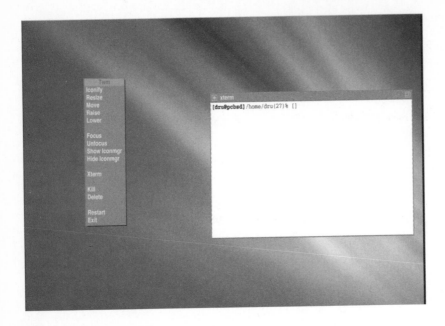

Figure 3-18. TWM desktop

When you first start TWM, all you will see is your wallpaper. Click on the desktop and hold down your mouse to see the green rectangular application launcher menu. If you drag your mouse down to Xterm, it will start a command prompt for you, but it expects you to drag the new window to the desired location. In other words, you'll see what looks like a grid, which will only turn into the white command window after you drag it to a location. As you can see from the limited choices in the application launcher menu, TWM is designed for the person who likes to type commands.

Switching to GNOME

Open source is known for providing many choices. Some users prefer the GNOME[7] (pronounced gi-nome) desktop environment. GNOME provides many of the same features as KDE, but uses a different layout. Like KDE, GNOME is an open source project with a large community of users. Many Linux desktops use GNOME instead of KDE.

While PC-BSD doesn't install GNOME for you, it is easy to install and try out GNOME on your PC-BSD computer. To install GNOME, make sure you are connected to the Internet. Click on the Software Manager icon on the Desktop or open Software Manager from Kickoff ➤ Applications ➤ System. Once you input the administrative password, a Software Browser tab will show the software that is available for install.

---

[7] See http://gnome.org

■ **Tip** Software Manager is discussed in detail in Chapter 8.

Type the word gnome into the Search bar, and you should receive search results similar to Figure 3-19. Note that the size of this PBI is large; like KDE, GNOME is a very feature-rich desktop.

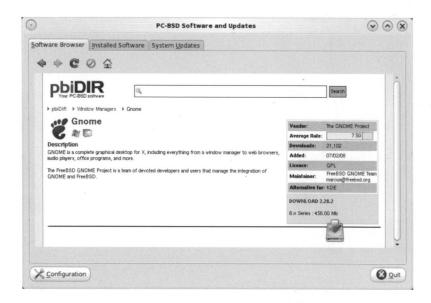

Figure 3-19. Using Software Manager to install GNOME

Click the download icon, then OK to the pop-up message that asks if you want to install GNOME. The status of your download will show in the Installed Software tab. When the download is complete, the installation of the GNOME PBI will start. Click Next through each of the installation screens to complete the install (the meaning of each installation screen is detailed in Chapter 8). Due to its size, it will take several minutes for the installation to complete.

Figure 3-20 shows the informational message you receive after GNOME is finished installing, indicating that you need to logout of your KDE session to start using GNOME.

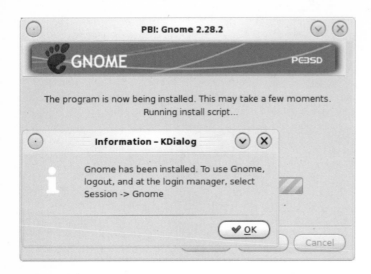

Figure 3-20. Installation of the GNOME PBI is finished.

To logout of your session, click Kickoff ➤ Leave ➤ Logout. When the login menu appears, click the button in the lower-left corner (it has three lines running through it), then select Gnome from the drop-down menu. Once GNOME is selected, input your username and password to login to a GNOME desktop. Figure 3-21 shows a default GNOME session; your desktop may vary if you have customized your KDE desktop since GNOME will show any desktop icons that you created in KDE.

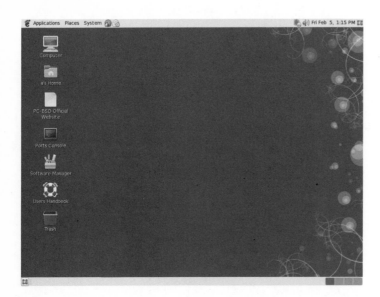

Figure 3-21. Default GNOME install on PC-BSD

GNOME provides two taskbar panels, one at the bottom and one at the top of the screen. The application launcher is located next to the GNOME foot in the upper left-hand corner. Like KDE, GNOME provides its own set of applications, meaning the Application menu will differ significantly from Kickoff's application menu.

This book does not cover how to use or customize the GNOME desktop. We recommend that interested readers refer to the GNOME User Guide.[8]

Other Desktop Managers

There are literally hundreds of open source desktop managers. Xwinman.org provides a list of the more popular desktops, including their descriptions and screenshots.

As of this writing, PC-BSD provides PBIs for the Enlightenment, KDE3, GNOME, and XFCE desktops. The x11-wm category of the FreeBSD ports collection provides nearly 150 desktops. Refer to Chapters 8 through 10 for detailed instructions on installing PBIs and software from the FreeBSD ports collection.

■ **Note** While you can install and run other desktop environments on your PC-BSD system, PC-BSD is optimized for KDE4. Most other desktops will not provide icons for PC-BSD specific graphical utilities, meaning you will have to access these utilities from the command line. Installing an alternate desktop from the FreeBSD ports collection is an exercise best left to power users or users who are experimenting on a test computer or within a virtual environment.

Summary

This chapter has introduced you to the components of the KDE4 desktop and how you can customize these components. It has also described alternative desktop environments for those users who would like to try non-KDE4 desktops.

In the next chapter, we'll learn how to launch applications using Kickoff as well as how to customize Kickoff's menus.

---

[8] http://library.gnome.org/users/user-guide/2.26/

■ ■ ■

## CHAPTER 4

Getting Around

In Chapter 3, we spent a fair bit of time customizing the look and feel of your PC-BSD system. In this chapter, we'll get down to work and show you how to find and access your files and applications. We'll include plenty of tricks and tips so you can find what you need quickly and in ways that are intuitive to you.

Dolphin File Manager

In Chapter 3, you learned how to create folder views to see and access the contents of a directory. But how do you get an overview of all of the files and directories on your system?

KDE4 provides a comprehensive file manager, known as Dolphin. To access Dolphin, click the Kickoff icon and select File Manager from the Favorites menu.

■ **Tip** Remember, you can also add Dolphin to your desktop or taskbar by right-clicking the word Dolphin in Kickoff and selecting Add to Desktop or Add to Panel from the pop-up menu.

Figure 4-1 provides a screenshot of Dolphin with a file selected.

Figure 4-1. Dolphin file manager

Note the red - next to the sometext.txt file, indicating that it is the currently selected file whose contents are displayed in the Information panel.

Directories in Dolphin are represented by the folder icon. If you use your mouse to hover over an icon, the Information panel will display its contents and give you some information about the selected file or folder. If you double-click an icon, you will either see its contents (if it is a folder) or launch an application capable of opening the file. Use the back and forward buttons to navigate between a selected folder and its contents.

Right-clicking an icon will open a pop-up menu with several options. The available options vary depending upon whether the icon represents a directory or file, and by type of file. Many of the options are intuitive so we will discuss only the ones you may not be familiar with. Here are options for directories:

Open in New Tab: Tabs provide a useful view to focus on a folder's contents and allow you to view several files or folders at once. You can open as many tabs as you wish. To close a tab, click on its orange X.

Add to Places: This will add the directory to the Places panel on the left, allowing easy access to that directory. For example, you may find it useful to add your Downloads or Music folder if you access these directories often.

Open with: Allows you to view the contents of a directory or open a file with the specified application. If the application you would like to use is not in the list, select Other and browse for the application.

The following actions are also available:

- **Subversion:** Subversion allows you to keep up-to-date with a "repository" of files on another system. Subversion is discussed in more detail in Chapter 15.[1]

- **Archive/Sign/Encrypt/Decrypt:** Chapter 5 will show you how to setup encryption keys so you can protect the contents of a folder. You can also perform these actions on individual files.

- **Open Terminal Here:** Will open Konsole so you can type into a command prompt.

- **Start a Slideshow:** Allows you to view the contents of a folder as a slideshow. Press Esc to end the slideshow and return to your original screen.

You should experiment with the Icons, Details, Columns, Preview, and Split buttons to see which view you prefer. For example, split view makes it easy to drag and drop contents between folders.

■ **Tip** The second column will be empty in Column view until you double-click an icon in the first column. You can use your mouse in Details view to change the width of the Name, Size, and Date columns. Right-click that area to select from a menu of possible details you can view.

Dolphin Menu Options

Dolphin provides additional options through the menus below the title bar. Most of these options are intuitive so we will highlight some useful features:

- File ➤ Properties ➤ General will show you how much free space is left on your hard drive.

- View ➤ Navigation Bar ➤ Editable Location opens a location bar where you can type in the name of the folder/file you would like to view.

- Tools ➤ Find File allows you to search using a variety of factors, such as a file's name, contents, date, size, or owner.

---

[1] To learn more about subversion, visit its website at http://subversion.tigris.org

- Tools ➤ Show Filter Bar allows you to type in text so you can just view the icons matching that text.

- Tools ➤ Compare Files allows you to see if there are differences between two files or the contents of two folders. Use Split view to highlight the icons to compare or hold down the Ctrl key to select two icons.

- Help ➤ Dolphin Handbook (or F1 while in Dolphin) will show you how to get the most out of Dolphin.

Dolphin Places

Places allow you to quickly access the data locations you use most frequently. You can right-click any folder and select Add to Places. Once a folder is added to Places, it is also added to the Kickoff ➤ Computer menu, allowing you to quickly access its contents.

The default Places include Home, Network, Root, and Trash. These are discussed below.

Home

By default, Dolphin will present you with the contents of your home folder. When you create your own files or folders, you should save them somewhere within your home folder. This makes it easier to find and backup your own data. It also prevents you from inadvertently modifying or deleting important files needed by the operating system. To create a new file or folder, simply right-click any empty area within the Home view and select Create New from the pop-up menu.

Network

If there are other computers in your home or work network, this portion of Places allows you to browse the resources being shared by those computers. Figure 4-2 shows a screenshot of Network Places. If you double-click the Network icon, you will see the computers in your network. If you double-click the Samba Shares icon, you'll see the network's workgroup; you can browse the workgroup to see which network shares are available.

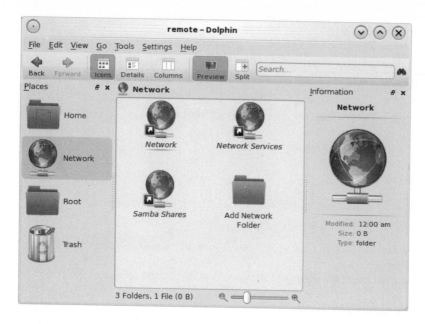

Figure 4-2. Network Places in Dolphin

If you hover over each icon in Network Places and read the text at the bottom of your screen, you'll see that each shortcut is actually a link to one of these three KIO slave protocols:

- network:/
- zeroconf:/
- smb:/

In KDE, a KIO slave controls one of nearly 50 supported protocols, with each protocol providing access to a type of resource. For example, the network KIO slaves seen in Network Places provide quick access to resources on different types of networks.

Another way to take advantage of KIO slaves in Dolphin is to check View ➤ Navigation Bar ➤ Editable Location. You can then type in a protocol name to access the associated resource.

Commonly used KIO slave protocols are listed in Table 4-1. It is worth spending some time typing each into Dolphin's navigation bar to see which protocols are useful to you. Don't forget to include the :/ after the name; for example, with an audio CD in your drive, type audiocd:/ to view the contents of the CD (don't just type audiocd).

Table 4-1. Useful KIO Slave Protocols

Protocol	Description
audiocd:/	Show tracks on an audio CD.
bookmarks:/	Display Konqueror (KDE's default web browser) bookmarks.
desktop:/	Access the files in the Desktop folder.
floppy:/	Access the floppy drive.
fonts:/	View installed fonts. This is a very quick way to access both your personal and system fonts.
ftp://	Note the double slash. Provides quick access to the files on a specified ftp server.
imap:/	Can be used by power users to connect to the specified IMAP mail server.
ldap:/	Can be used by power users to connect to the specified LDAP server.
mailto:/	Open a mail program (Kmail by default) to compose an email.
man:/	Can be used by power users to read system documentation. If you know the name of the command whose documentation you'd like to read, put it after the /. For example, type man:/ls to read the documentation for the ls command.
network:/	View other computers on the network.
nfs:/	Can be used by power users to connect to the specified NFS share.
nntp:/	Can be used by power users to connect to a specified news server.
programs:/	Quickly browse installed applications.
settings:/	Access advanced and general system settings.
sftp://	Can be used by power users to securely transfer files to/from the specified computer over SSH. Note the double slash. In Split view, you can drag and drop files between systems once the connection has been established.

Protocol	Description
smb:/	Browse Samba[2] and Windows shares.
trash:/	View contents of trashcan.
webdav:/	Can be used by power users to access shared files on a web server using WebDAV.[3]
zeroconf:/[4]	View other computers using zeroconf.

All of the protocols listed in Table 4-1 also work if you type them into KDE's web browser, Konqueror. More Konqueror tips are discussed later in this chapter.

■ **Tip** Once you have accessed a resource using a KIO slave protocol in Dolphin, if you find it handy, right-click on an empty space in its view and select Add to Places to create a shortcut to the resource.

Adding a Network Folder

The Add Network Folder in Network Places allows you to create your own network folders. If you double-click this icon, you will launch the Network Folder Wizard seen in Figure 4-3.

---

[2] Samba allows you to access shares on Windows computers. See `http://www.samba.org` for more information.

[3] The Wikipedia entry for WebDAV provides a good introduction: `http://en.wikipedia.org/wiki/Webdav`.

[4] The Wikipedia entry on zerofconf provides a good introduction: `http://en.wikipedia.org/wiki/Zeroconf`.

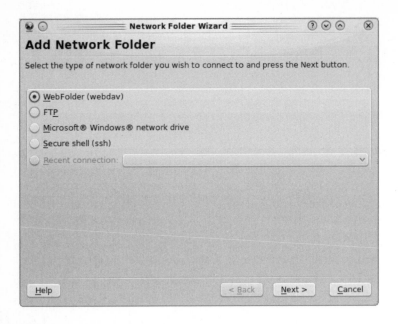

Figure 4-3. *The Add Network Folder wizard*

Select the type of network folder you would like to create and click Next. You will then be prompted for further information (such as the address of the server you would like to connect to). This is similar to mapping a network drive in Windows, but you are able to connect to a wider variety of network services.

Root

In Dolphin, Root Places refers to the root, or beginning, of the operating system's file system, not to the administrative user's home directory (the administrative user is also known as root). In other words, it allows you to see all of your system's parent folders. Figure 4-4 shows a screenshot of Root Places with the Icons view selected.

Figure 4-4. *Root Places in Dolphin*

Most of the folders are system folders, meaning their contents are needed by the operating system. You should leave these folders as-is unless you are an administrator and understand the changes you are making.

If you have used Linux before, you probably recognize some of the folder names. However, the contents of the folders may be different from what you are used to on your Linux system. man:/hier will explain the contents of all of the folders except PCBSD and Programs, which are unique to the PC-BSD operating system. Table 1 in the Appendix provides an overview of each folder and indicates which folders should be left as-is.

Trash

You probably recognize the concept of a trash or recycle bin. By default, any files you delete using Dolphin will be placed in Trash and stay there until you empty it. If you click on Trash, you can view your recently deleted files. Right-click a file to either Restore it or permanently Delete it, as seen in Figure 4-5:

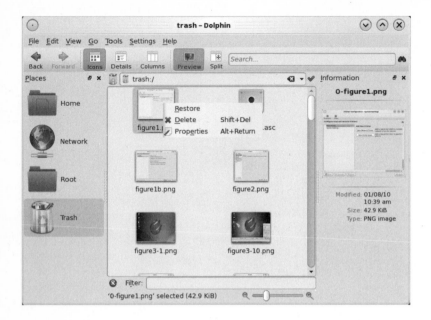

Figure 4-5. Right-clicking a deleted file in Trash Places

■ **Note** Any file you delete from the command line does NOT go into Trash, meaning it is instantly deleted.

You can also access Trash Places by double-clicking the Trashcan icon in your taskbar. If you right-click the Trashcan icon in the taskbar, you can quickly and permanently delete all of the files in Trash Places by selecting Empty Trashcan. Figure 4-6 shows the configuration menu you receive when you select Trashcan Settings from the Trashcan icon's right-click menu.

Figure 4-6. Trashcan settings menu

Konqueror

Konqueror is KDE's built-in web browser; it can be accessed from Kickoff ➤ Web Browser. Konqueror is much more than just a web browser and has features that allow you to quickly access and manipulate files. This section provides some useful tips for using Konqueror.

The first time you open Konqueror, you will see a screen similar to Figure 4-7.

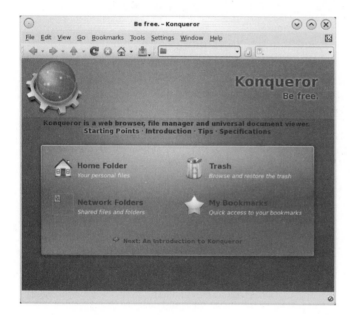

Figure 4-7. Main screen of Konqueror

The top portion of Konqueror looks like a web browser as it provides a toolbar of icons, a location bar where you can type in an Internet URL, and a search bar. The middle section provides links to quickly access your Home folder, trashcan, network folders, and your web bookmarks. In other words, anything you can do in Dolphin, you can also do in Konqueror. If this is your first time using Konqueror (or if you only have used Konqueror for web browsing), take a few minutes and click on the link entitled Next: An Introduction to Konqueror.

You can also access your files using Konqueror's location bar. Try typing file:/ . If you pause slightly after the slash, all of the folders on your system will appear in the scroll-down menu. You can either select one, or keep typing. The more you type, the more Konqueror narrows down the folder and file names that match the path you have typed. Once you have selected or typed the path to the desired file, Konqueror will display it for you using a plugin for an application that understands the file format. For example, if you select a text file, Konqueror will display the text and allow you to modify the text. Konqueror will add a Save and Save As icon to the toolbar so you can save your changes to the file. If you select a graphic, Konqueror will add Zoom icons to the toolbar to assist you in viewing the image. Konqueror has been designed to display many types of files and to modify the icons in the toolbar so that they make sense for the type of file being displayed. For some file formats, such as Office documents or PDF files, Konqueror will open the file in an external program.

If you explore Konqueror's menus, you'll find all kinds of intriguing options that deal with files and web browsing. Here are a few examples to get you started:

- If a website gives an error stating that your browser is unsupported, try setting Tools ➤ Change Browser Identification to a different value.

- If you have a bunch of tabs open that you aren't finished with, but you need to shutdown your system, click File ➤ Sessions ➤ Save As and give your session a name. You can reopen that session later as it will be added to your File ➤ Sessions menu.

- To translate a webpage, select the to and from languages from Tools ➤ Translate Web Page.

- To see your file system while you browse the Internet, select Settings ➤ Show Navigation Panel. You can then drag a download link from the web browser panel to a location in the Navigation Panel. Figure 4-8 provides an example of dragging the downloadable link labeled English to the Documents directory. Selecting Copy Here will download the file associated with the link. You can also view two websites simultaneously using the Split View options from the Window menu. Click on one of the panes to use the location bar.

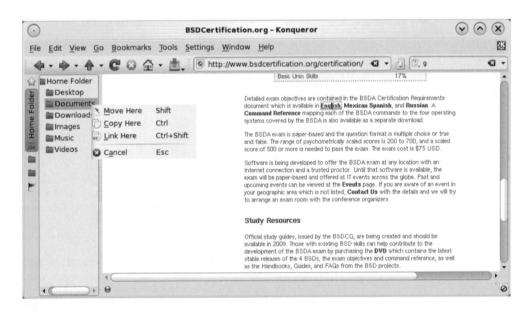

Figure 4-8. Dragging a download link to Konqueror's Navigation panel

We have barely scratched the surface of all of the cool things you can do in Konqueror. Spend some time poking about—you may find that you can access anything you want on your PC-BSD system from this one utility!

KRunner

KRunner is a handy way to start applications. Figure 4-9 shows the KRunner interface. While it looks quite simple, KRunner has some pretty nifty built-in features.

Figure 4-9. KRunner

Press Alt-F2 to launch KRunner. If you know the name of the application you would like to start, type its name into the dialog box. If you're not sure of the name of the application, start typing a search term and KRunner will present you with a list of applications that match, as seen in Figure 4-10. The down arrow to the right of the type-in box can be used to scroll through recently launched programs.

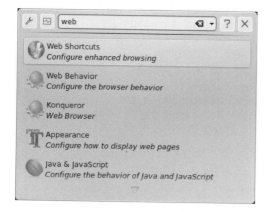

Figure 4-10. Using KRunner to find an application using a search term

KRunner isn't limited to just finding and launching applications. You can also use it as a

Calculator: Type in your equation using * for multiplication, / for division, + for addition, and – for subtraction. Put the = sign *before* the equation and don't use any spaces. Figure 4-11 shows the result of multiplying 12 and 1024.

Figure 4-11. Using KRunner to multiply 12 and 1024

Unit converter: Need to convert miles to kilometers? Try typing "100 miles in km." Typing "100 euros in ca" will convert euros to Canadian dollars. KRunner supports several types of unit conversions. Try typing the unit that you know and KRunner will respond with a list of what it is able to convert to.

Web shortcut: If you type gg:bsd, KRunner will open a tab in your default browser and display Google's (gg:) results for the search term "bsd." If you prefer to instead see the Wikipedia entry for the term bsd, type wp:bsd. You can view other existing web shortcuts and create your own in Konqueror ➤ Settings ➤ Configure Konqueror ➤ Web Shortcuts, as seen in Figure 4-12.

Figure 4-12. Configure Web Shortcuts menu in Konqueror's settings

To create a new web shortcut, click on New. Figure 4-13 shows the values you would input to map "fp:" to Freshport's search utility (Freshport is discussed in more detail in Chapter 9). Note that the Search URI always ends in \{@} as this tells Konqueror to add the search phrase you type after the shortcut. After pressing OK, the new shortcut will show up in the Web Shortcuts menu. Don't forget to check its box and press Apply in order to start using the shortcut in KRunner.

■ **Tip** If you check the Enable Web shortcuts box, web shortcuts will also work within Konqueror. Otherwise, they will only work with KRunner.

Figure 4-13. Creating a new web shortcut for KRunner

KRunner supports other operations using a plugins system. You can configure which plugins are available by clicking on the wrench button on the far left of KRunner. Figure 4-14 shows some of the available plugins. If one sounds interesting, click its informational button (to the right of the plugin name) to receive a short description of the plugin.

Figure 4-14. KRunner plugins

Click on the User Interface tab if you would like to preview an alternate KRunner interface.

The button next to KRunner's configure button that looks like a square with a squiggly line in the middle is the Show System Activity button. Clicking this button will show a screen similar to Figure 4-15—your screen will differ depending upon which applications you have running on your system.

Name	Username ▼	CPU %	Memory	Shared Mem	Window Title
kdeinit4	dru	5%	39840 K		
kdeinit4	dru		66436 K		System Activity
plasma-...	dru		59808 K		
ksnapshot	dru		32788 K		figure4-8.png – KSnapshot
kdeinit4	dru		65788 K		
knotify4	dru		42596 K		
kdeinit4	dru		38424 K		
ksnapshot	dru		36248 K		
kwin	dru		36040 K		
kgpg	dru		32040 K		
ark	dru		31244 K		
ark	dru		31204 K		
mysqld	dru		28928 K		
kdeinit4	dru		28024 K		
korgac	dru		27076 K		
kdeinit4	dru		26320 K		
kdeinit4	dru		26264 K		

Figure 4-15. KRunner's system activity window

If your system is running slowly, you can use this utility to determine if an application is slowing things down. Check out the CPU% column. Things are normal if the number is quite low. If the number is very high, that application is slowing your system down.

■ **Tip** You can also type ksysguard into KRunner. This will open up a similar window, but will add a System Load column, as seen in Figure 4-16.

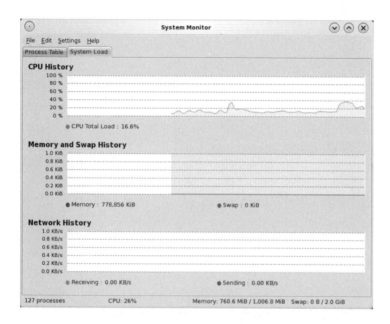

Figure 4-16. Viewing system load in ksysguard

Launching Applications with Kickoff

Kickoff, the right flame icon in the far left corner of your taskbar, provides another way to view and launch your applications.

■ **Tip** In addition to the Kickoff application that was pre-installed in the taskbar panel, there are two Application Launcher widgets (Kickoff style and traditional style) and a QuickLaunch widget. Any of these can be added to a panel or your plasma workspace. The Quicklaunch widget allows you to quickly launch the applications contained in your Favorites.

This section will concentrate on the Kickoff style application launcher. Figure 4-17 shows the menu you see when you click on Kickoff.

Figure 4-17. Kickoff menu

If you type in a search phrase, Kickoff will display any applications that match by name or description.

The bottom of Kickoff contains five icons:

> **Favorites:** If you right-click an item in Kickoff, you have the option of adding it to your Favorites menu. If you right-click an item in Favorites, you can add it to your Desktop or Panel or remove it from Favorites.

> **Applications:** This utility sorts your installed applications into categories, as seen in Figure 4-18. If you click on a category, the menu will slide in the direction of the arrow; use the arrows to browse back and forth between a category and its list of applications.

Figure 4-18. Kickoff's Applications menu

Computer: Provides quick access to System Settings, KRunner, and Dolphin's Places.

Recently Used: Provides quick access to recently used applications and documents.

Leave: Provides quick access to logout, lock, switch user, restart, and shutdown functions.

If you right-click the Kickoff icon, you will access a menu of the following choices:

Menu Editor: Allows you to customize Kickoff's categories and which applications appear in which categories. This is discussed further in the next section.

Switch to Classic Menu Style: Allows you to view and launch applications using the previous KDE style. Figure 4-19 shows the Classic Menu. The top five applications (without arrows) represent the past five applications used on this system.

Figure 4-19. *Classic menu style*

Application Launcher Settings: These allow you to change the Kickoff icon, switch tabs on hover, show applications by name, and set a keyboard shortcut to launch Kickoff.

Remove this Application Launcher: If you do so, you can re-add the Application Launcher widget at a later time.

■ **Tip** If you ever lose the PC-BSD flame icon and want to reapply it to Kickoff, use Application Launcher Settings ➤ Select Icon ➤ Other icons ➤ Browse ➤ /usr/share/skel/.fluxbox/icons/pcbsd.png.

Menu Editor

KDE provides the ability to modify the categories and applications that appear in Kickoff. Figure 4-20 shows a screenshot of Menu Editor, the utility provided for this purpose. Right-click the Kickoff icon to open the Menu Editor.

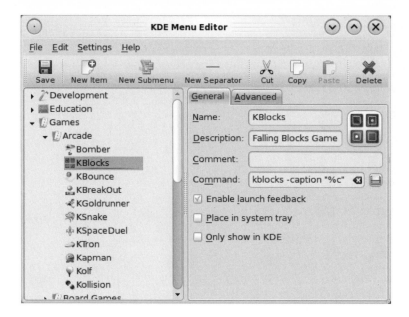

Figure 4-20. Menu Editor utility

Each of the categories found in Kickoff's Application panel will appear in Menu Editor's left frame. Click on the arrow next to a category to see its list of applications. If you highlight an application, the right frame will activate, allowing you to modify its settings. In Figure 4-20 the KBlocks application in Games ➤ Arcade is highlighted. The General tab allows you to configure the following items:

Name & Description: These are searched whenever you type a search phrase in Kickoff, so it can be useful to use descriptions that make sense to you. For example, if you have difficulty remembering the name of the software used to burn CDs, make sure its description contains "burn" so you can search for that term.

Icon Source: Click on the graphic to change the application's icon. Figure 4-21 shows the browse menu that opens for this purpose.

Figure 4-21. Using Menu Editor to change the icon that appears next to an application in Kickoff

Comment: Only shows in Menu Editor. This can be useful if you have multiple versions of an application.

Command: Power users can add switches to modify a program's behavior.

Enable launch feedback: If checked, you'll see a little bouncy icon while the application is starting.

Place in system tray: This will place an icon for the application in the system tray when you open the application.

Only show in KDE: If checked, the application will show in KDE application launchers but not in other desktop environments, such as GNOME.

The Advanced tab allows power users to configure these items:

Work path: The location where the application starts.

Run in terminal: Check this box if you are adding a command line application.

Run as a different user: Check this box and type in "root" if the application needs to start as the super user.

Current shortcut key: Allows you to set or change the shortcut key to launch the application.

While in Menu Editor, you can cut, copy, paste, or delete any category or application. You can also add a new item, submenu, or separator through the menus, icons, or by right-clicking. This allows you to customize Kickoff to meet your needs.

Summary

This chapter has shown you the many ways you can find files and launch applications within KDE. Chapter 5 will further explore the applications available on your PC-BSD system and demonstrate how to perform common tasks.

CHAPTER 5

■■■

Performing Common Tasks

Now that you know how to get around your customized desktop, it's time to start using PC-BSD! In this chapter, we introduce you to some of the software that is available for your day-to-day computing needs. We also show you how to perform various computing tasks such as encrypting or compressing files, importing your data from another system, accessing data on removable drives, configuring a printer, and sharing your desktop.

Which Built-In Application Do I Use?

If you've used only Windows operating systems, it can take some time to get used to the idea of having literally thousands of applications at your fingertips, all at no cost to you. For any given task, a choice of applications is usually available to suit the needs of any type of user. Some applications are barebones with command-line programs that get the job done, whereas others are feature-rich with a snazzy looking interface. Several other choices range between barebones and feature-rich.

You might find that the applications you are used to using and paying for are missing on PC-BSD. This doesn't mean that you can't use those applications on PC-BSD because you might still be able to use them. There is also a good possibility that an equivalent program is already installed or available for PC-BSD. In fact, there are probably several equivalent programs available, some of which might even contain features not provided by your original program. This is part of the open source experience—discovering the world of software choices and possibilities available to you.

PC-BSD installs many useful applications for you. Many start with the letter K, meaning that they come with the KDE desktop. These applications can be launched from Kickoff or KRunner.

■ **Note** If you use KDE on another operating system, it might include the applications mentioned here, depending upon which KDE components are installed with that operating system.

Many of these applications are intuitive to use. If one sounds interesting, start it and poke about its menus. Don't forget that each application should have its own handbook that is accessible if you click F1 in the application or go to its Help menu. The application's handbook is a good reference for learning more about how to use the features provided by the program.

■ Table 2 in the Appendix provides a summary of some of the built-in applications and where you can find them in Kickoff ➤ Applications. It also provides a handy reference when you're wondering which application is available to perform a certain task.

Which PBI Do I Use?

PC-BSD uses the PBI (Push Button Installer) system to make it easy to find, install, run, and uninstall commonly used applications. We demonstrate in detail how to use the PBI system in Chapter 8.

Table 3 in the Appendix lists some of the most popular software available using the PBI system. If you want to install additional software, spend some time perusing the websites listed in this table. You'll probably find what you're looking for, and the websites contain all of the screenshots, feature lists, and documentation you need to get started with using the application.

■ **Tip** If you have existing Windows applications you have already purchased, spend some time checking out Bourdeaux, Crossover Games, Wine, and Virtual Box, which are listed in Table 3 of the Appendix. If you can't find your favorite Linux application, refer to the "When You Can't Find Your Favorite Application" section in Chapter 8.

Windows Equivalents

If you are used to using the Windows operating system, you might want to know which specific applications provide similar functionality to the applications you have been using. If you don't have time to look for software, Table 4 in the Appendix contains a list of software available for the PC-BSD and the equivalent application for Windows.

These equivalents will get you to work on your PC-BSD system in no time. However, we still recommend that when you have more time, you look for other equivalents. A lot of great software exists, and you might not know what you're missing!

Importing Data

The last consideration when researching which software is best for you is how to get your existing data into the new application. Many applications have made it easy for Windows users to migrate their existing data. Table 5-1 lists some common data sources and websites that contain instructions about how to import that data into the listed application. Note that the data sources listed in this table are in formats that need to be imported into the new application, meaning that you can't just copy the files over to your PC-BSD system.

Table 5-1. *Import Instructions for Common Data Sources*

Data Source	New Application	Instructions
Accounting data	KMyMoney	`http://kmymoney2.sourceforge.net/online-manual/details.impexp.ofx.html`
Bookmarks	Firefox	`http://kb.mozillazine.org/Import_bookmarks`
	Konqueror	`http://docs.kde.org/stable/en/kdebase-runtime/faq/webbrowser.html`
MS Outlook email/contacts	Thunderbird	`http://kb.mozillazine.org/Import_.pst_files`
	Evolution	`http://library.gnome.org/users/evolution/stableimporting-mail-and-settings.html.en`

For data that doesn't need to be imported, several utilities make it easy to drag and drop existing files and directories from your old system to your PC-BSD system. If the existing data is on a network share, you can use Split View in Konqueror. In Figure 5-1, the user dru opens Konqueror, and then clicks Window ➤ Split View Left/Right. She then clicks the Home Folder link in the left frame to show the home directory of her PC-BSD system.

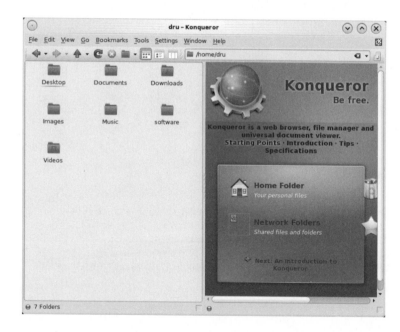

Figure 5-1. *Using Split View in Konqueror to copy between two systems over the network*

The user can now click on the Network Folders link in the left frame, and then click the Samba Shares icon to browse for the files to copy over the network. The user simply drags the file to copy from one pane to the other.

■ **Tip** This chapter assumes that the network share is already configured for you. Chapter 7 demonstrates how to create network shares on your PC-BSD system and discusses the basics of Samba shares.

If the existing data is on a system running SSH, use sftp:// in one of Konqueror's panes to connect to the other system. You can then drag and drop between panes. Figure 5-2 demonstrates a connection to a computer with the IP address 192.168.1.105 and the username dlavigne6. Before the connection is completed, a pop-up message prompts for the password of the user.

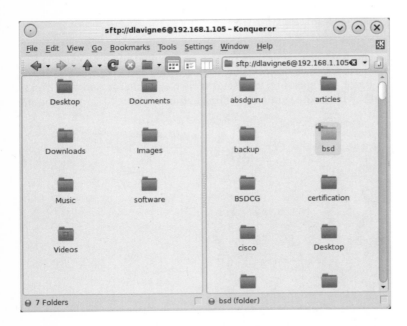

Figure 5-2. Using sftp:// within Konqueror to copy files between two systems.

■ **Tip** SSH is a secure method for transferring files. It is often seen on open-source systems and is what system administrators use most often to transfer files.

If you have backed up your existing data to an external USB drive, simply plug it into your PC-BSD system. It automatically displays in Dolphin's places. In the example shown in Figure 5-3, the user has opened Dolphin and clicked View ➤ Split. She highlighted the left pane and clicked Home, and then she highlighted the right pane and clicked Volume (ufs). She can now drag and drop files between her computer and the USB hard drive.

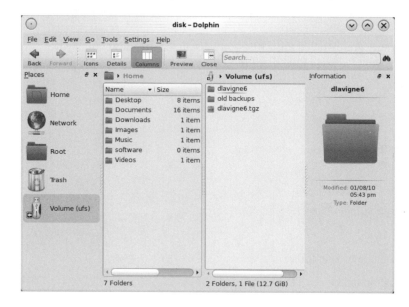

Figure 5-3. *Using Dolphin to copy files between a PC-BSD computer and a USB hard drive*

When finished using the USB drive, don't forget to right-click the USB media and select Unmount Volume (ufs) from the menu before physically unplugging the device. This is the safe way to eject the device and to let your PC-BSD system know that you are finished using the USB drive.

Web Browser

The rest of this chapter demonstrates how to perform some common tasks on PC-BSD. We start with some of the features users expect to see in their web browsers.

Flash and Java

Your PC-BSD system comes with Java and the latest version of Flash (as of February 2010, version 10) pre-installed and preconfigured for you. Multimedia websites such as Youtube, video.google.com, veoh.com, and moviefone.com should work in Konqueror and the Firefox PBI.

■ **Note** If you happen to come across a website that doesn't work, see Chapter 11 for instructions on how to get help from the PC-BSD forums.

MS TrueType Fonts

Your PC-BSD system comes with many pre-installed fonts (these are discussed in Chapter 6). If you wish, you can also use Software Manager to install the PBI for MS TrueType Fonts, which adds the following fonts to your system:

- Andale Mono
- Arial Black
- Arial (Bold, Italic, Bold Italic)
- Comic Sans MS (Bold
- Courier New (Bold, Italic, Bold Italic)
- Georgia (Bold, Italic, Bold Italic)
- Impact
- Times New Roman (Bold, Italic, Bold Italic)
- Trebuchet (Bold, Italic, Bold Italic)
- Verdana (Bold, Italic, Bold Italic)
- Webdings

Files

Chapter 4 introduced you to the Dolphin File Manager. This section shows you how to encrypt/decrypt and compress/uncompress your files, and how to access the contents of the clipboard.

File Encryption

When you encrypt and decrypt files, you use something known as a public/private key pair. As the name suggests, the public key is made available to others, the private key must be kept secret and available only to yourself, and the two keys are related as a pair. Wikipedia provides a good introduction to encryption concepts at `http://en.wikipedia.org/wiki/Public-key_cryptography`.

Before you can encrypt or decrypt files, you have to generate a public/private key pair. The next section shows you how to do this using KDE's Gpg Assistant. If you already have a key pair, you can skip ahead to the "Encrypting/Decrypting" section.

Creating a Key Pair for Encryption

KGpg Assistant can be used to generate your key pair. You can access this application using Kickoff ➤ Applications ➤ Utilities ➤ Encryption Tool.

The Assistant starts with some informational messages as it goes through the process of creating a key pair for you. You can accept the default locations for the GnuPG binary and configuration file and leave the boxes checked to generate the new key and start KGpg automatically at KDE startup.

The assistant then opens a tip message and the Key Generation - KGpg menu seen in Figure 5-4.

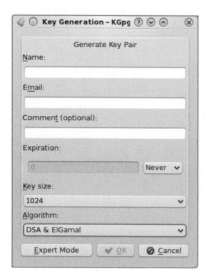

Figure 5-4. Generating a key pair with KGpg

You can complete this configuration screen as follows.

Name: Input your first and last name so others know to whom the key belongs.

Email: Input the email address you would like to associate with the key.

Comment (optional): This field is optional and can help remind you why you use the key.

Expiration: By default, your key never expires. You can select days, weeks, months, or years from the drop-down menu, and then type in the desired value.

Key size: The larger the key size, the harder it is to bypass the encryption provided by the key. You should select the largest key size available.

Algorithm: Unless you have a reason to change this to RSA, you can use the default.

Expert Mode: Power users can use this button to generate keys at the command line.

Tip The KGpg Handbook contains information about each of the menus contained in the KGpg program. You can access it by pressing F1 in the program or by selecting Help ➤ KGpg Handbook.

After you enter the values and click OK, a screen displays where you should type in your passphrase. It is *important* that you choose a passphrase that you can easily remember, but that is difficult for others to guess. The passphrase is needed to decrypt your files; if you lose it, you can't access the contents of your encrypted data. If someone else guesses it, he can access your encrypted data. After you input your passphrase two times, you will see a screen similar to the one shown in Figure 5-5.

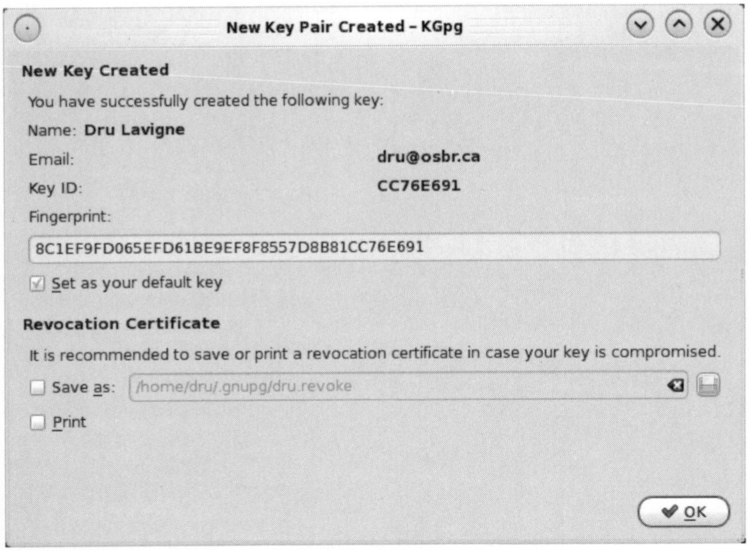

Figure 5-5. New Key Pair Created - KGpg confirmation screen

The fingerprint is unique to the key and can be used to determine that you are using the correct key. If you send your public key to others, they can use the fingerprint to verify that the key is correct. You should either save or print the revocation certificate. If you forget your passphrase or if your private key is compromised or lost, the revocation certificate is used to notify others that they should no longer use that public key. A revoked public key can still be used to verify signatures made by you in the past, but it cannot be used to encrypt future messages to you. It does not affect your ability to decrypt existing messages, assuming you remember your passphrase.

After you click OK, the new key pair displays in the Key Management screen. You're now ready to encrypt and decrypt your files.

Encrypting/Decrypting

Now that you have a key pair, let's go back to Dolphin. Right-click the file you would like to encrypt and select Actions. As seen in Figure 5-6, there are two Encrypt File actions; the first uses the KGpg utility, and the second uses the Kleopatra application. We demonstrate both utilities.

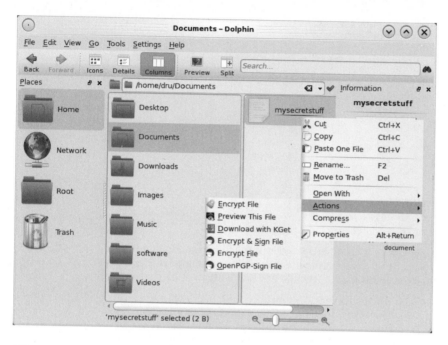

Figure 5-6. Encrypting file actions in Dolphin

To encrypt with KGpg, select the first Encrypt File option. KGpg presents the menu seen in Figure 5-7. Click the Options button to see the possible encryption options.

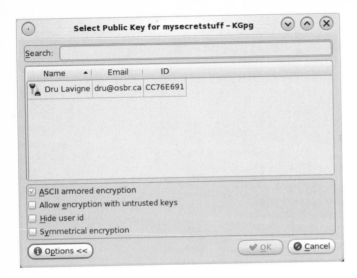

Figure 5-7. Using KGpg to encrypt a file

Before highlighting your key and clicking OK, review the options.

> *ASCII armored encryption:* This does not encrypt the file; instead, it adds an encrypted "envelope" that protects the file from getting mangled by email programs. If you choose this option, the file will end with an .asc extension.

> *Allow encryption with untrusted keys:* This option is not needed for encrypting your own files in Dolphin. If you are using KGpg to encrypt an email message, you need to use the recipient's public key to encrypt the message so he can use his private key to decrypt it. This means that you have to first import the recipient's public key into KGpg; at that time, you will have the option to indicate whether or not you trust the key.

> *Hide user id:* This option is useful only when using KGpg to encrypt email. It removes the recipient information; if the wrong recipient receives the email, he won't know the name of the key to use to decrypt the message.

> *Symmetrical encryption:* This is the option that actually encrypts the message. It prompts you to enter your passphrase twice.

Because your intent is to encrypt the file, select the Symmetrical encryption option. It is up to you to keep the ASCII armored encryption option selected or deselect it. If you're planning on emailing the file, it is good to keep this option. If you uncheck this option, the encrypted file will end with a .gpg extension instead of an .asc extension. The resulting file will be placed in the same directory and have the same name as the original file with the new extension added.

If you select the second Encrypt File action, the file is encrypted with Kleopatra instead. When Kleopatra first starts, it displays a self-test screen; if you don't want to see this screen, uncheck the Run these tests at startup box. Click the Continue button to see the screen in Figure 5-8.

Figure 5-8. Kleopatra encryption manager

Kleopatra offers the following options.

> *Sign and encrypt:* This option encrypts the file and proves that it came from you (was signed by you). This is useful when emailing a file.

> *Encrypt only:* This option is similar to the Symmetrical encryption option in KGpg.

> *Sign only:* This option does not encrypt the file, but proves it came from you; again, this is useful when emailing a file.

> *ASCII armor:* This option is similar to the ASCII armored encryption option in KGpg.

> *Remove unencrypted original:* Because this option removes the original file, don't forget your passphrase because you will need it to access the contents of the decrypted file.

After you select your option(s), click Next. The next menu prompts you to highlight the file you plan to encrypt. After you do this, you click Next.

The Recipients menu might seem strange if you are not sending the file to anyone (for example, you are only encrypting a file on your hard disk). Think of it this way: you want to be able to access the contents of the encrypted file, so you are its recipient. Click the Add Recipient button and highlight the recipient's key (that is, your key) in the Certificate Selection menu. Click OK, and then click Next. You can click OK after Kleopatra indicates that your encryption was successful. You should now have a file with the same name as the original and a .gpg or .asc extension. If you highlight the encrypted file, Dolphin indicates that it is PGP/MIME-encrypted and won't allow you to preview it in the Information panel.

If you right-click the encrypted file and click the Actions menu, you can choose one of the following options.

> *Decrypt/Verify File:* This action prompts you for a folder to save the decrypted file. After choosing the location, click the Decrypt/Verify button. You are prompted to enter your passphrase because you can't decrypt without it.

> *View file decrypted:* This option is for text files only. Choose this option if you want to view the file without saving a decrypted copy. It again prompts you for your passphrase. After you enter it, the file opens in an application capable of viewing its contents. If you make changes to the file, you have the option of saving your changes and re-encrypting the file.

■ **Tip** Kleopatra puts a red and white icon in your system tray. Double-click this icon to see the main Kleopatra window shown in Figure 5-9.

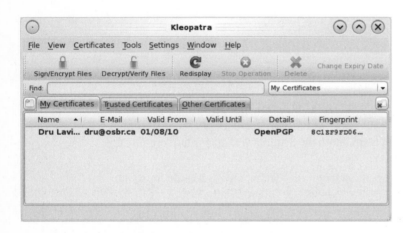

Figure 5-9. Main screen for Kleopatra encryption utility

Exporting Your Public Key

If you sign files or send encrypted emails, you need to export your public key so it is available to the recipients of the signed files and emails. You can export your public key using KGpg. Highlight your key in the Key Management screen and click the Export Key icon. The menu seen in Figure 5-10 displays.

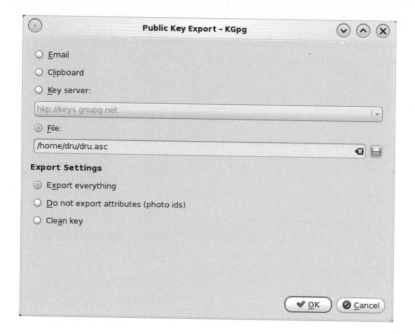

Figure 5-10. Exporting a public key in KGpg

■ **Tip** If you "lose" KGpg, click the arrow to expand your system tray. It is the icon that looks like a yellow lock.

If you select the Email option and click OK, your default email program (KMail, unless you change the default) opens, and the public key is pasted into the body of the email. Simply type in the recipient's address and a subject before sending the email.

If you want your public key to be available to many recipients, select a Key server from the drop-down menu and let everyone know which server you use. If recipients go to the URL of the server and search for the name associated with the key, they can download your key. Remind recipients to contact you to verify the fingerprint so you both know that they have the correct key.

You can also save your public key to a file and give that file to recipients as they need a copy of your public key.

■ **Note** After your friend has a copy of your public key, she will need to import it into her key management software before using your key to verify/decrypt the files and emails you send.

Compressing Files

You have probably downloaded or created .zip files. These are examples of compressed files—files that have been reduced in size (compressed) either to conserve disk space or to reduce download time. Compression utilities are built in to your PC-BSD system, making it easy to work with compressed files.

Using Ark

Ark is KDE's archiving application. Think of an archive as a container holding one or more compressed files. When you compress[1] a file, directory, or a number of files, you create an archive.

You can launch Ark from Kickoff ➤ Applications ➤ Utilities ➤ Archiving Tool.

■ **Tip** The Ark Handbook provides more usage information for this application. It can be accessed by pressing F1 in Ark or by selecting Help ➤ Ark Handbook.

Figure 5-11 shows the menu you see when you click the New icon in Ark.

---

[1] Interested in learning more about file compression? Check out Tom Harris's "How Stuff Works" article at http://www.howstuffworks.com/file-compression.htm.

Figure 5-11. Creating a new archive with Ark

This menu prompts you to indicate where you want to store the archive, the name of the archive you are creating, and the type of compression to use for the files to be stored in the archive. If you share or send the compressed files to a user on a Windows system, you can create zip archives. If you and the person you share the archive with are familiar with the other file formats, you can select another compression method. In the example shown in Figure 5-12, a zip file called test has been created. You add files to compress and store inside the archive with the Add File or Add Folder icons.

Figure 5-12. Ark interface for adding files to a new archive

As you add a file or directory, Ark automatically compresses it in the archive. Ark displays the contents of the archive in a tree view (any directories between the selected folder and the root of the filesystem are unnamed—you can click through these to expand to the view you want to use). If you highlight a file and click Preview, you can view the uncompressed version of the file or list the compressed directory's contents. Use the Extract button to browse to the location where you would like to save an uncompressed version of the highlighted file or directory.

If you download or someone sends you a compressed archive, use the Open button to browse to its path. You can then preview and extract the contents of the archive. Table 5-2 summarizes the compression formats that Ark supports.

Table 5-2. Compression Formats Supported by Ark.

Format	Extension	More information available from
Java	.jar	`http://en.wikipedia.org/wiki/JAR_%28file_format%29`
Zip	.zip	`http://en.wikipedia.org/wiki/ZIP_%28file_format%29`
Gzip	.gz	`http://en.wikipedia.org/wiki/Gzip`
RAR	.rar	`http://en.wikipedia.org/wiki/RAR`
XZ	.7zXZ	`http://en.wikipedia.org/wiki/Xz`
LZMA and 7-zip	.7z	`http://www.7zip.com/`
Debian	.deb	`http://en.wikipedia.org/wiki/Deb_%28file_format%29`
Tar	.tar	`http://en.wikipedia.org/wiki/Tar_%28file_format%29`
Tar (bzip compressed)	.tar.bz	`http://www.bzip.org/`
Tar (gzip compressed)	.tar.gz	`http://www.gzip.org/`

Using Dolphin

If you right-click a file or directory in Dolphin, the following options for Compress are available.

As ZIP Archive: This option creates a compressed .zip file with the same name as the highlighted selection in the same directory.

As RAR Archive: This option creates a compressed .rar file with the same name as the highlighted selection in the same directory.

As ZIP/TAR Archive: This option creates a compressed tar.gz with the same name as the highlighted selection in the same directory.

Compress To: This option opens an Ark menu where you can browse to the location to save the archive and select which compression method to use in the Filter drop-down menu.

If you right-click an existing archive in Dolphin, the following options are available.

Open with Ark: Allows you to preview the contents of and extract the archive.

Extract Archive To: This option takes you directly to the Extract screen in Ark where you can select the directory to which you want to uncompress the contents of the archive.

Extract Archive Here: This option extracts the archive contained in the underlying directory structure. For example, an archive named mystuff.doc.zip would be extracted to a folder called Home. That folder would contain dru ➤ Documents ➤ mystuff.doc.

Using the Clipboard

By default, KDE's clipboard tool Klipper is placed in your system tray and looks like a small black box on a larger box. If you ever remove it from the tray, you can start it from Kickoff ➤ Applications ➤ Utilities ➤ Clipboard Tool.

Klipper keeps a history of your copy and cut operations. If you click or right-click Klipper, you can see your last seven clipboard items and the following actions:

Enable Clipboard Actions: This option enables actions that allow you to associate an expression with an action. How to configure an action is discussed later in this section.

Clear Clipboard History: Occasionally, Klipper becomes confused if you have performed several recent copy operations; clearing the history should get you pasting again.

Configure Klipper: Figure 5-13 shows the Configuration options which are discussed next.

Help: This option launches the Klipper Handbook.

Quit: Klipper remains in your system tray until you select this option. If you do, it asks you if you want Klipper to start the next time you log in.

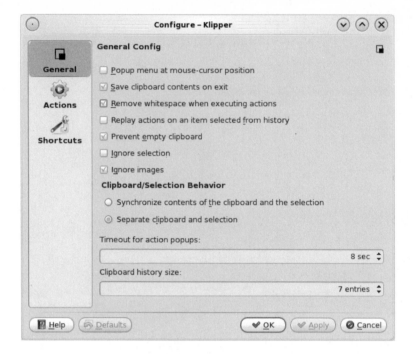

Figure 5-13. Klipper Configure menu

The General configuration screen enables you to configure many settings, including how many copy operations are saved to the clipboard. If you need to copy and paste images, uncheck the Ignore images box.

The Actions menu enables you to associate actions with regular expressions. Figure 5-14 shows the expression and action that will allow you to click a URL in the Clipboard History to open it in Konqueror. Note that this action does not work unless the Enable Clipboard Actions box is checked in Klipper.

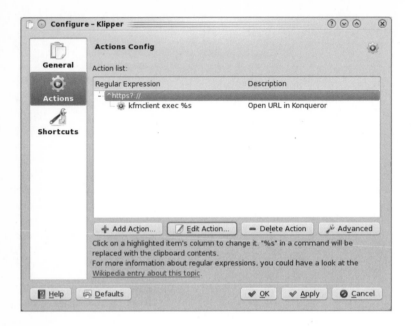

Figure 5-14. Associating an action with a regular expression in Klipper

---

■ **Tip** Regular expressions are definitely in the realm of power users. If you've created an Action that is useful to you, share it on the PC-BSD forums so less advanced users can benefit from your expertise. Chapter 11 introduces you to the PC-BSD community.

The Shortcuts tab enables you to view and create shortcuts to the options in the Klipper menu.

Removable Media

PC-BSD makes it easy to access the data on removable media as it can automatically notice the new data source and make it available to you. This section discusses dealing with CDROMs and DVDs, and USB devices such as thumb drives, USB hard drives, and digital cameras.

CDROM/DVD

If you insert a data CDROM or DVD disk containing data and wait a second or so, Device Notifier pops up and displays the label of the disc. You can click the Device Notifier icon (a blue square with white arrows) to remove the notification message. The label representing the disk then displays in the Places panel of Dolphin, allowing you to access its data. When you are done, right-click the label in Places, and then click Eject. This automatically opens the CD tray so you can remove the media.

To access the data in Konqueror, type /media into the location bar and double-click the icon representing the label name (it should be a blue folder).

If you insert a music CD and hover over its label in Device Notifier, you will see a screen similar to the one shown in Figure 5-15:

Figure 5-15. Device Notifier provides the option to play a music CD.

If you click the Play Audio square, Device Notifier launches the KsCD music player. If you click the round icon with an arrow (the Eject button), Device Notifier ejects the CD tray. The entry for the CD stays in Device Notifier until the CD is ejected; you can click the Device Notifier icon whenever you would like to access its menu.

If you insert a video DVD and hover over its entry in Device Notifier, it indicates that multiple actions are available for the device. Click the entry and select the option to Open with Video Player (Dragon Player).

■ **Tip** The Appendix contains descriptions of other software that can be used to play music or video.

Unfortunately, not all DVDs play "out of the box." This is not a problem with PC-BSD but with the Digital Millennium Copyright Act (DMCA) that "criminalizes production and dissemination of technology, devices, or services intended to circumvent measures (commonly known as digital rights management or DRM) that control access to copyrighted works."[2] This means that the PC-BSD and FreeBSD Projects are not allowed to distribute the software that is able to play DVD content that has been encrypted by the manufacturer. You will know that your DVD is encrypted if nothing happens when you press Play in a computer video player.

Software capable of bypassing the encryption on DVDs does exist and is known as libdvdcss. Due to distribution restrictions, if you decide you want to install this software, you need to compile it yourself and assume any legal responsibility for doing so. Chapters 8–10 tell you everything you need to know about installing and compiling software. If you think that being denied computer access to DVDs that you purchased is unfair, consider speaking to your local political representative or join a digital advocacy group such as the EFF (http://www.eff.org).

USB Devices

To access data on a digital camera or on a USB thumb or hard drive, insert the USB device and wait a second or two until Device Notifier pops up with the label. You can then access the data in both Dolphin and Konqueror. When you're finished, right-click the label name in Dolphin to safely Eject the media before removing it.

Printing

PC-BSD provides a Printer Configuration module that makes it easy to set up printing on your PC-BSD system. It does assume that you know how to physically connect your computer to a printing device or to a network and that you have already done so. Depending upon how you choose to connect to the printing device, you might have to perform some tasks before you configure your PC-BSD system to print.

Consider how your computer connects to the printer device.

- If your computer is physically cabled to the printer using a USB or printer cable, make sure the cable is plugged in and that the printer is turned on.

- If another computer in your network is physically cabled to the printer, check that it has been configured to share its printer.

- If you use a network printing device that is not physically cabled to any computer, you must first configure the network printing device using the manual that came with the device.

---

[2] http://en.wikipedia.org/wiki/DMCA

After you have verified your connection setup, you can use the PC-BSD Printer Configuration module to configure printing for any of these connection scenarios.

Configuring a Printer

After you have ensured that you are connected to the printer device either through a cable or a network connection, launch the Kickoff ➤ System Settings ➤ Printer Configuration module to install the printer on your PC-BSD system. After inputting the administrative password, you will see the initial Printer Configuration screen shown in Figure 5-16.

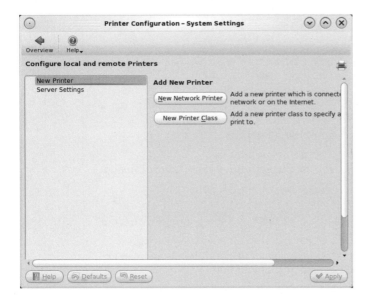

Figure 5-16. Printer Configuration system module

Before adding your printer, click Server Settings to see if the defaults are appropriate for your situation. This screen is seen in Figure 5-17.

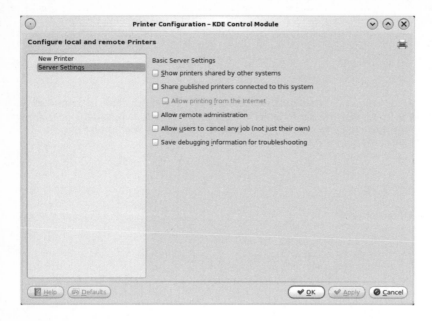

Figure 5-17. *Server Settings configuration for Printer Configuration – KDE Control Module*

The settings are

Show printers shared by other systems: Check this box if the printer device is not physically cabled to your computer.

Share published printers connected to this system: Check this box if you plan to share the printer that is physically cabled to your computer with other computers on your network.

■ **Tip** If there are other computers on your network, don't forget to check the Shared published printers box so other users on the network can print from the computer cabled to your PC-BSD system.

Allow remote administration: By default, you can administer the printer (for example, view the print queue or stop and start the printer) only from this computer. This box should be selected only by advanced users who know how to secure remote administration connections.

■ **Caution** For security reasons, it *is not* a good idea to check the box Allow printing from the Internet. Check this box only if you really know what you're doing and have a good reason to do so.

Allow users to cancel any job (not just their own): By default, users can cancel only their own print jobs. Check this box with caution, unless the users in your network play nicely together. Note that the administrative user always has permission to cancel anyone's print job.

Save debugging information for troubleshooting: Check this box if you have problems configuring your printer.

After you check the boxes you want to use, click Apply to save your changes.

If the printer is attached to another PC-BSD or Linux system that has already shared its printer using CUPS (Common Unix Printing System, `http://www.cups.org`), the connection is automatically created for you after you check the Show printers shared by other systems checkbox and click Apply. Figure 5-18 shows an example; in this example, the printer is physically cabled to a Linux system with an IP address of 192.168.1.107.

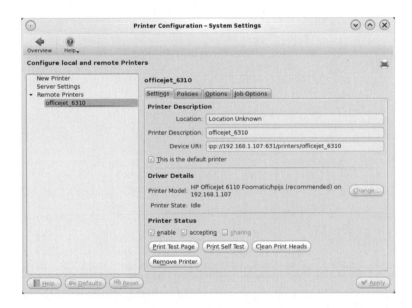

Figure 5-18. The Printer Configuration - System Settings module has automatically found a remote printer that has been shared using CUPS.

■ **Tip** If the remote CUPS printer is not automatically found for you, double-check that a firewall is not blocking port 631.

After the remote printer is found, you can highlight the remote printer and skip ahead to Figure 5-24.

If the printer is physically cabled to your computer or is shared by a Windows system, click the New Printer ➤ New Network Printer icon to create your printer. Despite the name of the button, it can be used to create printers of any connection type, even those cabled to your computer. It will pause for a few seconds while it looks for printers attached to your system, and if you configured it to do so, any printers available on the network. When it is finished, a screen similar to the one in Figure 5-19 displays.

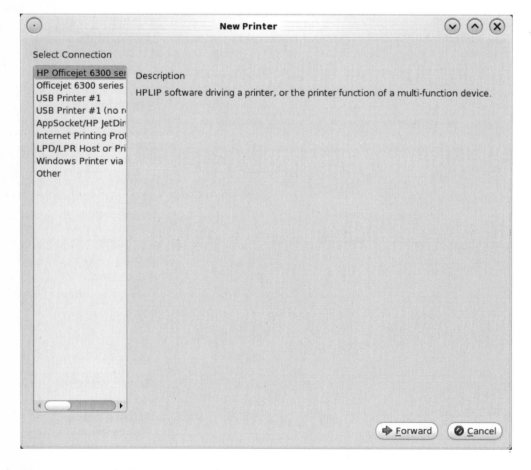

Figure 5-19. Results from Printer configuration module looking for available printers

In this example, the PC-BSD computer is physically cabled to an HP 6310 printer, and the printer configuration module has found the printer.

■ **Tip** If your computer is physically attached but the model is not showing in this screen, check that the cable is plugged in and the printer is turned on. If that's not the problem, search at `http://www.linuxprinting.org/printer_list.cgi` to determine whether an open-source printer driver exists.

If the printer is physically cabled to a Windows computer on your network, click the Windows Printer entry in the left frame, as shown in Figure 5-20.

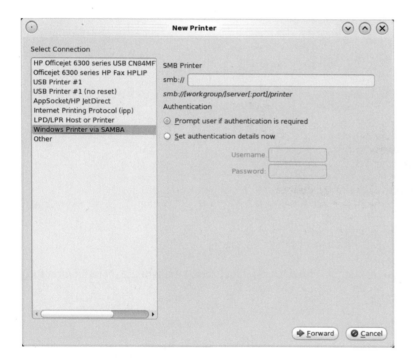

Figure 5-20. Selecting the Windows printing share

Input the name of the Windows workgroup, the name of the computer the printer is cabled to, and the name of the printer share. If the share requires a username and password, input those as well.

After you have highlighted the printer cabled to your system or configured the Windows share, click Forward, where you will the screen in Figure 5-21.

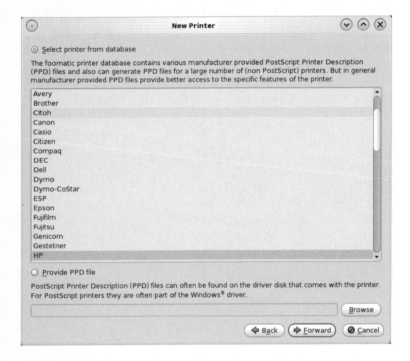

Figure 5-21. Printer manufacturer selection screen

The printer's manufacturer should be highlighted for you; if it is not, highlight the manufacturer for the printer and click Forward to the model screen, as shown in Figure 5-22.

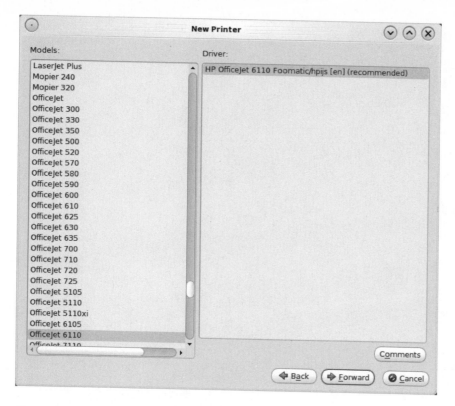

Figure 5-22. Printer model selection screen

The recommended print driver should already be selected for you. Otherwise, highlight the model of the printer; the number might not be exact, but it should be close. Click Forward to continue to the screen seen in Figure 5-23.

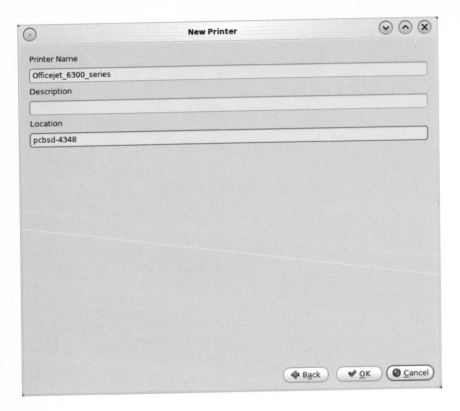

Figure 5-23. Configuring the printer's name and description

You can change the printer name and description to values that make sense to you, but do not change the Location. When you are finished, click OK, and the printer is created for you. You should see a screen similar to the one shown in Figure 5-24.

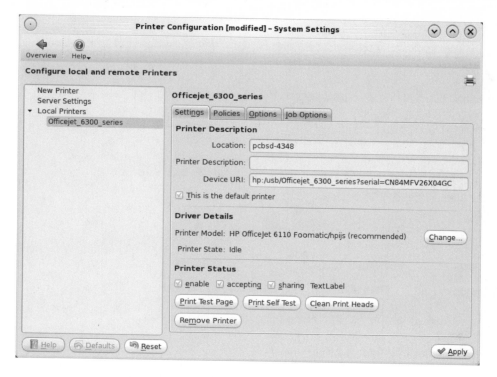

Figure 5-24. A local printer in the Printer Configuration module

Make sure there is some paper in the printer, and then click the Print Test Page button to confirm that your setup works properly.

If You Share Your Printer

If you checked the box to share your printer, your printer connection will be published to the other computers in your network. You need to double check that each computer is capable of printing a test page.

If the other computer runs PC-BSD, Mac OS X, or Linux, open its web browser and type in the URL "localhost:631/printers", as seen in Figure 5-25.

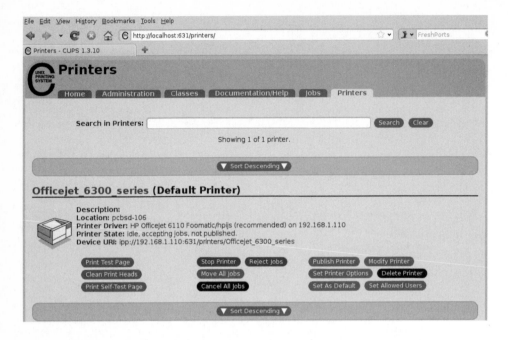

Figure 5-25. Viewing the shared printer in a web browser

That URL connects to the CUPS server that runs on the computer to display which printers are published (shared) on the network.

■ **Note** This assumes that the CUPS has been installed and is running on the Linux system; if it is not, refer to the documentation for your Linux system. CUPS starts automatically on PC-BSD systems.

In this example, the printer running on computer 192.168.1.110 has been found. Click the Print Test Page button to verify that printing works over the network.

If the computer runs Windows, you need to use the Add Printer Wizard on the Windows system. The easiest configuration uses IPP (for example, using the IPP Device URI seen in Figure 5-25). How to configure an IPP printer varies by the version of Windows. We recommend that you Google "IPP Windows" to find a how-to for your version of Windows.

Desktop Sharing with Krfb

Desktop Sharing enables you to share your current desktop with a virtual networking computer (VNC)[3] user on another machine. Typically, you do this when another user shows you how to perform a task or helps you troubleshoot a problem with your system.

Click Kickoff ➤ Applications ➤ Internet ➤ Desktop Sharing to launch Krfb, KDE's desktop-sharing application. Figure 5-26 provides an example of the invitation information you would give to the person with whom you wish to share your desktop.

Figure 5-26. Creating a personal invitation in Krfb

In this example, the Personal Invitation button has been clicked; it generates an invitation containing an IP address and port number, a unique password for the connection, and an expiration time of an hour for the password. Be sure that you give this information only to the person you trust to help you with your computer.

After you have created an invitation, it displays in the invitation menu with its creation and expire times. If you want to stop an invitation before it expires, highlight it and click Delete.

■ **Note** Before your invitee can connect, you need to open the port number (in this case, TCP and UDP port 5900) listed in the invitation. See the "Firewall" section of Chapter 7 for instructions on how to open a firewall port.

---

[3] The Wikipedia entry for VNC provides a good introduction, including links to VNC client software for other operating systems. Visit `http://en.wikipedia.org/wiki/Virtual_Network_Computing`.

After your invitee connects to your IP address and port number, a message similar to the one shown in Figure 5-27 displays on your desktop.

Figure 5-27. Connection request in Krfb

After confirming (by telephone, for example) the identity of the person trying to connect, decide whether or not you want the user to control your keyboard and mouse, and then click the Accept Connection button. After you do this, the other person is prompted to input the invitation password. After the password is accepted, the user can see your desktop and you can watch as she moves your mouse and interacts with your desktop. After she is finished assisting you, she can close the VNC session.

■ **Tip** After a session is closed, the user cannot connect again unless you send another invitation. Don't forget to remove the firewall rule for the VNC port and restart your firewall when you are finished!

Summary

This chapter introduced you to some of the software available on and for your PC-BSD system. It also showed you how to deal with encrypted and compressed files, the Clipboard, and accessing data on removable media.

In Chapter 6, you will learn how to configure the system to best suit your needs by starting with the system settings that are accessible to your user account.

CHAPTER 6

■■■

User System Settings

By now, you are probably comfortable enough with your PC-BSD system to start looking under the hood at some of your system's settings. Chapters 6 and 7 will introduce you to the System Settings utility and walk you through its configuration modules. These modules allow you to configure every aspect of your PC-BSD system's behavior.

Chapter 6 will concentrate on the general settings any user is allowed to make. Chapter 7 will concentrate on the more advanced settings that are usually performed by the superuser. It should be noted that most of the settings found in the Systems Settings utility apply to other operating systems running KDE4. We will let you know as we come across the configuration modules that are specific to PC-BSD.

System Settings can be launched from Kickoff ➤ Computer ➤ System Settings, or by typing **systemsettings &** in a command prompt.

Figure 6-1 shows the System Settings menu on a PC-BSD system.

Figure 6-1. System Settings menu

■ **Note** The order of the icons in the System Settings menu may vary depending upon your language settings, but the functionality will be the same.

The System Settings menu is divided into sections, with each section containing icons representing a configurable module. This chapter will discuss the modules in the Look & Feel, Personal, and Computer Administration sections. Chapter 6 will discuss the Network & Connectivity section as well as the sections found in the Advanced tab.

■ **Tip** Power users can launch individual modules from the command line. Type **kcmshell4 --list** to see the list of modules with brief descriptions; then type **kcmshell4 name_of_module** to launch the specified module's menu.

Look and Feel

The modules in this section allow you to change the appearance of your KDE4 desktop.

Appearance

Figure 6-2 shows the configuration screen you receive when you double-click the Appearance module.

Figure 6-2. Appearance configuration module

■ **Tip** Once you've entered a configuration module's menu, click the Overview button in the top-left corner if you want to go back to the main System Settings menu.

You can spend a fair bit of time previewing and trying out the various Appearance options. We'll provide a brief overview of each to get you started:

Style: A widget style controls the color and look of components such as tabs, radio buttons, check boxes, and status bars. Several widget styles are installed for you. If you select one from the drop-down menu, you'll see its effect in the Preview pane. If you don't like the new look after clicking Apply, try another style.

Colors: Several color schemes are installed for you, and you can watch their Preview as you go through the menu of choices. The Get New Schemes button will connect you to the Color Schemes section of `www.kde-look.org` so you can browse for additional schemes. The rest of the tabs in this section allow you to fine-tune the selected color scheme.

Icons: Several themes control the look of icons that have already been installed for you. A preview of each theme is shown above the selection menu. You also have the option to Get New Themes from the Icon Themes section of `www.kde-look.org`. Use the Advanced tab to control the size of the icons and to configure their effect and transparency.

Fonts: These font settings apply to every application you launch in KDE. You can set different fonts and sizes for toolbars, menus, window titles, taskbars, and desktops as well as configure your anti-alias settings. If you click Adjust All Fonts, it will apply the same font to all settings. If you don't like that, click Reset. If you really mess up your font selections, click Defaults to return to the original KDE settings.

Windows: Several window decoration themes are available for preview. You can also decide whether to show window button tooltips (the description you see when you hover over a button in a window's title) and adjust the location of the buttons on a window's title bar. Note that these settings apply to all windows. To apply to an individual window, see the Configuring Windows section in Chapter 3.

Splash Screen: When KDE starts, you see several icons bouncing in the middle of your desktop as it loads. This screen allows you to change that theme, as well as Get New Themes from the Splashscreens section of `kde-look.org`.

GTK Styles and Fonts: When graphical applications are created, they use something known as a widget toolkit to control the look of the window and its buttons. KDE4 applications use the QT toolkit, but many applications, such as Firefox and GIMP, use the GTK toolkit. If you find that some application windows look "ugly," see whether they look better to you after selecting another style from the drop-down menu. You can also install the Firefox and Thunderbird scrollbar fix in this menu.

Emoticons: Many applications, such as instant messaging and Skype, support emoticons. This menu allows you to configure and get new emoticon themes from the Emoticons section of kde-look.org.

Desktop

This module allows you to configure desktop effects, multiple virtual desktops, screen edge actions, screen savers, and launch feedback. Figure 6-3 shows the Desktop settings module.

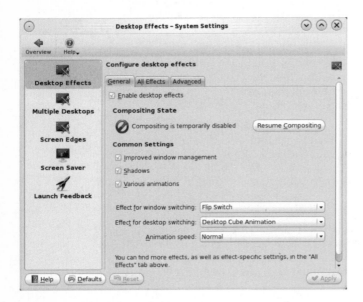

Figure 6-3. Desktop settings module

Following is an overview of the configuration options available in each of the icons in the left panel:

Desktop Effects: These were discussed in detail in Chapter 3.

Multiple Desktops: By default, four virtual desktops are created for you. This menu allows you to change and rename the number of virtual desktops. Accessing your virtual desktops is discussed in Chapter 3.

Screen Edges: This configuration screen allows you to enable active screen edges. Once activated, your screen edges will support actions such as switching between virtual desktops by hovering your mouse near the edge of your screen.

Screen Saver: Use this menu to select, configure, and test your screensaver. There are dozens of built-in screensavers that have been sorted into categories. You can choose to start the screensaver after a specified period of inactivity and to require a password to stop the screensaver. Advanced Options allow you to configure the screen to lock when you hover your mouse over a specified screen corner. Additional screen savers are available from the Screensaver section of kde-look.org.

Launch Feedback: This screen allows you to configure the cursor that appears while an application is launching. You can also configure the timeout before being notified that an application is taking too long to launch.

■ **Tip** You can disable the launch feedback cursor for a specific application in Menu Editor in the General tab of the application. Menu Editor is discussed in detail in Chapter 4.

Notifications

Figure 6-4 shows a screenshot of the Notifications module.

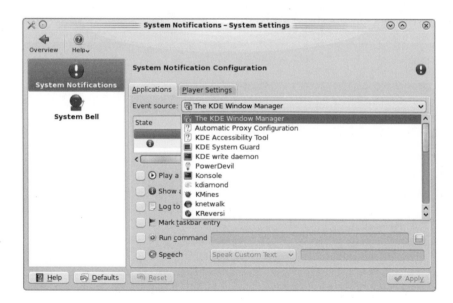

Figure 6-4. Notifications module menu

In the Applications tab, the Event source provides a drop-down menu to select the specific application to configure. Once selected, the configurable actions for that application are displayed in the State window of the screen. Select a state to configure which notification you would like to receive. For example, if you select PowerDevil ➤ AC adaptor plugged in, you'll see that the default notification is to play the KDE-Sys-App-Positive.ogg file and to show an informational popup message. Click the arrow icon next to Play a sound to hear the sound or click the browse icon to select a different sound. You can also configure the system to speak a default or customized message.

■ **Note** Speech-to-Text must be configured before the system can speak the message. See the Accessibility section later on in this chapter for instructions on how to enable and configure this feature.

The System Bell section allows you to use the system bell instead of system notification. If you check this option, you can then set the volume, pitch, and duration of the bell.

Window Behavior

This module provides another view of the settings discussed in detail in the Windows Actions section of Chapter 3. Figure 6-5 shows the layout of this configuration module.

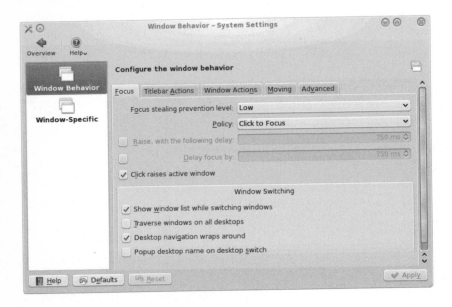

Figure 6-5. Window Behavior module

Personal

This section of System Settings contains modules to configure your personal, accessibility, and language preferences. These settings apply only to your user account, meaning that users sharing the same system can use different personal settings.

About Me

Figure 6-6 provides a screenshot of this module.

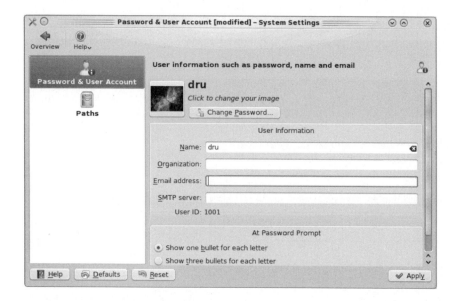

Figure 6-6. *About Me module*

The Password & User Account section allows you to associate an image with your name that will show in the login screen after you use the Leave button to log out or switch user accounts. You can browse for an image that KDE will automatically scale for you. This configuration section also allows you to change your password; it will prompt you for your current password first.

The information you provide in the User Information section is used by some programs, such as the default user created by KMail.

Have you ever noticed that bullets appear when you type your password into the login screen? Use the At Password Prompt option to configure KDE to show one, three, or no bullets for each character in your password.

The Paths menu is shown in Figure 6-7. You can change the default location that applications search through when looking for specific types of files. Any paths you change should remain somewhere within your home directory.

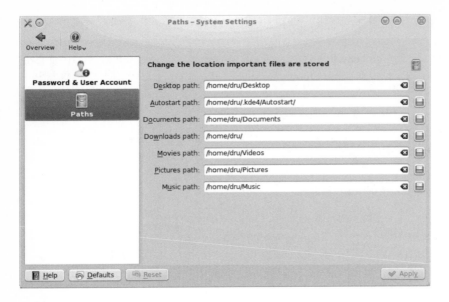

Figure 6-7. Default path locations in the About Me configuration module

---

■ **Tip** The contents of the Autostart directory are configured in the Autostart configuration module discussed in Chapter 7.

Accessibility

KDE4 provides many configuration options to ease the computing experience for disabled users. The KDE Accessibility Project (http://accessibility.kde.org/) provides a good overview of KDE's accessibility features as well as additional resources.

Figure 6-8 shows the configuration menu for the Accessibility module.

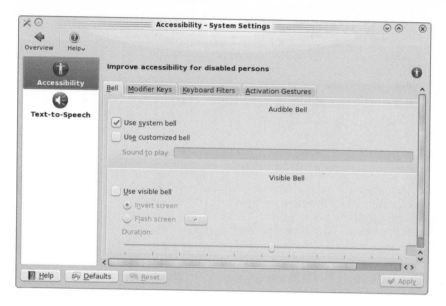

Figure 6-8. *Accessibility module*

The tabs in the Accessibility panel allow you to configure the following:

Bell: If you have difficulty hearing the system bell, use a customized bell that contains the path to a sound to play. Deaf users can configure a visible bell that will either invert or flash the screen. These settings will apply to any configured Notifications, as discussed earlier in this chapter.

Modifier Keys: This menu allows you to enable sticky keys. This is useful if you have problems holding down a modifier key (such as Ctrl, Alt, or Shift). Once sticky keys are enabled, you can let go of the modifier key and it will remain active until you press another key. For example, you can start KRunner by clicking Alt, letting go, and then pressing F2 instead of having to press Alt+F2 simultaneously. This tab also allows you to activate a bell whenever a locking key (Caps Lock, NumLock, or Scroll Lock) is toggled on or off.

Keyboard Filters: This tab allows you to activate and configure slow and bounce keys to assist users with limited hand mobility. Slow keys tell the computer to ignore unintended keystrokes because there is a configured time delay before a keystroke is accepted. Bounce keys tell the computer to ignore repeated keystrokes within a set time frame.

Activation Gestures: This tab allows disabled and nondisabled users to share the keyboard during the same session. Sticky and slow keys can be turned off after a period of inactivity, and notifications can be configured for when an accessibility feature is turned on or off.

The Text-to-Speech module contains the following tabs:

■ **Tip** The KTTS Handbook provides a detailed overview of using the text-to-speech subsystem and is available from `http://docs.kde.org/stable/en/kdeaccessibility/kttsd/index.html`.

General: By default, text-to-speech is disabled. Checking the box to Enable Text-to-Speech System will start the KTTSD service for you.

Talkers: Click the Add button to configure the language and synthesizer used by the text-to-speech talker. When selecting the Synthesizer, select either Festival Interactive or Festival Lite because FreeTTS is currently not supported. While Festival Lite supports only one voice, the Festival talker supports several voices.

Figure 6-9 shows the Select voice menu for the Festival synthesizer. Once you select a voice, click Test to see whether you like the sound of the voice.

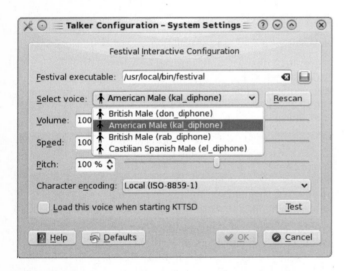

Figure 6-9. *Selecting a voice for the festival synthesizer*

Once a talker is configured, you can use the KMouth program to speak for you.

■ **Note** The KMouth Handbook at `http://docs.kde.org/stable/en/kdeaccessibility/kmouth/index.html` contains detailed instructions for configuring and using Kmouth.

Filters: Filters are advanced features that allow you to preprocess the text before it is spoken. The Filters section of the KTTS Handbook provides examples for creating your own filters.

Interruption: This tab allows you to set a message or sound to be played before and after interruptions (when a spoken warning interrupts the text being spoken, for example).

Audio: This tab allows you to set a location to store audio files. This means that KDE will store any text read by the text-to-speech reader as an audio file, allowing you to replay it again. Files will have names like kttsd-J-SS, where J is the job number and SS is the sentence number.

■ **Caution** Audio files can take up a lot of disk space, so take the time to periodically remove the files you don't use. Uncheck the Keep audio files box in the Audio tab to stop file creation.

Jobs: As seen in Figure 6-10, this screen can be used to speak the contents of the Clipboard or a text file. Buttons are provided to navigate to the previous or next sentence. When speaking, the contents of the text being spoken will be displayed in the Current Sentence panel.

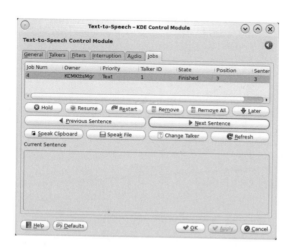

Figure 6-10. Using the Jobs tab of Text-to-Speech to speak text

Default Applications

Figure 6-11 shows the Default Applications module, which controls which applications are used for common tasks.

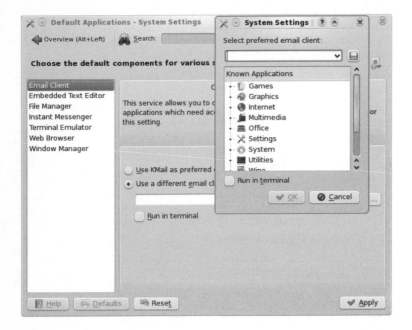

Figure 6-11. *Selecting a different e-mail client using the Default Applications module*

The default e-mail client is KMail. In this example, I've selected Use a different email client; then pressed the ... button to browse for the application I want to use instead.

Table 6-1 summarizes the default applications used by KDE programs that support the specified functionality.

Table 6-1. *Default Applications Used by KDE Programs*

Functionality	Default Application
Email client	KMail
Text Editor	Embedded Advanced Text Editor (Kate)
File Manager	Dolphin
Instant Messenger	Kopete

Functionality	Default Application
Terminal Emulator	Konsole
Web Browser	Konqueror
Window Manager	KWin

Regional and Language

This module allows you to configure your language, keyboard layout, and spell checker. These settings will be used by all applications in KDE. Figure 6-12 shows the module's menu.

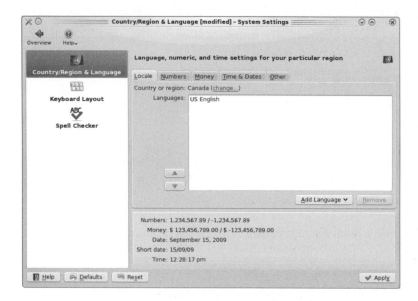

Figure 6-12. Regional & Language configuration module

The bottom portion of the Country/Region & Language section provides a preview of your currently applied settings. You can use this screen's tabs to change the following:

Locale: Either click the word change… next to the Country or region, or click Add Language to select the desired locale.

Numbers: Use this tab to change the decimal symbol, thousands separator, positive and negative signs, and to select the numbers set.

Money: Here you can change the currency symbol, its location to the numeric value (such as before or after), and the number of digits after the decimal symbol.

Time & Dates: Here you can select the calendar system, time and date formats, and first day of the week.

Other: Use this tab to select your paper format setting and the metric or imperial measuring system.

The Keyboard Layout section provides tabs allowing you to configure the following:

Layout: Your current keyboard layout was selected during the PC-BSD install. If you want to change it, click the Enable keyboard layouts button to select a different keyboard model or layout.

■ **Tip** The Kxkb Handbook at `http://docs.kde.org/kde3/en/kdebase/kxkb/index.html` contains more information and examples about the Keyboard Layout tabs. The Enable keyboard layouts button needs to be enabled to activate the Switching Options and Advanced tabs.

Switching Options: By default, the selected layout applies to all applications (Global). Use this tab if you want to configure the keyboard layout to affect only the current desktop, application, or window. You can also configure shortcuts for switching between layouts.

■ **Tip** KDE will not let you change some shortcuts, such as Ctrl-Shift and Alt-Shift. If you receive an error indicating that your shortcut is not supported by Qt, select another shortcut.

Advanced: This tab contains hundreds of keyboard behavior options sorted into categories. Spend some time browsing the options to see whether any interest you.

The Spell Checker section allows you to set the default language for editors that use spellcheck. It also provides options to skip uppercase and run-together words. To use spellcheck in an editor, select Spelling from its Tools menu.

Computer Administration

This section contains modules that allow you to configure items such as the date and time, your display and fonts, keyboard and mouse actions, and multimedia.

■ **Note** Most of the settings in this section can be modified using your regular user account. However, some settings, such as changing the system time, require you to input the administrative password.

Date and Time

A screenshot of this module is seen in Figure 6-13. The default settings were selected during the PC-BSD install.

Figure 6-13. Time and Date module showing Toronto as the current local time zone

If you check Set date and time automatically, your system will automatically adjust itself by syncing with a network time protocol (NTP) server on the Internet. You can select which server to use from the NTP server drop-down menu just above the clock.

Use the single forward and back arrows to scroll through the months in the selected year's calendar, and use the double arrows to scroll through previous and upcoming years. In the clock area, use the up and down arrows or your mouse scroll to change the hour, minute, and seconds; or type in the desired value.

Local time zones are listed alphabetically. You can scroll through the list to pick the city closest to your geographic area.

Display

Figure 6-14 shows a screenshot of the Display module. The Size and Orientation settings will vary according to the features provided by your video card driver.

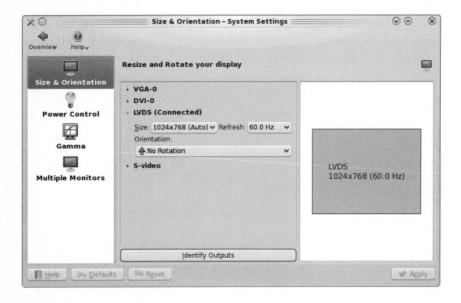

Figure 6-14. The Display module

This module allows you to configure the following:

Size & Orientation: This tab allows you to change the display size (currently shown as 1024x768), the refresh rate, and the orientation.

Power Control: If your laptop display or monitor supports it (most modern hardware does), you can check the Enable display power management check box and set the standby, suspend, and power off times.

Gamma: This tab provides sliders for red, green, and blue settings so you can calibrate your monitor's contrast and brightness settings.

■ **Caution** Don't calibrate your monitor unless you know what you are doing.

Multiple Monitors: If your system has multiple video cards connected to multiple monitors, you can use this tab to configure KDE to spread your desktop across all of the monitors.

> ■ **Tip** The site `www.dualmonitorbackgrounds.com/` has a large selection of wallpaper designed for dual monitors. To save a wallpaper, right-click its image and select Save Image As from the menu. Chapter 3 contains instructions for changing your desktop wallpaper.

Font Installer

This module allows you to preview, configure, and add fonts. Figure 6-15 shows a screenshot of this module. This system currently has 40 fonts installed.

Figure 6-15. Font Installer configuration module

Expand the arrow next to a font's name to view which fonts are installed—such as bold, italic, or regular. Right-click any font and you will have an option to delete, print, or open it in the font viewer application. If you purchase or download a font from the Internet, use the Add button to browse to the path in which you saved the font.

Input Actions

This module makes it easy for you to configure several useful responses to keyboard input. Figure 6-16 shows the initial Input Actions menu.

Figure 6-16. Input Actions module

This menu will change if you select an option in the left panel. Click the Settings button to return to the original menu. If you check the Gestures check box, you can associate mouse movements with actions.

Spend some time expanding each category to see which options it provides. If you click an action, the comment will provide a brief description. Depending upon the option, it may also provide a trigger tab where you can configure a keyboard shortcut and/or an action tab where you can launch a command or fine-tune the action.

An example of a useful Input Action is found under Preset Actions ➤ PrintScreen. The comment indicates that this action launches KSnapShot when the PrintScrn key is pressed. You could change the application that launches using this action's Action tab.

The Edit button ➤ New menu allows you to define your own global shortcuts, window actions, and mouse gesture actions. You can also group the actions you create into their own category (for example, MyShortcuts) using Edit ➤ New Group. You can save all your Input Actions to a file using Edit ➤ Export. You can restore your saved settings to another system or after a new installation using Edit ➤ Import and specifying the path to the file you saved.

Use the Reset button if you decide you want to return your system to the default Input Actions settings.

■ **Caution** Reset will delete any actions or groups you have created.

Keyboard & Mouse

This module allows you to configure keyboard and mouse behavior as well as keyboard shortcuts. Figure 6-17 provides a screenshot of this module.

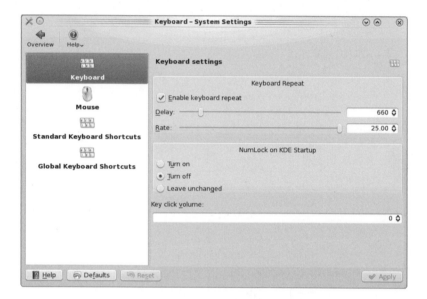

Figure 6-17. Keyboard & Mouse configuration module

This module provides tabs to configure the following:

Keyboard: If you tend to make mistakes as you type, you'll want to enable keyboard repeat. If you don't, you will have to press Backspace for every character you want to redo. You might have to experiment with the delay (not too slow) and the rate (not too fast) to find a speed that works for you when you hold down Backspace. If your keyboard has a NumLock section and you use it often, configure KDE to activate these keys for you. If you like to hear yourself type, adjust the key click volume.

Mouse: This menu allows you to specify right- or left-handed button order, reverse scroll direction, and specify whether a single or a double click opens files and folders. You can also preview and install mouse cursor themes, set various intervals, and configure the NumPad keys to act as a mouse.

■ **Tip** A useful setting for laptops with touchpads is to lower pointer acceleration to about 1.5 and pointer threshold to 0 in the Advanced tab of the Mouse panel.

Standard Keyboard Shortcuts: Allows you to view and customize default shortcut keys. In Figure 6-18, the Add Bookmark action has been selected. It shows that this action is currently using the default shortcut of Ctrl-B. If you select Custom, click the None button, which will change to Input. Press the keys you want to use for the shortcut, and the Input word will change to show your new shortcut.

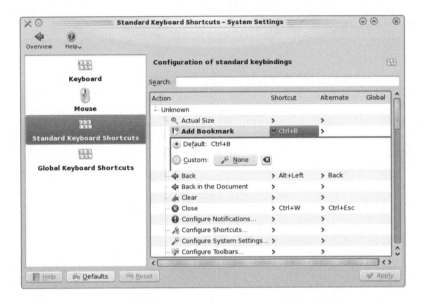

Figure 6-18. Changing a default keyboard shortcut in the Keyboard & Mouse configuration module

Global Keyboard Shortcuts: This section allows you to view and change the default shortcuts for specific applications. Click the KDE component scroll-down menu to select the application to configure. The File drop-down menu lets you select from additional component schemes, set all shortcuts in this section to none, and remove a component from this menu. A filter bar is included if you know which action you want to configure for the selected component.

Figure 6-19 provides a screenshot showing KWin as the currently selected component. You might want to spend some time browsing the actions available for each component to see whether any shortcuts would be useful to you.

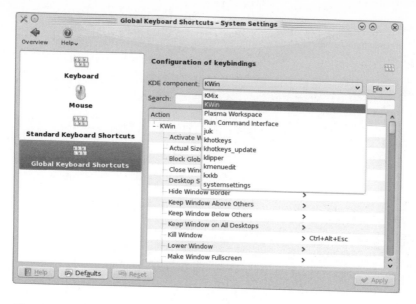

Figure 6-19. Default global keyboard shortcuts for the Kwin KDE component

Multimedia

This module allows you to view the sound card and backend driver being used by the multimedia subsystem. If you have multiple sound cards, you can specify their order for each category. For example, you can configure the card attached to your speakers for Video and another card attached to your headphones for Communication. Otherwise, these settings should "just work" and are typically left as-is.

Figure 6-20 shows that this PC-BSD system uses an Intel 82801AA AC'97 (snd_ich) sound card.

■ **Tip** On PC-BSD (and FreeBSD systems), sound card drivers start with snd_, and the man page for the driver name will tell you the type of sound card and the driver's capabilities. In the previous example, I could type **man snd_ich** in Konsole or **man:/snd_ich** in Dolphin's navigation bar or Konqueror.

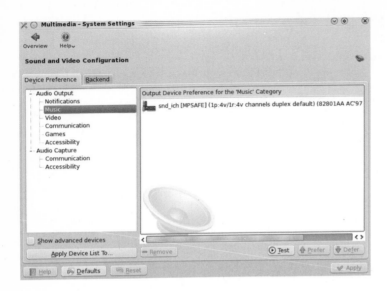

Figure 6-20. Multimedia configuration module

You can test your sound device by highlighting it and clicking the Test button. If you click the Apply Device List To... button, you can see which categories the device is applied to without having to click each category individually in the left pane.

The backend tab is seen in Figure 6-21. The KDE4 multimedia network is known as Phonon and it depends on a backend engine to play various audio and video formats. PC-BSD installs the Xine backend engine for you. If you are curious about interlacing, its Wikipedia entry (http://en.wikipedia.org/wiki/Deinterlacing) provides a good introduction.

■ **Note** See www.xine-project.org/home for more information about Xine.

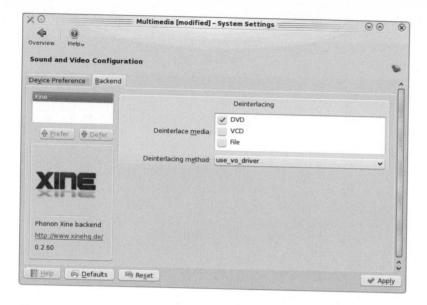

Figure 6-21. PC-BSD system using the Xine backend for multimedia applications

Summary

This chapter introduced you to several of the configuration modules in the System Settings utility. You learned how to customize the look and feel of your system, configure accessibility features, customize your keyboard layout and language, and manage your fonts. You've also learned how to customize your display, input actions, and keyboard and mouse.

We'll discuss the rest of the configuration modules in the next chapter.

CHAPTER 7

Administrative System Settings

Chapter 6 concentrated on system configuration settings available to any user. This chapter focuses on the system settings usually performed by the administrative user. Many of these configuration modules will prompt you for the superuser password.

We'll start by finishing up System Settings' General tab by discussing the modules in the Network & Connectivity section, as well as the remaining modules in the Computer Administration section. We'll then move on to the sections in the Advanced tab of System Settings.

Network and Connectivity

The modules in this section allow you to configure the built-in firewall, various network settings, connections to Windows shares, and your network interfaces.

Firewall

This module is specific to PC-BSD and is used to configure the pf[1] firewall. It requires administrative access. Figure 7-1 shows the Firewall configuration module.

■ **Caution** A firewall affects the security of your operating system. If you are not familiar with TCP/IP ports or firewall rules, you should leave your firewall settings as-is. If you want to practice creating firewall rules in order to learn more about firewalls, use a test system that does not contain any of your data.

---

[1] pf is unique to BSD operating systems. See the pf Guide (`http://www.openbsd.org/faq/pf/`) if you want to learn more about this firewall.

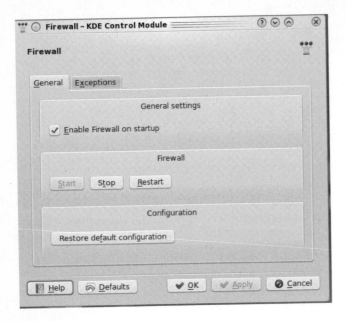

Figure 7-1. Firewall configuration module

The General configuration screen allows the firewall to be enabled or disabled at system startup. You can tell that the firewall is currently running on this system because the Start button is greyed out. If the firewall was not running, the Stop and Restart buttons would be greyed out. If you ever mess up your firewall configuration, click the Restore default configuration button to return to the original working configuration. If you make a change to your firewall settings, don't forget to click Restart (or Start) for your changes to take effect.

Figure 7-2 shows the screen for the Exceptions tab.

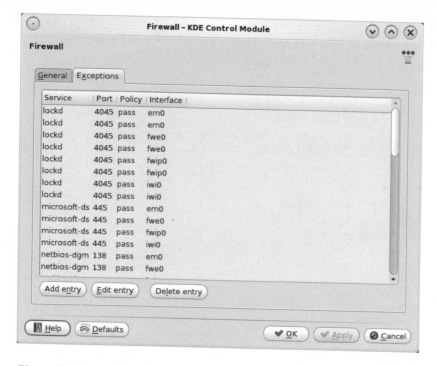

Figure 7-2. Firewall rules in Exceptions tab of Firewall configuration module

The Exceptions tab provides a graphical interface for viewing, adding, modifying, and deleting firewall rules. Each rule (or exception) contains the following information:

Service: The name of the application affected by the firewall rule.

Port: The TCP/IP port associated with that service. The file /etc/services contains a list of common applications and their default port.

Policy: Whether that application is allowed to pass through or is blocked by the firewall.

Interface: The BSD name of the network interface.

Users already familiar with pf can view the underlying configuration file, /etc/pf.conf using Konsole. Figure 7-3 shows that configuration file from the same system. It should be noted that /etc/pf.conf shows all the underlying firewall rules. The default rules support network address translation (NAT[2]), allow you to access the Internet and run the ping and traceroute utilities, and accept NetBIOS packets on the interface attached to the internal network.

---

[2] http://en.wikipedia.org/wiki/Network_address_translation

> ■ **Tip** The default Exceptions show that the NetBIOS ports are open, allowing your computer to share files over a Windows or Samba network. Samba is discussed later in this chapter.

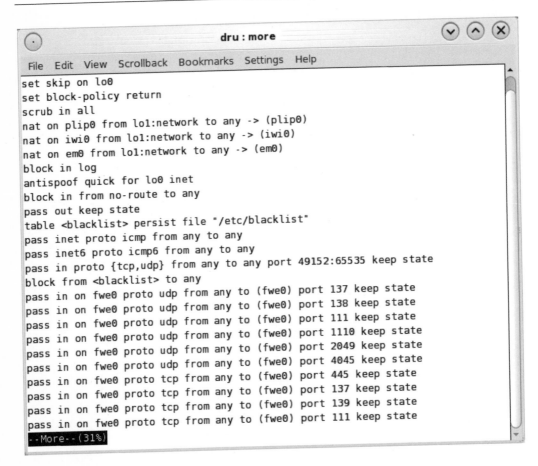

Figure 7-3. /etc/pf.conf configuration file showing the same firewall rules

Power users can change their firewall rules using either the graphical Firewall module or by editing /etc/pf.conf directly.

Figure 7-4 shows the menu that appears if you click Add entry in the Exceptions tab. In this example, a firewall rule is being added to allow for incoming Doom connections over TCP port 666 on the em0 network interface.

Figure 7-4. Adding a firewall rule to allow incoming Doom connections

When creating a rule, use the drop-down Service menu to select an application by name. You can choose to either allow or block connections over the port. Protocol choices are TCP or UDP, and the drop-down Interface menu will allow you to select from the interfaces installed on the system. Once you press Ok, the rule will be added and will show in /etc/pf.conf.

■ **Note** While the new firewall rules will appear, they won't be used until you restart the firewall.

Network Settings

Figure 7-5 shows the Network Settings configuration module.

Figure 7-5. Network Settings configuration module

■ **Caution** The menus in this module are for advanced users. Don't change them unless you have good reason to and you have researched your changes.

The menus within this module allow you to configure the following:

Proxy: If you need to go through a proxy to access the Internet, your service provider or network administrator will tell you which proxy settings you need to use. If you're curious, the Proxies document from `http://docs.kde.org/stable/en/kdebase-runtime/kcontrol/proxy/index.html` gives an overview of each proxy setting.

Connection Preferences: This menu allows you to change network timeout values and enable useful FTP options. It is rare that you would change the default values and you should leave them as-is unless you really know what you are doing.

Service Discovery: Service discovery is also known as zeroconf[3] and is designed to let a computer configure itself for networking with no user intervention. KDE uses Avahi to provide service discovery. It will search the local domain to see which resources are available. This screen allows you to add additional service discovery domains.

Sharing

Figure 7-6 shows the Sharing configuration module which is used to set the default username and password for Windows shares. This allows you to browse Windows network shares using Konqueror without being prompted for the share username and password.

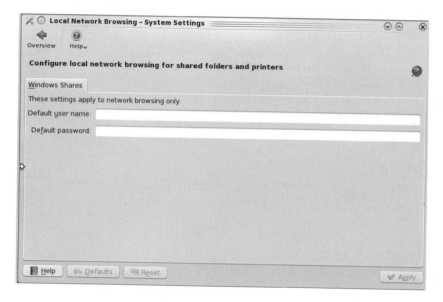

Figure 7-6. Sharing configuration module

System Network Configuration

The System Network Configuration module is provided by PC-BSD and understands BSD network interface settings. You will need administrative access to change any of the settings in this module.

---

[3] Wikipedia provides a good introduction to zeroconf (`http://en.wikipedia.org/wiki/Zeroconf`).

■ **Tip** Your PC-BSD network settings should "just work." For example, if you plug in an Ethernet cable or insert an external wireless card, its network settings should be automatically configured for you. Should you have a problem with a network interface, you can use this module to configure the interface manually.

Figure 7-7 shows a screenshot of this module. This system contains a RealTek Ethernet card (rl0), a firewire (fwip0) interface, a wireless card (wlan0), and the loopback interface (lo0). The IP address for the highlighted wireless interface is 10.13.0.13.

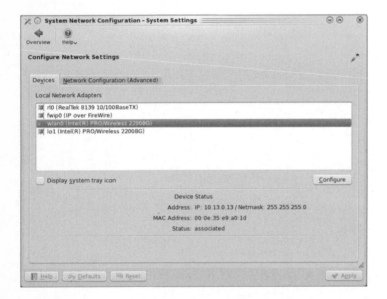

Figure 7-7. System Network Configuration module showing an Ethernet, firewire, wireless, and loopback interface

■ **Tip** BSD Ethernet device names differ from Linux. On BSD systems, the interface name is associated with its driver; on Linux systems, Ethernet drivers always start with *eth*. To read the details of a driver, look at the man page for the interface name (without the number). In this example, I could type **man:/rl** into Konqueror to learn more about the RealTek driver.

The Devices tab allows the administrator to view and configure the network interfaces. If you highlight an Ethernet, firewire, or loopback interface and click Configure, you have the option of obtaining the IP address automatically using DHCP or manually typing in the IP address and subnet mask.

If you highlight a wireless interface and click Configure, in addition to the options mentioned for the other interfaces, you have the ability to add, edit, and remove wireless network profiles. The Wireless configuration menu is shown in Figure 7-8.

■ **Tip** A quick way to access an interface's configuration is to highlight it and check the Display system tray icon. Once in the system tray, you can double-click the icon to open the System Network Configuration module. Hover over the icon to get a summary of the interface's current settings.

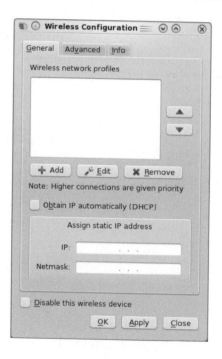

Figure 7-8. Configuring a network interface

If you click the +Add button, you have the option to scan for available wireless networks. You can also choose the appropriate security setting of disabled, WEP, WPA personal, or WPA enterprise[4]. Click the Configure button in the Network Security section to type in the key required by the wireless network.

Back to the main menu, the Network Configuration (Advanced) tab will show the DNS server and hostname received from a DHCP server. If you are manually configuring the interface, click the Change Configuration button so that you can enter the DNS servers, hostname, and default gateway settings. If you use PPPoE to connect to the Internet, you can configure the username and password you use to connect, as well as select the network interface from a drop down menu. PPPOE also provides check boxes to configure an always-on connection and Internet connection sharing.

Computer Administration

Chapter 6 covered most of the modules in this section. We finish this section by describing the remaining modules.

Password & User Account

This module allows the superuser to easily add and remove users, configure who has administrative access, and change the administrative password or the password of the selected user. Figure 7-9 provides a screenshot of this module.

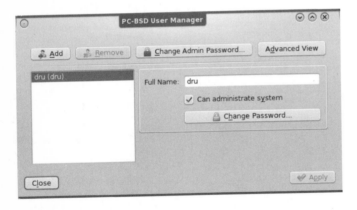

Figure 7-9. Password & User Account module

---

[4] These settings are needed if security has been configured on the wireless router. Ask your Internet provider or the person who set up the wireless configuration settings if you cannot connect to the wireless network.

In this example, the only regular user account on this system is "dru" and this user has superuser access because the Can administrate system check box is checked. The Change Password button can be used to reset the user's password. Because this utility is run as the superuser, you don't have to know the user's old password in order to change it.

The Change Admin Password can be used to reset the superuser password.

The Advanced View button allows you to view and modify all the user accounts and groups on the system. Figure 7-10 provides a screenshot with the dru user account selected.

Figure 7-10. The Users tab of the Advanced View of Password & User Account system settings module

This advanced view allows you to change the user's Full Name, Home Directory, default shell, and primary group.

■ **Caution** Even the superuser shouldn't change the settings for the system user accounts unless there is a good reason to do so. System user accounts are all the accounts needed by the operating system and are created for you. In this example, it is every account except for the dru account.

The Groups tab allows you to easily create (add) new groups and add or remove members from groups. Again, be cautious about changing the settings for system groups—it is recommended that you modify only the settings for the groups that you have created.

Printer Configuration

This module is used to configure printing on your PC-BSD system. It supports printers that are physically cabled to the system, connecting to print shares over the network, and printing to a network printer. Using this module to set up printing is discussed in detail in Chapter 5.

Services Manager

This module requires the superuser password and is unique to PC-BSD. It allows the administrator to control the startup settings of PC-BSD services and to stop or start these services. Figure 7-11 provides a screenshot of this module.

Figure 7-11. Services Manager configuration module

■ **Tip** Later in this chapter, we will discuss Service Manager, which is provided by KDE and shows KDE services.

Each entry in this menu shows the following:

Service Name: The name of the service.

Running: Whether the service is currently running or stopped.

AutoStart: Indicates whether the service is set to start automatically when the system boots up. Use the Enable Startup or Disable Startup buttons to change the current setting.

Description: A brief description of what the service does.

■ **Tip** Don't change the startup setting for a service unless you understand what the service does.

If you highlight a service, the appropriate buttons will activate. For example, if a service is currently running, the Stop and Restart buttons will activate. If a service is currently set to start at boot time, the Disable Startup button will activate.

Software & Updates

This module is unique to PC-BSD and requires superuser privileges to access. Figure 7-12 shows a screenshot of this module.

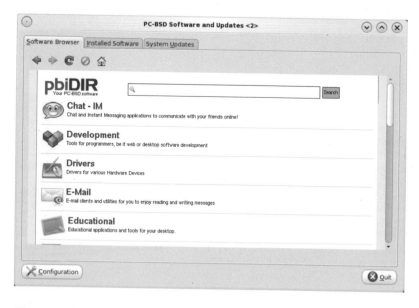

Figure 7-12. Software & Updates module

How to use this module to install software and to keep your installed applications and operating system up-to-date is described in detail in Chapter 8.

System Manager

The System Manager module is unique to PC-BSD and requires the administrative password. Figure 7-13 provides a screenshot of this module.

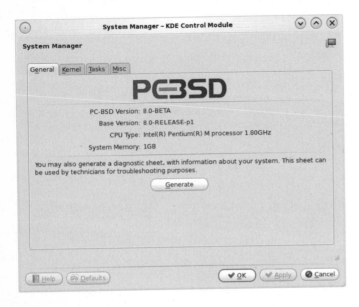

Figure 7-13. System Manager configuration module

The General tab can be used to view the version of PC-BSD, the version of FreeBSD it is based upon, the system's CPU type and frequency, and the amount of installed memory. The Generate button allows you to create a diagnostic report and will prompt you for the name and location of the file to generate. This allows you to easily send a file of diagnostic information to a mailing list or another user who is helping you to troubleshoot your system.

The Kernel tab, seen in Figure 7-14, allows you to enable ATAPI DMA mode. This mode is off by default as it can cause hardware on some systems to hang. If you feel that the transfer mode on your disk drives is less than optimal, you can try checking this box to see whether it makes a difference. If it results in system freezes, go back and uncheck the box. You can also reduce the boot delay in this tab. Boot delay is how long the system waits for you to select an option from the boot menu you see when the system starts up; it is set to 10 seconds by default. It's probably not a good idea to set a value lower than

3 seconds to give you time to select another boot option;[5] for example, if you ever need to go into single-user mode to repair your system. Finally, the Kernel tab allows a power user who has compiled and installed another kernel[6] to select which kernel to boot.

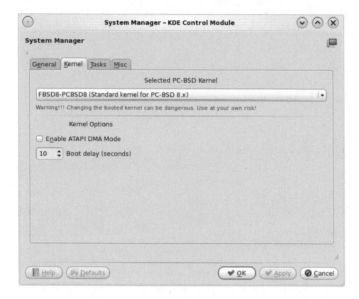

Figure 7-14. Kernel tab of System Manager configuration module

The Tasks tab is shown in Figure 7-15.

---

[5] If you find that the boot menu goes by too quickly to read it, press the spacebar. It will pause the menu until you make a selection.

[6] How to do so is beyond the scope of this book. See `http://www.freebsd.org/doc/en_US.ISO8859-1/books/handbook/kernelconfig.html` for more details.

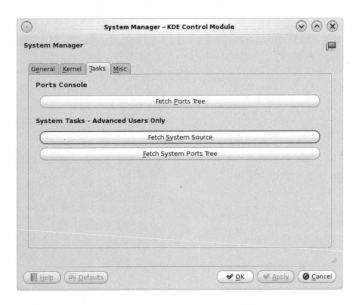

Figure 7-15. Task tab of System Manager configuration module

This tab is divided into two sections. The Ports Console section allows you to fetch the ports tree into Ports Console. (Ports Console and the Ports Tree are discussed in detail in Chapters 9 and 10.) The System Tasks section allows advanced users to fetch system source and the system ports tree; it is discussed in Chapter 14.

The Misc tab allows you to configure the language used in the system boot screen. The custom button allows you to select a custom image to display at boot time. This image will appear as the kernel starts to load and will hide the boot messages (you can press any key to leave the image and view the boot messages). The image must be in .pcx format; you can use the GIMP or KolourPaint applications to create pcx files.

■ **Note** .pcx images are not graphic intensive. If you receive an error about the size or color depth of the image when you try to add it using the Custom button, that image will not load at boot time.

Advanced User Settings

As the name suggests, the modules in the Advanced tab of the System Settings module tend to require more configuration knowledge and most require administrative access in order to make configuration changes. The Advanced User Settings section contains over a dozen modules dealing with various system services and hardware.

Akonadi Configuration

In KDE, Akonadi is the storage architecture behind the Kontact[7] Personal Information Management (PIM) application. A PIM application can be used to manage information such as your calendar, events, address book, and bookmarks. Figure 7-16 shows the menu for this configuration module. In this example, the Add button was selected.

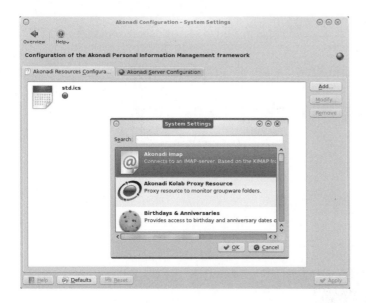

Figure 7-16. *Akonadi configuration module*

Akonadi can store personal information from a variety of sources, and this menu is used to add and configure these resources. Unfortunately, the documentation on Akonadi is still a work in progress,[8] so you might have to resort to trial and error and asking questions within the KDE community. Chapter 11 describes in more detail how to get help when you are having trouble figuring something out.

The Akonadi Server Configuration tab will show the database settings. Akonadi uses the MySQL database application to store your personal information and preconfigures the database for you. You should leave these settings as-is. However, you might find the Test, Stop, and Restart buttons useful if you are having problems with the MySQL database.

---

[7] See the Kontact User Guide `http://docs.kde.org/stable/en/kdepim/kontact/index.html` for more information on how to configure and use Kontact.

[8] Start your research at `http://pim.kde.org`.

■ **Tip** If you don't use Kontact, you can reduce startup time by disabling the Akonadi service by unchecking Contacts in KRunner ➤ Plugins.

Audio CDs

Figure 7-17 shows the Audio CDs configuration module that is used to set the default settings used by applications that play audio CDs. You can override most of these settings in the configuration menus provided by a specific CD player application. It should be noted that your audio settings should "just work" as-is; this module is for audiophiles who want to tweak their settings.

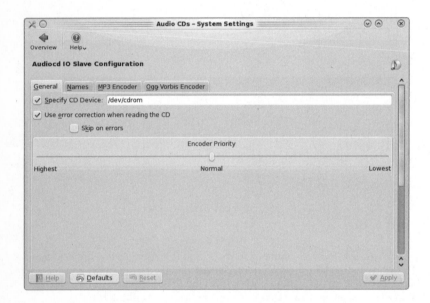

Figure 7-17. The Audio CD configuration module

The tabs in this module allow you to configure the following:

> **General:** Specifies the device name of the CD player, whether or not to use error correction and to skip on errors, and the encoder priority used when ripping CD tracks.

> **Names:** The track and album information that is displayed by the CD player is set in this tab. The default is to show the track artist, track number, and song title for each track and the album artist followed by the album title for each album. This information is gathered using CDDB, which is discussed later on in this chapter.

MP3 Encoder: Various settings for encoding MP3 files can be set here. A good introduction to understanding the terminology used in these settings is at `http://arstechnica.com/old/content/2007/10/the-audiofile-understanding-mp3-compression.ars`.

Ogg Vorbis Encoder: Wikipedia has a good introduction to some of the terms used in this tab: `http://en.wikipedia.org/wiki/Ogg_vorbis`.

Autostart

KDE allows you to specify which scripts are executed when KDE starts up. PC-BSD comes preconfigured with scripts in the Autostart module that set up your system's network interfaces, check that sound is working correctly, and check that the system is up-to-date. Figure 7-18 shows the Autostart configuration module. The computer in this example has an Ethernet (em0) network interface which is configured to be enabled at KDE startup. The drop-down menu for startstrigi.sh is selected to demonstrate that Script Files can be run at KDE startup, KDE shutdown, or before KDE starts up.

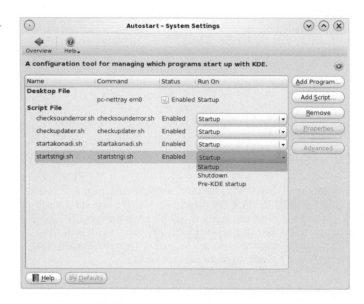

Figure 7-18. Autostart configuration module showing PC-BSD specific scripts

If you want your favorite programs, such as Firefox or Akregator, to start with KDE, click Add Program and select the program from the menu. Power users can also run their own custom scripts by clicking Add Script to browse to the script. The script will be added to the Script File section with its own drop down menu to select when the script will be run.

CDDB Retrieval

The Compact Disc Database (CDDB[9]) is an Internet database of track information for music CDs. Figure 7-19 shows the CDDB Retrieval configuration module. CDDB is enabled by default, meaning that track information should be available in all your CD playing utilities.

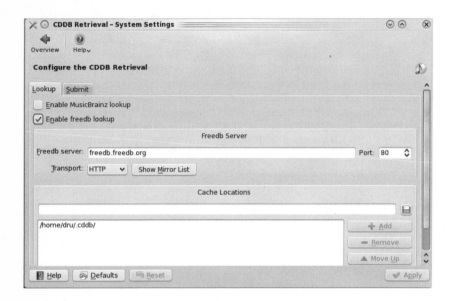

Figure 7-19. CDDB Retrieval configuration module

Two popular databases of CDDB information are MusicBrainz (`http://musicbrainz.org`) and freedb (`http://www.freedb.org`). freedb supports both the HTTP and CDDB protocols; HTTP is a good default because it is allowed through most firewalls. If track information is not available for your favorite CD, and freedb is enabled, you can use the Submit tab to configure the e-mail address used to submit the track information to the database using a CDDB-aware application such as xmms. Instructions on how to submit can be found at the freedb FAQ (`http://www.freedb.org/en/faq.3.html#21`).

---

[9] Wikipedia provides a good introduction to CDDB (`http://en.wikipedia.org/wiki/Cddb`).

Desktop Search

The Desktop Search configuration module allows you to enable the Networked Environment for Personalized, Ontology-based Management of Unified Knowledge (Nepomuk) semantic desktop and the Strigi desktop search feature. Nepomuk allows you to tag, rate, and comment your files through Dolphin and to browse tagged files in Gwenview. Strigi[10] is a fast desktop search utility.

The Basic Settings tab, seen in Figure 7-20, allows you to see whether the services are running and to enable them if they are not.

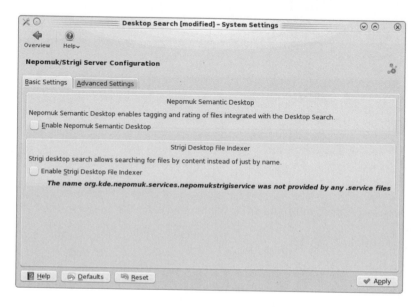

Figure 7- 20. Desktop Search configuration module

The Advanced Settings tab can be used to check off the directories you want Strigi to index for your searches. Your home directory will already be selected for you.

Nepomuk is the backend that allows Comments and Tags to appear in the right frame of Dolphin. In Figure 7-21, the Downloads folder has been selected. The Add Comment link is no longer seen on the right because it has been replaced by a text box containing the comment. A tag of "stuff" was previously added, and the user has clicked Change Tags to open the Create New Tag menu. Note that tags also allow you to change the icon and to add a detailed description.

---

10 See http://strigi.sourceforge.net/ for more information about Strigi.

Figure 7-21. Creating a new tag in Dolphin

Strigi allows this user to type the word **stuff** in Dolphin's Search bar and receive search results for both the comment and the tag.

Desktop Theme Details

Figure 7-22 shows the Desktop Theme Details configuration module.

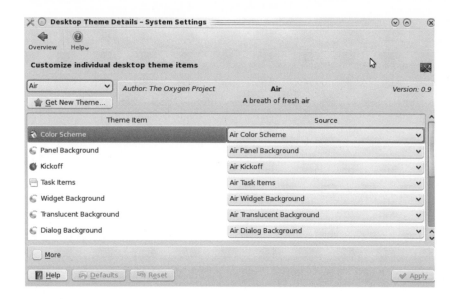

Figure 7-22. Desktop Theme Details configuration module

This configuration module allows you to fine-tune your theme settings by theme item. For example, the Color Scheme could be Air, while the Panel Background scheme could be Heron, and the Kickoff scheme could be Aya. You can get a preview of each scheme by clicking the drop-down menu above the Get New Theme button. The Get New Theme button provides easy access to the Plasma Themes section of kde-look.org.

Check the More box if you want to remove a theme or save it to a file. If you don't like your changes and want to return back to the defaults, click the Reset button.

Device Actions

KDE4 uses the Solid[11] hardware architecture to control access to hardware devices. Figure 7-23 shows the Device Actions module. This module is intended to be used by developers to set conditions to ensure that hardware is properly accessed by applications. Unless you are developing an application that requires access to hardware, you should leave the settings in this module as-is.

---

[11] See `http://techbase.kde.org/Development/Architecture/KDE4/Solid` for a description of Solid.

Figure 7-23. The Device Actions configuration module

If you highlight an action and click Edit, a menu will open where a developer can view the conditions that must be met in order for the selected action to be applied to the device.

■ **Caution** Unless you are a developer familiar with the Solid architecture, you should leave the settings as-is. Documentation on Solid is still pretty sparse. The curious can learn more about this architecture at http://solid.kde.org.

File Associations

The File Associations module allows you to configure which applications are used to open files according to their file extension. Figure 7-24 shows this module with the image section expanded and the .bmp file type selected. In this example, Gwenview is the preferred application, followed by KolourPaint and Okular.

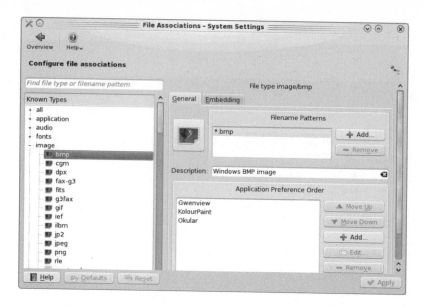

Figure 7-24. *Viewing the .bmp file association in the File Associations configuration module*

Use the Add button if your favorite application, capable of opening the highlighted extension, is not listed. If you highlight an application, you can move it up or down in the Application Preference Order. You can also remove applications that you don't want to associate with the specified file type.

The Embedding tab can be used to set the default left-click action. You can select one of the following:

- Show file in embedded viewer

- Show file in separate viewer

- Use settings for group (where group is the parent group for the file extension)

- Ask whether to save to disk instead

KDE Resources

This configuration module allows you to set which locations, or resources, can be used as data sources for Contacts, Calendar, Notes, and Alarms. Figure 7-25 shows the possible resources for Calendar. This menu was accessed by selecting Calendar from the drop-down menu and clicking the Add button.

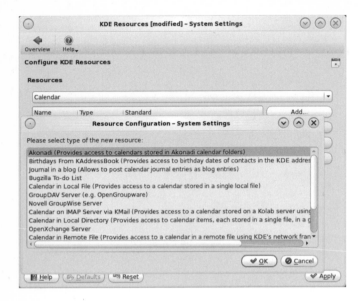

Figure 7-25. Adding a Calendar resource in KDE Resources configuration module

In this example, possible data sources for the Default Address Book containing your personal Contacts include KDE's Akonadi, OpenGroupware, Novell GroupWise, KMail, and OpenXchange. If you select a resource, it will attempt a connection to that type of server and will provide a resource settings configuration menu so you can select the correct location containing your contacts. You can have multiple resources, but only one can be selected as the Standard.

Spend some time browsing the possible resources for each item—you might be surprised how many types of resources are supported!

■ **Note** This module assumes that you already understand the possible configurations for the resources you select. For example, if you select the Novell Groupwise Server module, it will prompt you for the resource settings needed to successfully connect to an existing account on a Groupwise server.

KDE Wallet

KDE Wallet is a tool to store your passwords, web form data, and cookies in an encrypted format. The first time you enter private information into a KDE utility, it should ask you if you want to store it in your KDE wallet. The wallet itself is protected by a password so other users don't have access to its contents.

The KDE Wallet configuration module, seen in Figure 7-26, allows you to configure your wallet preferences.

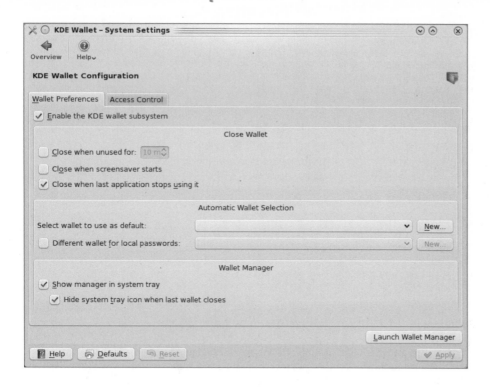

Figure 7-26. *KDE Wallet configuration module*

The Close Wallet section in the Wallet Preferences tab allows you to configure when the wallet closes. Note that once a wallet is closed, you need to input the wallet's password to reopen it.

The Automatic Wallet Selection allows you to select which of your wallets to use by default. You can store local passwords in a separate wallet from your Internet passwords. If you have never been prompted to make a KDE wallet, you can launch the wallet creation wizard by clicking New. You will be asked to choose a name for the wallet and then if you want to perform a basic setup (recommended) or advanced setup. Figure 7-27 shows the wizard screen after selecting the basic setup.

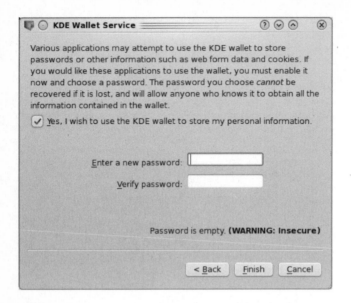

Figure 7-27. Using the create wallet wizard to set the password on a new wallet

Once you enter a password and click Finish, the KDE Wallet Service will re-prompt you for the password and provide a strength meter for the password. After clicking Create, your new wallet will show in the Automatic Wallet Selection drop-down menu.

The Wallet Manager allows you to view the information stored in your wallets. If you double-click a wallet within Wallet Manager, it will prompt you for the wallet password before displaying its contents.

The Access Control tab within Wallet Manager allows you to view which applications have access to the wallet (the list will be empty until an application uses it). If you no longer want to have an application use the wallet, you can delete its access here.

Service Manager

The Service Manager configuration module, seen in Figure 7-28, allows you to view which KDE services are currently running and which are configured to start with KDE.

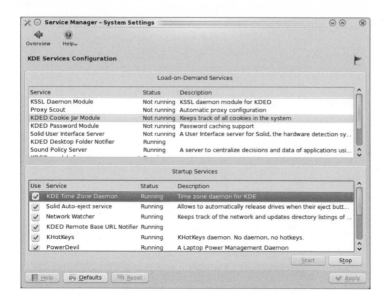

Figure 7-28. Service Manager configuration module

If you uncheck a box in Startup Services, that service will no longer be started with KDE. It will, however, continue to run in your current KDE session until you highlight it and click Stop. If there are services that you know you don't use, you can reduce KDE's startup time by not starting those services. If you are unsure, you should leave the services as-is. If you mess up your configurations, press Defaults to return to the system defaults.

■ **Caution** Don't change the status of a service unless you understand what the service does.

The Load-on-Demand services are automatically loaded whenever another application requires that service. This means that you can't use this interface to stop or start the services in this section.

■ **Tip** Power users can remove an unwanted Load-on-Demand service by editing the X-KDE-Kded-load-on-demand=true line to =false in the appropriate *.desktop file. These files are located in /usr/local/kde4/share/kde4/services/kded/. Make sure you understand the ramifications before editing a service's *.desktop file.

Session Manager

The Session Manager module, seen in Figure 7-29, allows you to configure which icons appear in the Kickoff ➤ Leave menu.

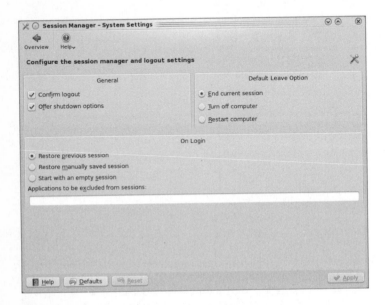

Figure 7-29. Session Manager configuration module

If you don't like receiving the extra 30 seconds confirmation dialog when you click one of the options in the Leave menu, uncheck the Confirm logout box. If you uncheck the Offer shutdown options box, the Restart and Shutdown options will be removed from the Leave menu. This can be useful if you share your computer with others and don't want them to have access to those options. You can still safely restart or shut down the system manually by typing **restart** or **halt** at the command line or by changing the Default Leave Option to Turn off computer or Restart computer.

If you have applications running when you leave a session, the On Login section determines whether they are restored when you start your next session. If you select Restore manually saved session, a Save Session option will be added to the Leave menu, allowing you to decide on a session-by-session basis. Once you have saved your session, you can then log out, restart, or shut down the system.

System

This section of the System Settings' Advanced tab provides modules that deal with managing logins to scheduling when to run specified tasks.

Login Manager

KDM,[12] the KDE Display Manager, is the software that is used to provide the PC-BSD login screen. The Login Manager configuration module, seen in Figure 7-30, allows you to configure various aspects of KDM.

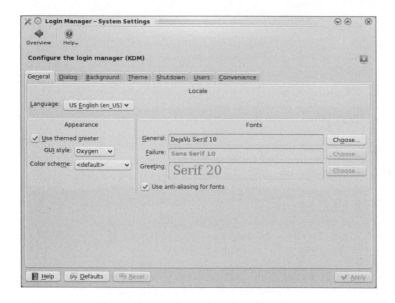

Figure 7-30. *Login Manager configuration module*

The options available in each tab are as follows:

> **General:** Here you can set the language, theme, color scheme, and fonts used by KDM.

> **Dialog:** If the Use themed greeter box is checked in the General tab, you will receive a message indicating that there is no dialog window. If you uncheck that box, this tab allows you to create your own greeting and show a logo, a clock, or nothing but the greeting.

> **Background:** Allows you to set the background wallpaper or a slideshow of pictures that appear behind the login screen.

---

[12] See the KDM Handbook at `http://docs.kde.org/stable/en/kdebase-workspace/kdm/index.html` for more information about configuring KDM.

Theme: This mode will be disabled unless the Use themed greeter box is checked in the General tab. Here you can select and preview preinstalled themes. Click Get New Themes to browse for more themes from `kde-look.org`.

Shutdown: This tab allows you to configure who is allowed to perform local (this computer) and remote (other computers on the network) shutdowns. The choices are Everybody, Only Root, and Nobody. By default, Everybody can perform a local shutdown and Only Root can perform a remote shutdown. The actual commands should be left as is, but you can view which commands are used to perform those operations. If you have installed the Grub boot manager, change the Boot Manager from None to Grub. Grub is most often seen on systems which dual boot with Linux.

Users: If you want to choose from a list of users when you log in, check any usernames that you do not want to appear from the Excluded Users list and make sure that the Show list check box is checked. For security reasons, you should leave the System UIDs setting as-is; this will prevent the root user and system accounts from being used at login time. In the User Images section, you can select a user in the drop-down list; then click the icon to select which picture appears next to that username. If you prefer the more secure but inconvenient setting of manually typing in the username without seeing a list of users and their icons, uncheck the Show list check box.

Convenience: This section comes with a big red Attention Read help warning message as changing these settings can affect the security of your system. During installation, you were asked if you want the primary user to automatically log in. If you change your mind, you can enable or disable that option and select the primary user in this tab. You can also check the insecure setting of Enable Password-Less Logins and select which users have this ability. You can specify which username is pretyped in for you in the Preselect User section; options are none, previous, or a specified user account. If the Focus password check box is checked, the cursor will place itself in the password type-in box. You can also choose whether or not to be automatically logged in should an X server crash abruptly end your current session.

PolicyKit Authorization

PolicyKit[13] is a framework for managing which user level processes are allowed to interact with processes running with system privileges. This means that it would be rare for anyone other than a KDE application developer to make changes within this configuration module. Any changes should be well researched and made at your own risk as they could affect the operation and security of your computer.

Figure 7-31 shows a screenshot of the PolicyKit Authorization configuration module with some of its options expanded.

---

[13] See `http://techbase.kde.org/Development/Tutorials/PolicyKit/Introduction` for more information about PolicyKit.

Figure 7-31. PolicyKit Authorization configuration module with expanded trees and an item selected

---

■ **Caution** Don't change any of these settings unless you know what you are doing!

Power Management

KDE4 uses PowerDevil to manage laptop power management. The Power Management module, seen in Figure 7-32, is used to configure the laptop's power settings.

■ **Tip** If you aren't running PC-BSD on a laptop, you can prevent the PowerDevil service from starting in System Settings ➤ KDE Services.

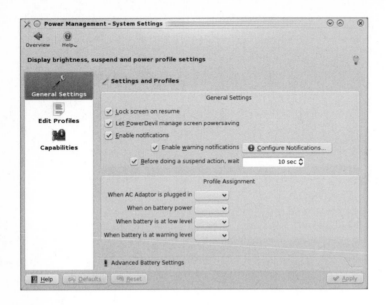

Figure 7-32. Power Management configuration module

The General Settings tab allows you to configure warning notifications and to assign profiles to specific actions. If you click Configure Notifications, you will see the screen in Figure 7-33. For each action in the Title column, you can configure a variety of events.

Figure 7-33. Configuring laptop power warning notifications in the Power Management configuration module

By default, the only profile that shows in the Profile Assignment drop-down menus is the performance profile that has been created for you. You can view and edit the default profile as well as create your own in the Edit Profiles menu, seen in Figure 7-34.

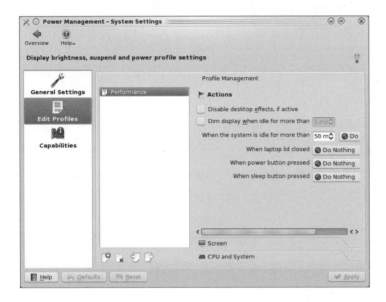

Figure 7-34. Viewing the default performance profile's settings in Power Management

This screenshot shows the Actions settings. You can also click the Screen and CPU and System tabs toward the bottom of the menu to view and modify their settings. The four icons in the lower-left corner of this menu allow you to create a new profile, delete the selected profile, and import or export the selected profile.

The Capabilities menu shows you what PowerDevil thinks your laptop hardware is capable of. A screenshot from a laptop is seen in Figure 7-35; your laptop's capabilities may differ.

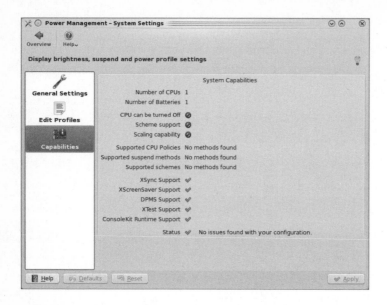

Figure 7-35. System Capabilities taken from a laptop

Samba

Samba allows PC-BSD, Linux, Mac OSX, and Windows systems to share files and printers. Samba can also allow your PC-BSD system to act as a Windows domain controller or a member of an Active Directory domain. Samba uses the smb.conf configuration file to control access to the network's shared resources. The Samba configuration module, seen in Figure 7-36, provides a frontend to this configuration file, allowing you to quickly browse and enable the options you need for your network. Note that you still need to understand the configuration file to get the most out of the available options.

■ **Note** Entire books have been written about Samba because it is a powerful tool with a lot of configuration possibilities. We provide only a brief introduction to the configuration tool in this section. To actually understand the configurations, you will want to spend some time reading the documentation available from http://www.samba.org/.

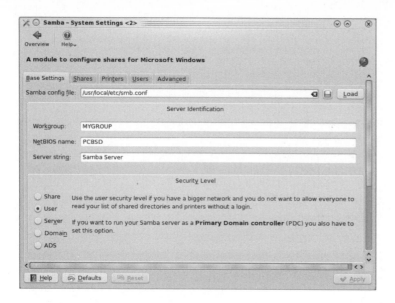

Figure 7-36. Samba configuration module

■ **Tip** If the options in this module are greyed out, restart the module from Kickoff ➤ Samba Manager. This should prompt you for the administrative password.

PC-BSD creates a MYGROUP workgroup for you; if your system is part of an existing Windows workgroup, change this setting to the workgroup's name. If there are other computers in the same workgroup, you can browse the workgroup's resources by typing **smb:/** into Konqueror or Dolphin. You should understand the available Security Levels in a Windows network before changing from the default setting of User.

The Shares tab allows you to fine-tune what gets shared in the network. By default, a homes share is created for you. If you double-click the share, a very comprehensive Add/Edit Share menu becomes available, as seen in Figure 7-37. Remember: change these settings only if you know what you are doing.

■ **Tip** You can create additional shares in Dolphin, using the instructions for sharing a folder in the "Installing from Another PC-BSD System" section in Chapter 8.

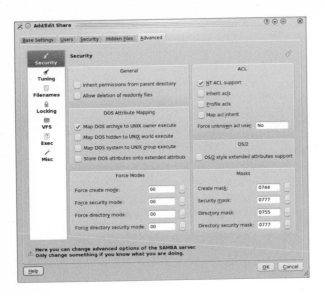

Figure 7-37. Editing a share's settings in Samba configuration module

The Printers and the Users tabs are expected to work in a future version of PC-BSD. They will allow an administrator to fine-tune the permissions of printer shares and Samba users.

The Advanced tab, seen in Figure 7-38 literally contains hundreds of Samba options. If what you want to configure isn't in any of the other tabs, it is probably here.

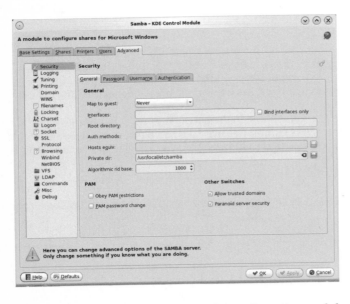

Figure 7-38. Advanced options of Samba configuration module

Task Scheduler

PC-BSD uses the cron service to schedule tasks. cron understands two types of scheduled tasks, or *crontabs*: tasks a user wants to schedule and tasks that are used to maintain the operating system. Operating system maintenance tasks are known as *system cron*. Only the superuser can edit the system cron and rarely does so. Users can schedule their own tasks.

■ **Tip** Systems that use the cron scheduler read "crontab" files to determine which tasks to run at what time. Power users can edit these files directly. Task Scheduler provides an easy to use interface for editing the underlying crontab files.

Figure 7-39 provides a screenshot of Task Scheduler.

Figure 7-39. Task scheduler configuration module

By default, the Personal Cron area will be empty until you add a task. If you click the System Cron button, you can view the scheduled operating system tasks. The tasks will be greyed out to remind you that you should not modify the system cron.

To schedule a personal task, click New Task to see the menu shown in Figure 7-40.

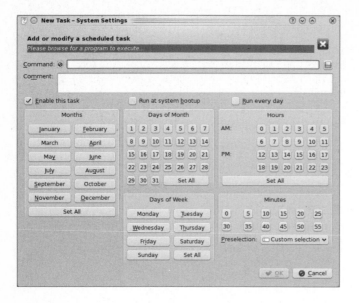

Figure 7-40. *Adding a new task to one's personal cron*

This menu makes it easy to browse to an application or custom script to run. You can then fine-tune which months, days, hours, and minutes the task will run. Note that you can select multiple items. For example, you can set the task to run at 1:15 AM as well as 19:15 PM. If you click the Custom Selection drop-down menu, you can choose to run the task at the specified time intervals.

Summary

This chapter concludes Part 2, which covered every aspect of using PC-BSD. You now know how to customize your desktop, find and launch applications, perform common computing tasks, and use all the System Settings configuration modules.

Part 3 concentrates on software: getting it, keeping it up-to-date, and uninstalling it. We'll start with the software management system that is unique to PC-BSD: the push button installer.

Software

CHAPTER 8

■ ■ ■

Push Button Installer System

Chapter 5 discussed some of the software that is available to perform common tasks using your PC-BSD system. Part 3 of this book will show you all the ways you can find, install, and manage software. This chapter covers the Push Button Installer (PBI) system.

What Is a PBI?

PBI is the name of the software management system that is unique to PC-BSD. An application that you can install using this software management system is also called a PBI. For example, you might see references to someone installing the Firefox PBI. If you ever come across a file with a .pbi extension, it is an application that can be installed using the PBI software manager.

As you go through Part 3 of this book, you'll discover that there are many different ways to install software on your PC-BSD system. Whenever possible, you should use the PBI system because it provides the following advantages:

- PBI software is easy to install. You simply find the application in Software Manager and click it to install.

- PBI software is easy to uninstall using Software Manager.

- Software Manager will tell you when newer versions of your installed applications become available and it will allow you to easily upgrade to the new versions.

- PBI software has been pretested to run on PC-BSD, meaning it should "just work."

- Software Manager ensures that no other applications are affected when you install or uninstall PBI software. This means that you won't accidentally overwrite or delete libraries or dependencies needed by the operating system or other applications.

The rest of this chapter demonstrates how to use Software Manager to manage PBIs.

Software Manager

To access the PBI system, simply double-click the Software Manager icon on the default Desktop.

■ **Tip** You can also find Software Manager in Kickoff ➤ Applications ➤ System ➤ Software Manager.

When starting Software Manager, you will be prompted for the superuser password because only the administrative account can install software. You also need to be connected to the Internet because Software Manager will attempt to connect to the PC-BSD software repository at pbidir.com. Figure 8-1 shows a screenshot of Software Manager.

Figure 8-1. *Software Manager*

If the connection to pbidir.com is successful, you will see the available software categories loaded in the Software Browser tab.

Software Manager contains the following tabs:

> **Software Browser:** Allows you to browse for PBIs. Using its built-in search feature is discussed in the following section, "Installing a PBI."

> **Installed Software:** Shows you which PBIs are already installed, and allows you to update or remove installed PBIs.

> **System Updates:** Allows you to check for, review, and install operating system updates. They are discussed in more detail in the "Update Manager" section later on in this chapter.

Software Manager also provides a Configuration button that contains the following tabs:

Mirrors: Specifies which PBI server on the Internet to connect to. You can also specify a custom mirror if you have created your own web server to host PBIs.

Software: Allows you to keep a copy of downloaded PBIs after installation. This is discussed further in the section titled "Installing from Another PC-BSD System."

System: Allows you to automatically install available updates.

Misc: Allows you to specify an alternate temporary directory to store downloaded PBIs.

The next section will demonstrate how to install a PBI using Software Manager.

Installing a PBI

The Software Browser tab of Software Manager can be used to browse for and install PBIs. In the example seen in Figure 8-2, the user has entered a search phrase of **firefox**, and the search results show that there are two Firefox PBIs available.

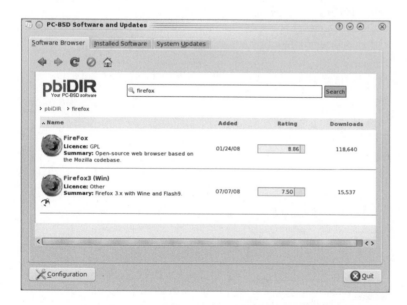

Figure 8-2. Using Software Manager to search for a Firefox PBI

If you don't know the name of the application you want to install or want to get an idea of which PBIs are available, you can instead click a software category. In the example shown in Figure 8-3, the user clicked the left arrow to return to the software categories screen. The user then clicked the Web Browsers category to see which web browsers were available.

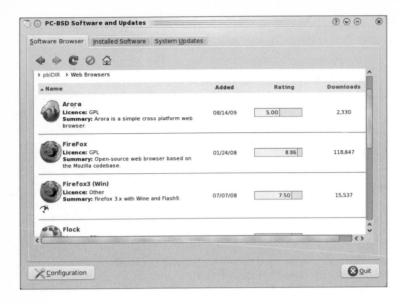

Figure 8-3. Browsing for software in the Web Browsers category

If the user clicks an application, they will see more information. Figure 8-4 shows the information for the Opera web browser.

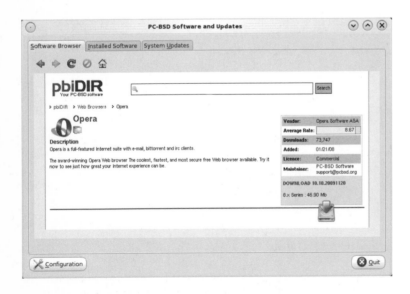

Figure 8-4. Information about selected PBI

Each PBI contains a description, the name of the organization (vendor) that creates the software, its rating among PBI users, the number of downloads since the PBI became available, the date the PBI was added to the repository, the license the software is released under, the e-mail address of the person who created the PBI, and the version number of the PBI. If you want to install the software, click either the DOWNLOAD hyperlink or the download icon that contains the green arrow.

■ **Tip** PBIs tend to be large because they contain everything needed to run the application. If you have several PC-BSD systems in your network, consider downloading the PBIs you need to a shared folder on one system. Instructions on how to do so are in the section called "Installing from Another PC-BSD System" later in this chapter.

When you click to install the application, a pop-up message will ask if you want to install the selected PBI. Click OK and the Installed Software tab will open, showing the progress of the installation. Figure 8-5 shows that the gtkpod PBI is currently downloading.

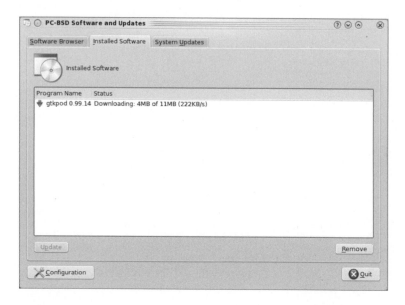

Figure 8-5. Software Manager downloading the gtkpod PBI

■ **Tip** Should the Internet connection fail during the download, the message in the Installed Software tab will change to "Download failed! Please try again later." When you regain your Internet connection, right-click the message and select Retry Download to resume the installation. The message will remain until either the installation is complete or you use the Remove button to remove it.

Once the download is complete, the installer will begin, as seen in Figure 8-6.

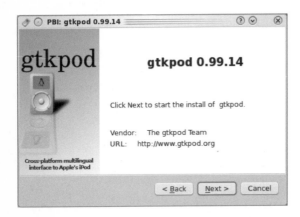

Figure 8-6. Initial screen of PBI installer

Click Next to continue. The installer will tell you where the application will be installed, how much disk space it requires, and how much space is available, as seen in Figure 8-7.

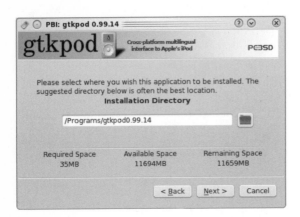

Figure 8-7. PBI installer showing amount of disk space needed and available for application installation

Click Next to start the installation. A progress meter will display while it is installing. When finished, the PBI will indicate its location in the Kickoff menu, as seen in Figure 8-8, and then will provide you with an installation complete message, as seen in Figure 8-9. The default is to start the application when the installer exits.

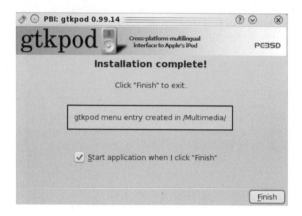

Figure 8-8. gtkpod installed into the Multimedia Applications category of Kickoff

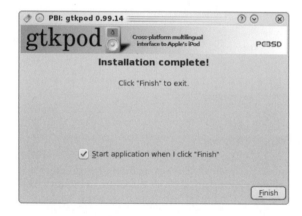

Figure 8-9. PBI installation is complete

gtkpod, along with its version number, will now show in the Installed Software tab of Software Manager.

Installing from a DVD

During the installation, you were asked if you wanted to install any software from the installation DVD. If you didn't install then, but want to now, simply insert the DVD and wait until Device Notifier pops up with the label of the DVD. You can then access the contents of the DVD from Dolphin.

While in Dolphin, click the DVD's label name in the Places panel. You will find the applications that came with the DVD in the extras ➤ PBI folder. Right-click the PBI you want to install and select Open with PBI Launcher from the menu. After entering the administrative password, the PBI will install as described in the previous section.

Installing from Another PC-BSD System

By default, Software Manager will download and install PBIs without permanently saving a copy of the downloaded PBI. If you want to save a copy of the PBI so it is available to other PC-BSD systems in your network, you will need to change this default. You can do so by clicking the Configuration button in Software Manager and then clicking the Software tab, as seen in Figure 8-10.

Figure 8-10. Software tab in Configuration button of Software Manager

Check the box Keep downloaded software in Temporary Directory. The location of that directory is in the Misc tab and by default is set to /usr/local/tmp. If you change this default directory to a folder in your home directory, you can easily share your PBIs with other PC-BSD users in your network. In the Misc tab, click the folder icon next to the Temporary file directory to browse to a folder you want to share.

In Figure 8-11, I highlighted dru's home directory and then clicked the New Folder button to create a new folder called software. Once I click OK, /home/dru/software will show as the new temporary file directory.

Figure 8-11. Creating a new directory in the Misc tab to store downloaded PBIs

To share this directory so it is accessible to other PC-BSD computers in the network, open up Dolphin. Click Home in the Places panel; then highlight the software folder. Right-click and select Properties from the menu. Click the share tab and then the Configure File Sharing button. You will be prompted for the administrative password, and then you will see the menu shown in Figure 8-12.

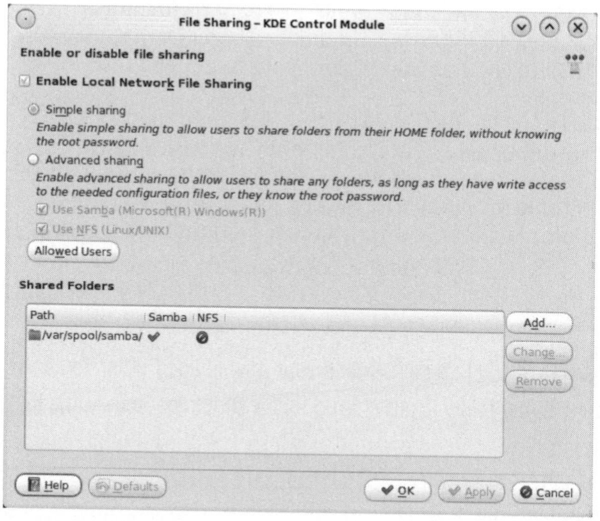

Figure 8-12. Configuring file folder sharing

Because the folder you want to share is in your home directory, you can keep the default of Simple sharing. Click the Add button to open the Share Folder screen seen in Figure 8-13. You can then browse to the folder you want to share (in this example, /home/dru/software).

Figure 8-13. Sharing a software folder in Dolphin

Once the folder is selected, check the box to Share with Samba (Microsoft(R) Windows(R)). This will add the Name of the folder—it will be capitalized, and if the original name was greater than eight characters, it will be reduced to eight characters. This will allow the folder to be shared with any computer that understands Samba. You should leave the Writable box unchecked unless you want other computers to be able to add files to this folder. When finished, press OK, and your folder will show in the Shared Folders list.

You can check that your changes worked from Dolphin. Click Network in Places and then Samba Shares ➤ Mygroup. You should have an icon with your hostname; in my example, the icon's name was Pcbsd-3228 (Samba Server). If you click that icon, you will see your software folder and its contents. The other PC-BSD users in your network should now be able to access your shared folder from Dolphin or Konqueror. If they use Konqueror, they can type **smb:/** to browse to your group, computer, and shared software folder.

■ **Tip** We have demonstrated sharing a folder so other PC-BSD users can access your downloaded PBIs. You can use the folder-sharing instructions to share the contents of any folder. Your shared folder should be accessible to any computer running PC-BSD or any version of Microsoft.

Installing from the Temporary Directory

If you already have a copy of a downloaded PBI saved in the temporary directory, you can install it directly from Dolphin without downloading it all over again within Software Manager. You might run across this situation if you install a PBI, remove it, and then decide you want to install it again.

Open up your PBI temporary directory in Dolphin, right-click the PBI, and select Open with PBI Launcher from the menu. After typing the administrative password, the PBI installation will proceed as usual.

Removing a PBI

To uninstall a PBI, highlight it in the Installed Software tab and either right-click and select Uninstall or click the Remove button. You will receive a warning asking if you want to remove this application. Once you press Yes, the application will be uninstalled, removed from the Installed Software tab, and removed from its location in the Kickoff menu. Its entire directory will be removed from /Programs. If the application stored data in your home directory, it might ask if you want to remove it when the application is uninstalled.

Updating PBIs

The Installed Software manager tab in Software Manager can be used to update PBIs whenever a newer version becomes available. The Status section will indicate which versions are available. Figure 8-14 indicates that this system can upgrade from Firefox version 3.5.5 to version 3.5.6.

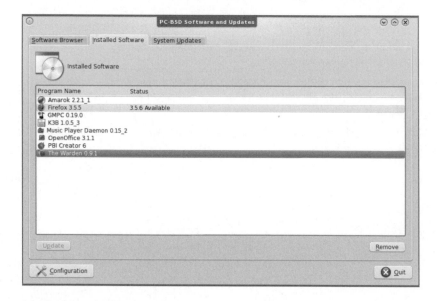

Figure 8-14. Updating a PBI in Software Manager

If an update is available, simply highlight the PBI you want to update and click the Update button. It will uninstall the old PBI for you and then download and install the newer version. When finished, the new version number will show in the Program Name.

■ **Tip** If you ever accidentally remove the desktop icon for an installed PBI, right-click the application in the Installed Software tab of Software Manager. Click Install Desktop Icons, and it will re-add the icon to your desktop.

Update Manager

Update Manager is used to notify you when newer versions of PBIs become available and when patches are available for your operating system. The system tray includes an icon for Update Manager. When your PBIs and operating system are up-to-date, the icon for Update Manager appears as a green shield with a white checkmark. If updates are available, the icon changes to a red shield with a white X.

If you right-click the Update Manager icon in the system tray, you can do the following:

> **Start the Update Manager:** Launches Software Manager. You can then use the Installed Applications tab to update any PBIs whose status shows that there is a newer version available and use the System Updates tab to update the operating system, as discussed in this section.

> **Check for updates:** Causes the icon to change to a green circular arrow as it connects to the PC-BSD update server to see whether any updates are available. When finished, a pop-up menu will indicate if your system is completely up-to-date or if updates are available.

> **Run at startup:** If checked, Update Manager will automatically check for updates whenever you start KDE. If unchecked, you can manually check whenever you want by clicking Check for updates.

> **Quit:** This will remove Update Manager from the system tray. You can still manually start Update Manager from Kickoff ➤ Applications ➤ System ➤ Online Update Notifier.

The System Updates tab of Software Manager is used to install operating system patches. Figure 8-15 shows that the SSL Security Update is available for a PC-BSD system.

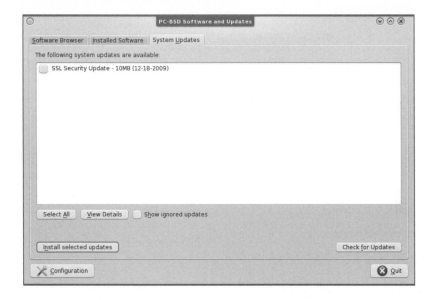

Figure 8-15. Installing a system update using Software Manager

If you highlight the entry, the View Details button will explain the reason for the update. An example of an older update is seen in Figure 8-16.

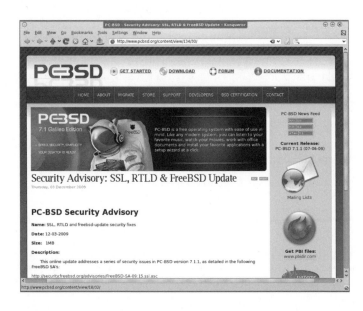

Figure 8-16. Viewing the details of a security update

To apply the update, check the box next to it or click the Select All button to apply all security updates. A progress bar, seen in Figure 8-17, will show you which update is currently being downloaded or applied.

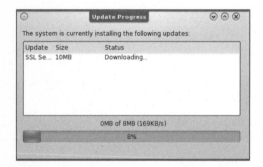

Figure 8-17. Update progress for a system update

Some updates will require the system to reboot, and Update Manager will present a pop-up message to remind you to reboot for those changes to take effect. Update Manager will not automatically reboot for you. This means that you can continue to do other things with your computer while the system is being updated, without worrying about losing the data you are currently working on.

When a PBI Doesn't Exist

We mentioned at the beginning of this chapter that the PBI software management system is the best way to install applications on your PC-BSD system. While the PBI system offers many of the most popular software applications, not every application will have a PBI. If you can't find a PBI of your favorite application, you have a few choices available to you:

- Install its FreeBSD package, as described in Chapter 9.

- Install its FreeBSD port, as described in Chapter 10.

- Ask that someone within the PC-BSD community create the PBI. Chapter 11 discusses how to ask for help within the community.

- Create the PBI yourself. How to do this is demonstrated in Chapter 12.

Summary

This chapter introduced you to PC-BSD's PBI system. Its Software Manager makes it easy to find, install, remove, and update software. The next two chapters will introduce you to FreeBSD's packages and ports collections. Both of these collections allow you to access a much larger collection of software, but also require a bit more knowledge on your part.

CHAPTER 9

■ ■ ■

FreeBSD Packages

Chapter 8 introduced you to the PBI system of installing and managing software. While this is the preferred way to handle software on your PC-BSD system, it is not the only method available to you. This chapter will introduce you to FreeBSD packages, the second easiest way to manage software on your PC-BSD system. Chapter 9 will introduce you to FreeBSD ports, which allow advanced users to customize their software installations.

■ **Caution** Chapter 9 and Chapter 10 require you to use the command line to manage software. If you prefer to use a GUI or don't have the time right now to learn new commands, use the instructions in Chapter 8 to find, install, and manage your software. You can always come back to these chapters later when you have more time and want to advance your software management skills.

What Is the Ports Collection?

The Internet contains literally hundreds of thousands of free applications. Many can be found at free software websites such as Sourceforge.net (which hosts more than 200,000 applications); others, such as openoffice.org and gimp.org, have their own websites. Some are stable and well documented; others are buggy, and you have to guess how they work. With so much out there to choose from, how do you find the software you need and how do you know it will work on your PC-BSD system?

The FreeBSD Project maintains something known as the ports collection.[1] This is a large collection of software that has been "ported" for FreeBSD. In a nutshell, ported means that someone did a fair bit of work to make the necessary changes needed for the software to run on FreeBSD. If you're curious as to what is involved, the *Porter's Handbook*[2] contains the instructions for making a port. The person who makes the port is known as the port's maintainer.

---

[1] See http://www.freebsd.org/doc/en_US.ISO8859-1/books/handbook/ports.html for more details.

[2] http://www.freebsd.org/doc/en_US.ISO8859-1/books/porters-handbook/

To make sure that all the ports in the ports collection work, the FreeBSD Project uses a build farm known as pointyhat.[3] A build farm is a cluster of machines that constantly rebuilds the ports in the ports collection. This is important because an application that is known to work can sometimes stop working (for example, if a software library it uses changes). Sometimes an application that works on one version of FreeBSD won't work on a newer version of FreeBSD without some modification. Pointyhat will e-mail the maintainer if there is a problem with the port until the maintainer fixes the problem.

The FreeBSD Project is also concerned about software security. It maintains a database of known vulnerabilities, known as VuXML,[4] and provides tools you can use to determine if any of your installed software is vulnerable.

The ports collection is the collection of ported software. However, you have two choices in how you install an application from the collection. The first choice is to install the package. Think of a package as a command-line installer program that knows how to install the application, all its dependencies, and any documentation and configuration files associated with the application. The second choice is to compile (or build) the port yourself. This chapter concentrates on packages; Chapter 10 will show you how to compile a port.

What Is a Package?

Like a PBI, a FreeBSD package represents an application that has been pretested for you so that it can be easily installed and used on your PC-BSD system (remember, PC-BSD is really FreeBSD "under the hood"). Similar to a PBI, a package contains instructions to install everything it needs to work on your system. FreeBSD's package management system allows you to see if newer versions of the package are available and provides a way to upgrade or uninstall applications. While the end result is the same, in that both the PBI system and the FreeBSD package management system allow you to install and manage software, the commands you use to do so are different. The major difference is that the PBI system provides a graphical Software Manager, whereas the FreeBSD package system requires you to type commands at a command prompt.

Why Use Packages on PC-BSD?

If the PBI system provides a graphical Software Manager, why would you want to use a command-line system to install software? The most compelling reason is the sheer number of FreeBSD applications that are available. As of February, 2010, there are more than 21,000 applications in the FreeBSD ports collection, meaning that there is a very good chance that the application you are looking for is available as a package. It is also pretty cool that PC-BSD gives you the choice of how you install and maintain your software, rather than forcing you to use one software management system.

---

[3] http://pointyhat.freebsd.org

[4] http://www.vuxml.org/

Finding Packages

The easiest way to find FreeBSD packages is to point a web browser to `http://www.FreshPorts.org`, as seen in Figure 1. FreshPorts provides an easy-to-use interface to the information available within the FreeBSD ports collection. If you're wondering what software is available to install on your FreeBSD or PC-BSD system, FreshPorts is the place to go!

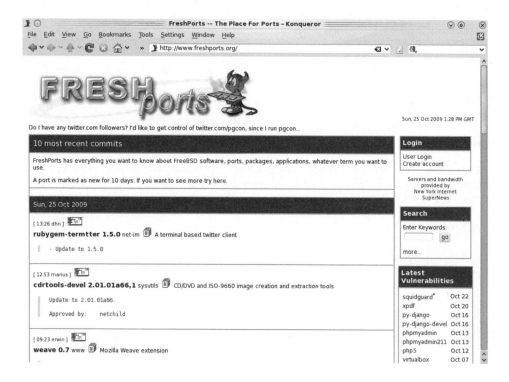

Figure 9-1. FreshPorts website

If you use the Firefox web browser, you can access this website quickly using a FreshPorts search plugin available from `http://www.searchplugins.net/pluginlist.aspx?q=FreshPorts&mode=title`. While in Firefox, go to that website and click the I to install the plugin (see Figure 9-2).

■ **Tip** There are two Is to choose from. The first one will use the default search engine icon, and the second one will install the Beastie icon. If you change your mind about which to install, use the Manage Search Engines menu in the Firefox search bar drop-down menu to remove the plugin.

Figure 9-2. *Installing the FreshPorts Firefox plugin*

A pop-up Add Search Engine message will ask if you want to Add this plugin. Check the box Start using it right away; then press Add. You can then click the drop-down arrow in the search engine bar in the upper-right corner of Firefox to select the FreshPorts search utility, as seen in Figure 9-3. To search for an application using the plugin, simply type the name of the software into the FreshPorts search bar and it will show you the results from FreshPorts.org.

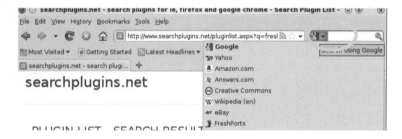

Figure 9-3. *Firefox search plugin menu showing FreshPorts search plugin*

■ **Tip** If you don't use the Firefox web browser, you can still search for software using the Search utility at the FreshPorts.org website.

FreshPorts provides a lot of useful information that can assist you in deciding which software to install. If you have no idea where to start and want to get a feel for what software is available, click the Categories hyperlink, located about halfway down the page in the right frame. This will show you a view of all available software divided into categories, as seen in Figure 9-4. Click a category to browse all its applications.

FreshPorts - list of categories

This page lists the categories and can be sorted by various criteria. Virtual categories are indicated by *.

You can sort each column by clicking on the header. e.g. click on **Category** to sort by category.

Category	Count	Description	Last Update
accessibility	24	Ports to help disabled users.	01 Sep 2009 23:19:47
afterstep*	35	Ports to support the AfterStep window manager.	06 Sep 2009 07:41:59
arabic	10	Ported software for the Arabic market.	01 Sep 2009 23:19:47
archivers	188	Utilities for archiving and unarchiving data.	22 Oct 2009 14:27:20
astro	108	Applications related to astronomy.	20 Oct 2009 19:27:50
audio	839	Audio utilities - most require a supported sound card.	24 Oct 2009 20:38:20
benchmarks	64	Utilities for measuring system performance.	18 Oct 2009 21:16:13
biology	94	Software related to biology.	01 Oct 2009 08:34:28
cad	84	Computer Aided Design utilities.	14 Oct 2009 12:38:16
chinese	136	Ported software for the Chinese market.	18 Oct 2009 07:41:22
comms	157	Communications utilities.	25 Oct 2009 01:04:04
converters	126	Format conversion utilities.	25 Oct 2009 00:45:06
databases	686	Database software.	23 Oct 2009 16:33:43

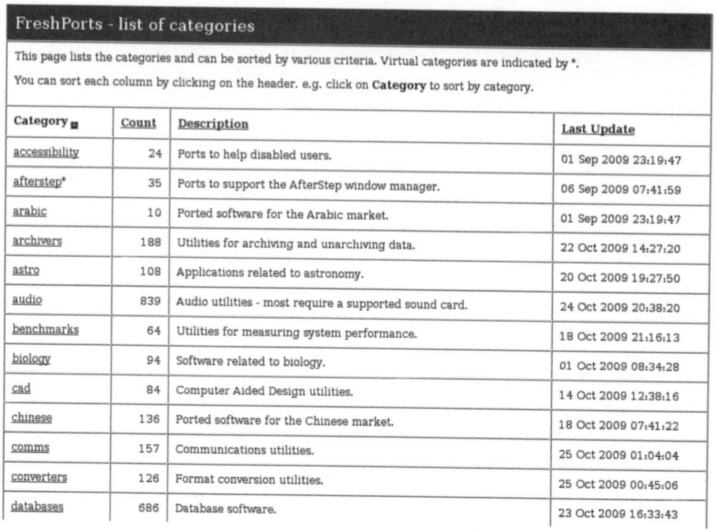

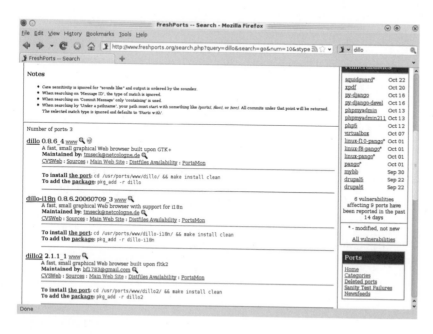

Figure 9-4. *Using FreshPorts to browse software categories*

Let's take a closer look at the type of information that is available for a port within the ports collection. Figure 9-5 shows the results from a FreshPorts search for the phrase "dillo".

Figure 9-5. *Search results for "dillo"*

From the output, you can see that dillo is "a fast, small graphical Web browser" and that there are three versions available within the ports collection. Version 0.8.6_4 has a skull icon, indicating that it has had a known security vulnerability in VuXML. If that vulnerability has not been fixed yet, a package will not be available. You can click the skull icon to read details about the vulnerability (click the dillo hyperlink in the page that opens up).

Each FreshPorts entry contains the following information about the software:

Name: The name of the application, followed by its version number and category. Click the magnifier icon to determine whether any other software depends upon this application.

Maintained by: The e-mail address of the person responsible for making sure the software works on FreeBSD. Click the magnifier icon to see what other applications they are responsible for.

CVSWeb: Contains the complete history of the application since it first became available within the FreeBSD ports collection. CVSWeb will be discussed in more detail in Chapter 10.

Sources: Shows the original source location of the software that was ported, as well as the checksums and size of the software source. Note that this is for informational purposes because the package system will fetch the software for you (that is, you shouldn't download it yourself).

Main Web Site: This is the primary site of the application. This website often contains screenshots, documentation, and more information about the software.

Distfiles Availability: Shows the availability of the software source for that category. This will be discussed in more detail in Chapter 10.

PortsMon: Shows a report on the status of the FreeBSD port. See http://portsmon.freebsd.org for more information about the PortsMon project.

Installation instructions: Provides the commands used to install the software using the FreeBSD ports system (discussed in Chapter 10) and the FreeBSD packages system (discussed in the "Installing a Package" section of this chapter).

In addition to the information about each port, the FreshPorts website contains lots of other useful information. The Latest Vulnerabilities section (in the right frame) can be used to browse through software with known existing security vulnerabilities. The Ports section contains hyperlinks to the software categories, the list of deleted ports, and the FreshPorts RSS newsfeeds.

The Statistics section contains graphs; counts for the total number of ported applications; and the number of broken, deprecated, and vulnerable applications. It also contains hyperlinks to lists of software added within the last 24 or 48 hours, 7 days, fortnight, and month. The FAQ in the This Site section includes explanations of packages and ports and descriptions of all the icons used on the website.

Ports Console

Beginning with version 8, PC-BSD provides a Ports Console utility to use when installing FreeBSD packages. An icon for this utility can be found on the desktop. It is also available in Kickoff ➤ Ports Console.

■ **Tip** Curious power users can read the underlying shell script that sets up the environment for Ports Console in /PCBSD/portjail/portjail.sh.

If you have ever installed packages before on a FreeBSD system, you know that there are several **pkg_*** commands that are used to manage FreeBSD packages. You will use the same commands on a PC-BSD system. Never use any **pkg_*** command directly from a PC-BSD command prompt! Instead, always use these commands within PC-BSD's Ports Console tool.

■ **Caution** Just in case you missed the warning in the preceding paragraph, you really don't want to use any commands that start with pkg_ outside of the Ports Console on a PC-BSD system. Ports Console ensures that the packages you install and manage don't interfere with the software already installed with the PC-BSD operating system.

Ports Console provides a safe environment for installing and managing FreeBSD packages. It does so by creating a jail[5] that separates the applications you install from the PC-BSD operating system. This means that you can install, update, and uninstall all the FreeBSD packages you like, without worrying about accidentally deleting applications that are needed by the PC-BSD operating system. This separation also means that Software Manager (described in detail in Chapter 8) has no idea which FreeBSD packages you have installed. FreeBSD packages will not show up in Software Manager's Installed Software tab and Update Manager will not notify you if new versions of your installed FreeBSD packages become available. As you go through this chapter, you'll learn how to use the command-line tools to manage your packages—meaning you can still manage your installed packages; you just won't be doing it with Software Manager.

When you start Ports Console, it looks like any other Konsole prompt. In reality, you have connected to a jail. Take a look at the difference between Figure 9-6 and Figure 9-7.

---

[5] Wikipedia provides a good introduction and references to FreeBSD jails http://en.wikipedia.org/wiki/FreeBSD_jail.

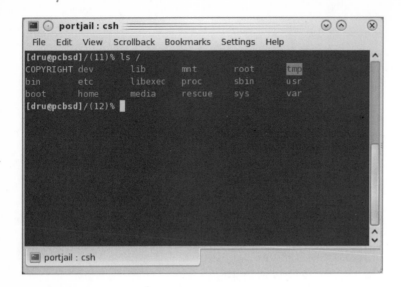

Figure 9-6. Listing of the / directory in Ports Console

Figure 9-7. Listing of the / directory in Konsole

Notice that the Ports Console is missing the /PCBSD directory, which contains programs used to maintain the operating system, and the /Programs directory, which contains the software installed using the PBI system. You will see even more of a difference if you try the **pkg_info** command, as demonstrated in Figure 9-8 and Figure 9-9. (Yes, I know I told you never to run a pkg_* command outside of Ports Console—we'll do it just this once with a view-only command to demonstrate the difference.)

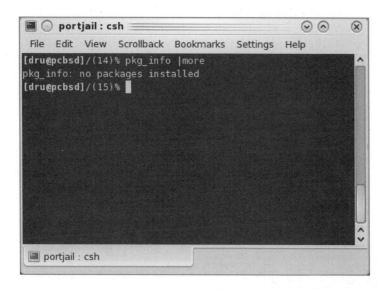

Figure 9-8. pkg_info output in Ports Console before installing any FreeBSD packages

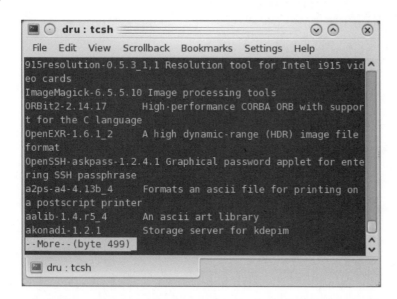

Figure 9-9. pkg_info output in Konsole on a default installation of PC-BSD

The **pkg_info** command is used to view which non-PBI applications (e.g., FreeBSD packages) are installed. Notice that Ports Console indicates that no packages are installed because we haven't installed any yet. However, if you press your spacebar to scroll through the output of **pkg_info** within Konsole, you'll see that hundreds of applications were installed with PC-BSD. These are the applications you don't want to mess up. This is why you use Ports Console to maintain that separation between whatever software you're playing with and the software that PC-BSD needs to keep your system humming happily along.

Installing a Package

Okay, now that we're in Ports Console, how do we add an application? Let's return to the dillo example we saw at FreshPorts in Figure 9-5. FreshPorts indicates that you can install dillo2 (version 2.1.2_1) using the command **pkg_add -r dillo2** (the **-r** means to fetch the remote package from the FreeBSD ports collection on the Internet). Double-check that you're in Ports Console (the title of your window should say portjail: csh) and that you are connected to the Internet. Become the superuser with the **su** command and type the **pkg_add** command, as seen in Figure 9-10. Note that the title bar at the top of the screen has changed to portjail: pkg_add, indicating that the package is being fetched. The informational messages in the Ports console screen let you know what is happening with the installation.

Figure 9-10. Installing the dillo2 package using Ports Console

When the installation is complete, you will receive your prompt back.

You probably noticed that dillo requires a lot of additional software, known as dependencies, to install and run. **pkg_add** found and installed all these dependencies for you. This "just works," thanks to the hard work of the maintainer of this port. If you ever want to know who to thank for making a favorite software application available for your system, check the port's Maintainer section at FreshPorts. Send a thank you e-mail or buy them their beverage of choice if you ever meet them in person to let them know that you appreciate their effort.

If you now repeat the **pkg_info** command, you'll get a listing of all the software that was installed, as seen in Figure 9-11.

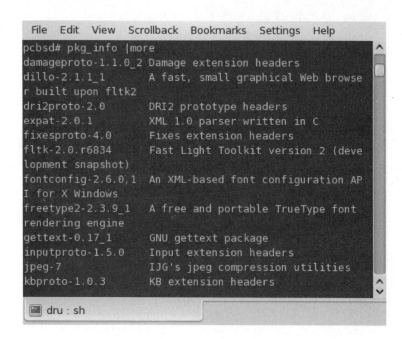

Figure 9-11. Viewing the software that was installed with dillo2

Determining what was Installed

Now that you have an installed application, you'll want to use it. **pkg_info** can be used to determine the path to the application. Use the **-Lx** switch to receive a list of what was installed, and filter your search using **| grep bin**. This tells **pkg_info** that you're interested only in the path to the binary (another name for the application's executable). The output indicates that this package installed three binaries, as seen in Figure 9-12.

File Edit View Scrollback Bookmarks Settings Help

```
[dru@pcbsd]/(5)% pkg_info -Lx dillo |grep bin
/usr/local/bin/dillo
/usr/local/bin/dpid
/usr/local/bin/dpidc
[dru@pcbsd]/(6)% whatis dillo
dillo(1)                  - web browser
[dru@pcbsd]/(7)% whatis dpid
dpid: nothing appropriate
[dru@pcbsd]/(8)% whatis dpidc
dpidc: nothing appropriate
[dru@pcbsd]/(9)% pkg_info -Lx dillo |grep dpid
/usr/local/bin/dpid
/usr/local/bin/dpidc
/usr/local/etc/dillo/dpidrc.dist
[dru@pcbsd]/(10)%
```

portjail : csh

Figure 9-12. Using pkg_info to find the location of the dillo2 binary

---

■ **Tip** Note that I asked pkg_info about dillo, not dillo2. The x in -Lx tells pkg_info to look for a package with the specified name (in this case, dillo). By not including the number, pkg_info will search for all versions of dillo and will let me know if multiple versions of dillo are installed.

It's a good bet that dillo, located in the /usr/local/bin directory is the executable you are looking for. You can double-check this with the **whatis** command. Note that in this example, the original creator of the dillo application (not the port maintainer) has not created any documentation (man pages) for the dpid or dpidc applications because the **whatis** command can't find anything appropriate. To see if any documentation was installed at all, I filtered the **pkg_info** output for the word *dpid*. The results show only the two binaries and a configuration file (config files live in a path containing /etc/). Looks like I'll have to go to the dillo website to see if there is any information at all about these binaries.

So, how do you start the dillo web browser? The short answer is to type **dillo** and press Enter. But take note of the longer answer:

- Type **exit** to leave the superuser account. Remember that you install applications as the superuser but run them as your regular user account.

- Once you are back to your regular user account, type **rehash**. If you don't, your shell doesn't know that you've just installed a new application, meaning that it won't find it and will give you a "command not found" error message.

- Occasionally, a binary will be installed outside of the path your shell searches when it is looking for an application, so it can start it for you. If this happens, you have to type the full path to the binary rather than just the binary name. If you're not sure what your path is, type **$PATH** to view it.

- Always run the application from Ports Console.

This last point is a biggie on a PC-BSD system. Because FreeBSD packages are installed into their own jail, they are available only from within the jail. This means that they can be started only within Ports Console and, for example, can't be added to the Kickoff menu. If you find yourself installing FreeBSD packages because the software you need isn't available as a PBI, it probably means that there should be a PBI for that software. If you're a power user, consider making the PBI yourself using the instructions in Chapter 14. If you're not confident enough to tackle creating a PBI, see Chapter 11 to learn how to interact with the PC-BSD community to see if someone else can create the PBI.

What to Do if Something Fails

Packages usually work flawlessly by using the instructions in the previous section. But occasionally something goes wrong. Sometimes **pkg_add** stops with a message saying that it can't fetch the package. Sometimes **pkg_add** complains that it can't find a dependency and refuses to finish the installation without it. Sometimes the package installs, but you get an error message when you try to run the application.

If **pkg_add** tells you it can't fetch the package, double-check that you are the superuser and that the **pkg_add** command FreshPorts told you to use was typed correctly into Ports Console. If you see a typo, fix it and try again. If it still won't fetch, double-check that you're connected to the Internet by pinging a website name. If it still won't fetch or still refuses to install or run, you'll have to do a bit of research to see what is going wrong.

Go back to that port's entry in FreshPorts. Does it have a skull icon or a message indicating that it is broken, forbidden, or restricted? If so, there probably isn't a package available. If you really want that version of the software, consider trying to build its port instead. Otherwise, try another version of the port or another application that provides similar functionality.

You can also browse the FreeBSD ports mailing list archives[6] to see if other users are experiencing the same problem. If you want to discuss the error on that mailing list, be sure to read the Frequently Asked Questions About The FreeBSD Mailing Lists[7] document first so that your e-mail contains all the information needed to get a useful response from the mailing list.

Updating Packages

Before you can update a package, you have to be aware that there is a newer version to update to. This section will show you how to create a customized watch list. We will then show you how to update to the newer version.

---

[6] http://lists.freebsd.org/pipermail/freebsd-ports/

[7] http://www.freebsd.org/doc/en_US.ISO8859-1/articles/mailing-list-faq/article.html

Automatic Notifications with FreshPorts

While Update Manager won't tell you when newer versions of FreeBSD packages become available, you can configure FreshPorts to send you an e-mail when changes are made to your installed ports.

To do so, you'll have to first create an account with FreshPorts. Once you have activated your account and are logged in, a Watch Lists section will appear in the right frame of the FreshPorts website. Click the Upload hyperlink, which will open the page seen in Figure 9-13.

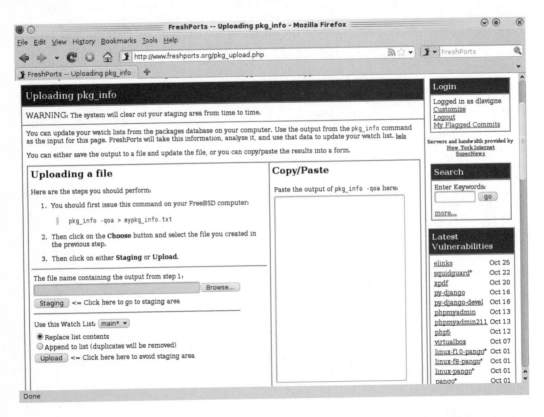

Figure 9-13. Creating a FreshPorts Watch List to be notified of changes to your installed ports

From within Ports Console, type **pkg_info -qoa|more**. This will create a list of the ports you have installed. Depending on what you have installed, this list may be several pages long. Cut/paste the list of ports you see in Ports Console into the Paste box seen in Figure 9-13. Then, return to Ports Console and press the spacebar to go to the next page so you can copy/paste its ports. Repeat until you get your prompt back in Ports Console. When finished, double-check that your pasted list contains only ports (e.g., not the word More); then click the Upload button. You should receive a message that your watch list has been updated. You can then configure how often you want to be notified by going back to Watch Lists ➤ Report Subscriptions. This page is seen in Figure 9-14.

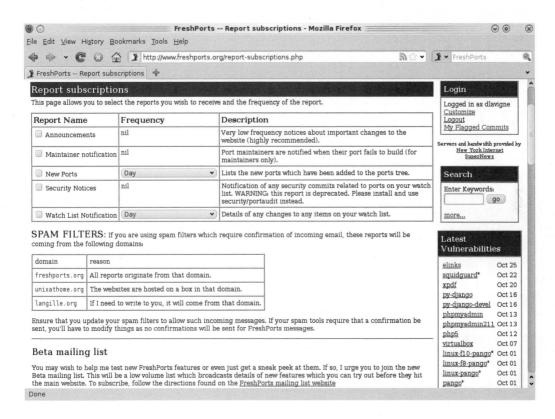

Figure 9-14. Configuring how often to be notified of changes to your installed ports

Check the box next to Watch List Notification. If you don't want to receive a daily e-mail, click Day to choose another selection from the drop-down menu. When finished, press the update button at the bottom of the page. You'll now receive an e-mail regarding any changes to your ports at the frequency that you configured.

■ **Tip** Don't forget to update your watch list whenever you add new packages. You can choose to replace or append (add to) your list.

Performing the Upgrade

The easiest way to upgrade to a newer version of a package is to remove the old one first (see the next section, "Removing a Package"); then use **pkg_add** to install the new version.

Power users can also use the **portupgrade** application to upgrade all or some of their FreeBSD software at once. **portupgrade** is discussed in detail in Chapter 10.

Removing a Package

While **pkg_add** is used to install (add) FreeBSD software, **pkg_delete** is used to uninstall (delete) FreeBSD software. Figure 9-15 shows an example of uninstalling the dillo package installed earlier. Note that this command is run within Ports Console and that you have to become superuser in order to uninstall a package. Again, the **-x** indicates that you have not given the version number of the port, just its name. **pkg_delete** will remove any software containing the name you specify—in this example, any software containing "dillo".

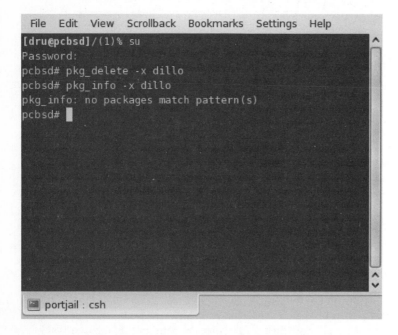

Figure 9-15. Using Ports Console and the pkg_delete command to uninstall the dillo package

In this example, **pkg_delete** didn't have any informational messages when it removed the dillo package. Sometimes you will see informational messages when you delete a package. You can verify that the package did uninstall by running **pkg_info**, as seen in Figure 9-15.

pkg_delete will not let you delete a package if another application needs it. Figure 9-16 shows an example of this. In this example, dillo is still installed and I tried to uninstall the wget package that installed with the dillo package as a dependency.

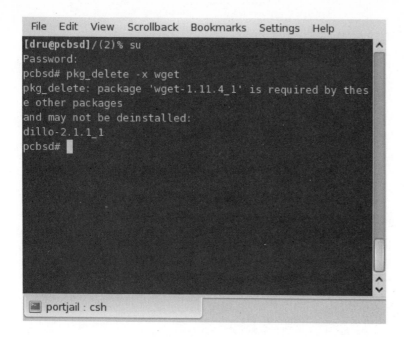

File   Edit   View   Scrollback   Bookmarks   Settings   Help

```
[dru@pcbsd]/(2)% su
Password:
pcbsd# pkg_delete -x wget
pkg_delete: package 'wget-1.11.4_1' is required by thes
e other packages
and may not be deinstalled:
dillo-2.1.1_1
pcbsd#
```

portjail : csh

Figure 9-16. pkg_delete will not let you uninstall software needed by another application

If you receive an error message that "no packages match pattern(s)", double-check that you don't have a typo in your **pkg_delete** command. If the command looks good, use **pkg_info** to double-check that the package you are trying to uninstall is indeed installed.

Summary

This chapter introduced you to the FreeBSD ports collection and demonstrated how to work with FreeBSD packages. While FreeBSD packages are fairly easy to work with, they do require you to use command-line utilities and to occasionally deal with error messages. The Ports Console provided on your PC-BSD system means that you can experiment with FreeBSD packages without worrying about messing up the software that came with your operating system.

The next chapter is definitely for power users as it will show you how to build your own customized applications. If that sounds like fun, read on! If it sounds a bit intimidating, skip to Chapter 11, in which we will introduce you to the PC-BSD community.

CHAPTER 10

■ ■ ■

FreeBSD Ports

Chapter 9 introduced you to Ports Console, which provides a safe environment for installing software that has been ported to FreeBSD on your PC-BSD system. Chapter 9 also demonstrated how to find, install, and manage FreeBSD packages. Although FreeBSD packages are managed from the command line, they are relatively easy to use and are considered the recommended way to install additional software that is not currently available within the PBI system.

This chapter teaches you how to compile and manage FreeBSD ports.[1] This chapter is intended for power users who want to customize their software applications. Much of the information in Chapter 9 applies to this chapter as well. For example, you can use FreshPorts to find the software you would like to compile, you still issue all of the commands within Ports Console, and **pkg_info** will tell you what was installed. However, you will use the **make** command to compile and install FreeBSD ports instead of the **pkg_add** command.

Package or Port?

If you're wondering whether you should install the package or compile a port for a given piece of software, you probably want to install the package. If you find yourself compiling ports without passing any **make** targets (that will make more sense as this chapter progresses), you definitely should be installing the package instead of compiling the port. Packages provide several advantages over ports:

- They are quick to install. With the exception of very large packages such as KDE or GNOME, most packages install in under a few minutes. Depending on the number of dependencies and your hardware, the same port may take several hours to compile.

- If you aren't customizing the port, you will end up with the same binary as the package would have installed, meaning you needlessly waited longer to install the software on your system.

---

[1] See `www.freebsd.org/doc/en_US.ISO8859-1/books/handbook/ports-using.html` for further information about managing ports.

However, at times you do want to install the port, when, for example, the following occur:

- A package is not available.

- You want to compile a binary with a known security vulnerability.

- You want to override a license restriction. For example, the license may allow you to compile the binary for personal use but does not allow the FreeBSD project (an organization) to distribute the binary package.

- You need to customize the options that are compiled into the binary; this is often done with server applications such as Apache or PostgreSQL.

What is Compiling a Port?

So what exactly is compiling a port? Software applications are created from source code,[2] or text files written in a programming language. Those files are considered human readable, at least for those humans who understand the syntax of the programming language used. The source code must be converted into a form that the computer understands by using a program known as a compiler; the end result is the binary executable of the program. When compiling a FreeBSD port, you use the following components:

- The **gcc**[3] compiler.

- The **make**[4] program to manage the dependencies that are needed when a binary is compiled.

- A Makefile that contains all of the instructions needed to compile the FreeBSD port.

- A directory structure, known as the ports tree, containing a subdirectory for each port. Each subdirectory includes the port's Makefile, a working area, any needed patches, the post-installation message, the package description, and the checksums for the archive containing the source code.

gcc and **make** were installed with your PC-BSD system. However, before you can compile any ports, you have to install the ports directory structure.

---

[2] http://en.wikipedia.org/wiki/Source_code

[3] http://en.wikipedia.org/wiki/GNU_Compiler_Collection

[4] See *make for Nonprogrammers* for more information: http://onlamp.com/pub/a/bsd/2005/03/24/FreeBSD_Basics.html

■ **Caution** Remember, all of the commands in this chapter need to be run from Ports Console to ensure that you are working within the safe environment of the ports jail.

Installing the Ports Collection

To install the ports collection, choose Kickoff ➤ System Settings ➤ System Manager. After inputting the administrative password, click the Tasks tab, as seen in Figure 10-1. In the Ports Console section, click Fetch Ports Tree.

Figure 10-1. *Installing the FreeBSD ports collection from System Manager to Ports Console*

Note that this operation will take some time because the ports collection is a very large tar file that needs to be downloaded and untarred to /usr/ports.

What Does a Port Contain?

This section will familiarize you with the contents and layout of the ports directory structure. After you have the ports collection, open Ports Console and become the superuser. Figure 10-2 shows a listing of /usr/ports/.

Figure 10-2. Contents of /usr/ports/

The files and directories highlighted by the yellow square contain the information needed for the ports collection to work. If you are interested in the inner workings of the FreeBSD ports process, read Mk/bsd.port.mk (the master file used by the ports system). You will also find useful information in **man ports**.

The remainder of the listing is composed of directories that represent the same categories found at FreshPorts. If you list a directory, you'll find that it contains subdirectories. Each subdirectory represents a port that can be compiled, and it contains all of the information needed to compile that port. Figure 10-3 shows a listing of the /usr/ports/databases/couchdb directory.

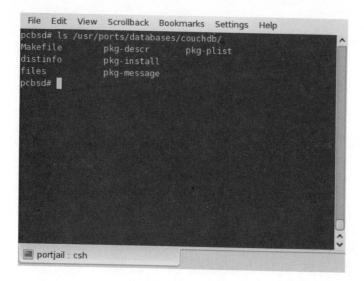

Figure 10-3. Contents of a port subdirectory

This directory contains the following:

Makefile: Contains the instructions[5] **make** needs to compile the application.

distinfo: Contains the MD5 and SHA256 checksums, the size, and the name of the archive containing the source code that will be fetched from the Internet. For security reasons, the ports system will refuse to fetch an archive that doesn't match the information in this file.

files: This directory contains patches the software requires to compile.

pkg-descr: Contains the description of the software. **pkg_info**[6] **-d** can also be used to display the contents of this file.

pkg-install: Optional script used during the installation. **pkg_info -i** can also be used to display the contents of this file.

---

[5] A Makefile's contents are described in more detail in `www.freebsd.org/doc/en/books/porters-handbook/book.html#MAKEFILE`.

[6] man pkg_info is well worth reading. Try each of its switches to discover which are useful to you.

pkg-message: Optional message (usually containing post-installation configuration information) that will be displayed at the end of the installation. If you missed the message or wish to reread it, you can find it here. **pkg_info -D** can also be used to display the contents of this file.

pkg-plist: Contains the paths to the files that are installed with the application. /usr/local is assumed to be at the beginning of each path. For example, if the file gives a location of bin/couchdb, the actual path is /usr/local/bin/couchdb.

Let's compare this information to Figure 10-4, which shows the CVSWeb page for couchdb at FreshPorts.

Figure 10-4. CVSWeb for /usr/ports/databases/couchdb

Note that FreshPorts contains the same files, enabling you to research your ports online before compiling them. CVSWeb has an added advantage in that it shows the entire history for each file. For example, if you click the Makefile link, you will see a history of the Makefile for every version of the port, along with the commit messages that indicate which changes were made and when. If you want to see only the current Makefile, click on the number in the Rev. (revision) column instead—in this example, the Makefile is at revision 1.7.

make Targets

To compile a port, simply **cd** to its subdirectory and type **make**. Wait until the messages stop, and if all goes well, you'll receive your prompt back without any errors.

To understand what actually happened and how you can customize what happens, you should know a bit about **make** targets. Targets are the words that follow the make command. The most commonly used targets[7] are summarized in Table 10-1. Note that targets are optional but very useful. For example, if you just type **make**, the port will compile, but it won't install unless you add the install target (that is, type **make install**).

*Table 10-1. Useful **make** Targets*

Target	Description
clean	**make** will create a work subdirectory when you compile a port. This target tells **make** to remove that directory before returning your prompt. Use the **clean-depends** target if you also want to clean out the work directory for each dependency.
config	Some ports provide a menu of options that enable you to choose which features to compile into the application (see Figure 10-5 for an example). Your original selection is saved in a subdirectory of /var/db/ports/. If you want to change your selection, use this target to access the port's menu screen. Use the **config- recursive** target if you want to see all the menus for each dependency.
deinstall	If you try to install a port that is already installed, you will receive an error message. Use this target first to uninstall the port. For example: **make deinstall && make install**.
fetch	This target downloads the source code and patches for the port but does not compile anything. The source code will be saved to /usr/ports/distfiles/. Use **fetch-recursive** if you want to also fetch the source for the port's dependencies.
install	This target tells make to install the files listed in pkg-plist to their locations in /usr/local/. This can take some time because they need to be compiled first.
package	Creates a FreeBSD package in the current directory (the file will end in .tbz). This is useful if you need to install the same software on multiple machines because you have to compile it only once. If you would like to compile all of the package's dependencies as well, use the **package-recursive** target instead.

Figure 10-5 shows the configuration options for /usr/ports/www/apache22. Those options with an X will be compiled into the application. Use your arrow key to highlight an option and the Enter key to toggle between X and a blank. When finished, use the Tab key to jump to OK and press Enter.

---

[7] The complete list of targets is listed in /usr/ports/Mk/bsd.port.mk and man ports.

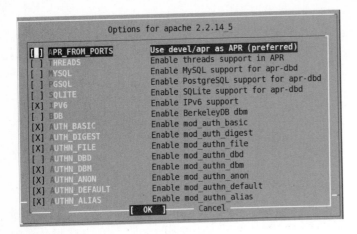

Figure 10-5. Example options menu for the apache22 port

■ **Tip** If you run **make config-recursive** and don't receive any menus, you might as well save yourself some time and install the package because there isn't anything to customize for that port.

The TARGETS section of **man ports** indicates that some targets build upon each other in order. For example, **make install** is equivalent to **make config fetch checksum depends extract patch configure build install**. In other words, if you use a target within that ordered list, it will "automagically" include all of the targets that precede it. This means that if you type **make config**, **make** will only display the port's options menu, if it exists. It will not fetch or build any source because those targets come after the config target. However, if you type **make install**, **make** will go through all of the targets, starting with config, then fetch, all the way up to install.

You may have noticed that each category directory also has a Makefile. This means that you could (if you had a lot of time) install every port in that category by typing **make install**. For example, to build all www ports, issue the command **cd /usr/ports/www && make install**.

■ **Tip** **make** reads only the Makefile in the current directory. If there is no Makefile in your current directory, **make** will give the error "make: no target to make." This means you should **cd** to the desired directory and try again.

There are **make** targets that are useful within a category directory or the /usr/ports/ directory itself. One is **make readmes**, which creates a local HTML copy of the specified ports structure. Figure 10-6 shows the resulting web page from running the **make** readmes command from the /usr/ports/ directory. You can click on each category to see a listing of its ports.

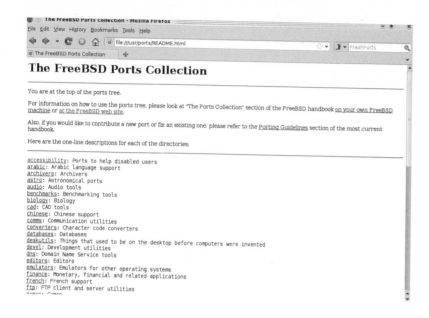

*Figure 10-6. /usr/ports/README.html generated from typing **make readmes** at /usr/ports/*

Another useful target to use from /usr/ports/ is search. The first time you run **make search**, you may be asked to run **make fetchindex** first. Figure 10-7 shows the results from running **make search name=youtube | more** from /usr/ports/.

*Figure 10-7. **make search** results*

The name= keyword in this command tells **make** to search for port names matching your search pattern. The search results will show the following:

Port: The name and version of the port

Path: The port's location within the ports directory

Info: A one-line description of the port

Maint: The e-mail address of the port's maintainer

B-deps: The names and version numbers of the dependencies required to build the port

R-deps: The names and version numbers of the dependencies required to run the application compiled by the port

WWW: The URL to the website for the software

■ **Tip** If you are interested in seeing only the Port, Path, and Info sections, use **make quicksearch name=** instead.

Troubleshooting Errors

Like packages, ports have been pretested for you and should compile on your system without errors. Occasionally you will receive an error message indicating that the port did not compile. If you receive the error almost immediately, one of the variables in Table 10-2 is probably set in the port's Makefile.

Table 10-2. Makefile Variables You Should Be Aware Of

Variable	Description
BROKEN=	This line in the Makefile will indicate the reason why the port is considered broken. You should probably look for a newer version or another port with similar functionality as this port is waiting for the maintainer to fix the problem.
CONFLICTS=	The Makefile will indicate which application the port conflicts with. If you uninstall the conflicting software, the error will disappear.
DEPRECATED=	This won't stop the compile but will give the message "This port is deprecated; you may wish to reconsider installing it." This typically means that there is a newer version of the port that you should be using instead.
EXPIRATION_DATE=	This won't result in an error, but you should check for this in a Makefile. If this line exists, consider another version of the port or a similar port because this one will be disappearing soon.

Variable	Description
FORBIDDEN=	The Makefile will indicate why the port is forbidden.
RESTRICTED=	This won't result in an error, but you should read the message if this line is in the Makefile because it may indicate a patent or license restriction that affects your use or distribution of the application.

Of course, you can remove the offending variable from the Makefile to force the port to compile, but that won't change the underlying reason for including the variable.

If you receive a "Couldn't fetch it - please try to retrieve this port manually into /usr/ports/distfiles/ and try again" error, double-check your Internet connection and try again.

■ **Note** Ports Console assumes you are running the default pf firewall. If you have disabled pf, you will have to type **pfctl -ef /etc/pf.conf** in Konsole in order to have Internet connectivity within Ports Console.

If your error does not seem to be connected with the Makefile or Internet connectivity, try googling the error message to see if there is a known fix. Or try installing another version of the port. If you're still not having any luck, send an e-mail to the FreeBSD ports mailing list.[8] If this is your first e-mail to the list, be sure to read How to Get Best Results from the FreeBSD-Questions Mailing List[9] first as the information it contains applies to all of the FreeBSD mailing lists.

Keeping the Ports Tree Updated

The ports collection is constantly being updated, with new ports being added daily, broken ports being fixed (and sometimes working ports becoming broken), and ports being updated to newer versions of the software. The csup utility enables you to sync with the current version of the ports tree whenever you wish.[10] In order to use csup, you need a configuration file. A well-commented configuration file is located in /usr/share/examples/cvsup/ports-supfile. If this is your first time using csup, take the time to read through the comments in the example file because they explain the meaning of each line in the file. Figure 10-8 demonstrates a customized configuration file saved as /root/cvs-supfile, as well as the csup command used to connect to the specified mirror (in this case, cvsup.FreeBSD.org) to sync the local ports tree with the latest release version (RELENG_8) of the ports tree.

---

[8] http://lists.freebsd.org/mailman/listinfo/freebsd-ports

[9] www.freebsd.org/doc/en_US.ISO8859-1/articles/freebsd-questions/article.html

[10] The FreeBSD Handbook covers this utility in more detail: www.freebsd.org/doc/en_US.ISO8859-1/books/handbook/cvsup.html.

```
File  Edit  View  Scrollback  Bookmarks  Settings  Help
pcbsd# more /root/cvs-supfile
*default host=cvsup.FreeBSD.org
*default base=/usr/local/etc/cvsup
*default prefix=/usr
*default tag=RELENG_8
*default release=cvs delete use-rel-suffix compress
ports-all tag=.
pcbsd# csup -L2 /root/cvs-supfile
Parsing supfile "/root/cvs-supfile"
Connecting to cvsup.FreeBSD.org
```
```
ports : csup
```

*Figure 10-8. Using **csup** and a custom configuration file to update the local ports collection*

Once connected, **csup** will compare the files on the mirror with your local copy of the ports collection and will download only the files that have changed or are missing.

■ **Tip** Power users who would like to keep their ports tree updated on a regular basis should consider adding that **csup -L2** command to their crontab within Ports Console.

Updating Ports

If you keep your ports tree up-to-date with **csup**, you can use the **portupgrade** application to update your installed ports to their latest versions. But first you need to know which ports have newer versions. In this section, you'll create a notification script and then learn how to use **portupgrade**.

Creating Your Own Notification Script

Although PC-BSD's Software Manager won't tell you when newer versions of FreeBSD ports or packages are available, it is easy to create a custom script to do this for you. First, you should install some useful packages by using **pkg_add**:

> **portaudit:** Used to compare your installed software to the VuXML database of software vulnerabilities. (Chapter 9 discussed VuXML.)

> **portupgrade:** Used to upgrade both your installed ports and packages to their latest versions.

Figure 10-9 shows an example script, and Figure 10-10 shows the results of running the script.

Figure 10-9. Custom script to determine which software has a newer version available

Figure 10-10. Results of running custom script

In this example, none of the installed software has any known security vulnerabilities, as **portaudit** indicates "0 problem(s) in your installed packages found." If there was a known vulnerability, **portaudit** would have displayed the name of the software and a description of the vulnerability. Two ports, however, need upgrading: portaudit and ruby.

Using portupgrade

If you have software that needs updating, you can use **portupgrade** to upgrade it. It doesn't matter whether you installed the software from a package or compiled it from a port—it can still be upgraded. Table 10-3 shows the most common switches used with **portupgrade**. See **man portupgrade** for a description of all available switches.

Table 10-3. *Commonly Used portupgrade Switches*

Switch	Description
a	Upgrade all installed software that has a newer version. Otherwise, specify the name of the software to upgrade.
b	Make a backup package of the old version. This is very handy should something go wrong and you need to revert to the original version. You'll find the package in /usr/ports/packages/All.
n	Allows you to do a "dry run" as it creates a report of what would be upgraded without actually upgrading anything.
P	First tries to upgrade by using a package, meaning the upgrade process will be quicker if a package is available. If there is no package, **portupgrade** will compile the port.
r	Also upgrades any software that depends on the software being upgraded.
R	Also upgrades any software required by the software being upgraded.

portupgrade switches can be stacked, and order does not matter unless the switch requires that it is followed by a variable (add those switches and their variables individually after your stacked switches). For example, you can type **portupgrade -an** instead of **portupgrade -a -n**. It is recommended that you always include **-rR** to make sure all dependent software is also upgraded. If you don't, over time you may run into dependency issues. It is also recommended that you include **-b** just in case something goes wrong. If you have problems with the new software, use **pkg_delete** to uninstall the new version and **pkg_add** to install the backed-up package of the original software.

> ■ **Caution** *Never* upgrade a port without first reading /usr/ports/UPDATING to see if there are any known gotchas or upgrade hints for that software. Always follow any instructions in this file that apply to the software you are trying to upgrade.

The upgrade process usually goes like this:

1. Use your notification script to get the latest version of the ports tree and ports index and to determine which software is vulnerable or has a newer version.

2. Decide whether you want to upgrade all of your outdated software or only a specific application.

3. Read /usr/ports/UPDATING to see whether there are any special instructions for the software you wish to upgrade.

4. If you have customized configuration files for the software being updated (for example, a customized httpd.conf for Apache), make sure you have a backup of those files.

5. Run a command such as **portupgrade -abrR** to upgrade all software, or **portupgrade -brR name_of_software** to upgrade only the specified software.

Your software upgrade should "just work." If you run across an error, double-check your Internet connectivity, check that you didn't miss anything in /usr/ports/UPDATING, or try googling the error. You can also try waiting a day or so and rerunning **csup** because sometimes a missing patch will be added to the ports tree. On the off chance that the new version doesn't work, you'll be glad that you saved a backup package of the old version. This last scenario is rare, but it is always best to be safe rather than sorry!

Uninstalling a Port

To uninstall a port, **cd** into its directory and type **make deinstall**. FreshPorts or **pkg_info -ox** will tell you the port's location in the ports tree.

Alternately, you can delete the port by using **pkg_delete**. Either way, you can then use **pkg_info** to verify that the software has been uninstalled.

> ■ **Caution** The **pkg_delete** command will not let you uninstall software that is required by other applications. However, **make deinstall** will. If you're worried about inadvertently uninstalling dependencies, use **pkg_delete** instead.

Summary

This chapter covered the basics of the FreeBSD ports system. Power users seeking additional information should read through the resources mentioned in the footnotes of this chapter. This chapter also concludes the "Software" section of this book. The next section deals with community, and Chapter 11 will introduce you to the PC-BSD community.

## PART 4

Community

CHAPTER 11

■ ■ ■

Getting Help

At the beginning of this book, we mentioned that PC-BSD is more than an operating system. It is also a community of other PC-BSD users who share their tips and tricks, answer questions, and discuss which features and applications they want to see added to PC-BSD. In other words, this community of other PC-BSD users is an excellent resource when you are looking for help with your PC-BSD system.

Learning how to effectively interact with a community is a lot like learning how to use your operating system. Some things might seem strange at first and you will have to learn some basic skills. But as you become more comfortable with how things are done, it becomes easier, and you even start to have some fun. And over time you find yourself showing others how to do things.

This chapter begins by introducing you to netiquette, the rules of the road that will help you get the most out of any online community. It will then concentrate on the various resources that are available to you through the PC-BSD community.

What Is Netiquette?

If you've ever been the new kid at a school or a new employee at a large company, you know what it is like to be a stranger in an existing community. Somehow you have to introduce yourself, figure out any unwritten rules of conduct, learn how to fit in, and discover who your friends are and what authority to go to when you need help with something.

Interacting with an online community, such as the PC-BSD community, is similar, but there are a few differences. For one, most of your interactions are online, meaning you rarely (if ever) meet the people you interact with in person. Second, community members can live anywhere in the world and represent a mix of age, gender, economic and educational backgrounds, and cultures. Third, English is not everyone's first language. Add these factors up and there is opportunity for misunderstood communications. For example, was a response rude, written in a hurry, written by someone who wasn't sure how to say a phrase in English, or written by a usually nice person who happened to be having a bad day?

Netiquette[1] is a set of conventions designed to help reduce the number of online miscommunications. Just like etiquette teaches you not to talk with your mouth full and not to interrupt others while they are talking, netiquette teaches you the proper way to behave and respond when you are communicating with others online.

---

[1] http://en.wikipedia.org/wiki/Netiquette

Netiquette also reminds everyone how to deal with new people in a community. If you are that new person, netiquette helps you to start off on the right foot rather than irritate the other people in the community. If you see a new person, netiquette reminds you to welcome them and get them oriented so that they can start to fit in.

While every community will have its own set of conventions, there are some universal rules of netiquette, including the following:

Use the proper method of communication: Every community provides multiple ways for members to communicate with each other. Some communication methods are very technical and formal, while others are informal and chatty. It is your job to figure out which is which and to communicate using the expected tone and technical level. This chapter introduces you to all the PC-BSD communication channels and what you can expect from each.

Do your homework before posting a technical question: If you have a problem with your system, there is a very good chance that someone else has already asked the same question and received the answer. In an online community, all these questions and answers are saved on the Internet, so you should research your question first.

Don't be rude: No one wants to deal with a rude person, and you don't want to inadvertently be rude. If a community has a set of rules they ask you to read before asking a question[2] and you don't follow those rules, you are being rude. Rude questions are usually ignored, but sometimes they get a nasty answer in reply. If this is happening to you, check your original question.

Be helpful: People do not want to be ignored, especially when they are looking for help. If you see an unanswered question that you know the answer to, respond.

Don't assume malice: If you see a nasty response, don't send a nasty reply. That type of interaction can escalate badly into something known as a flame war.[3] Perhaps the original response was misunderstood; if you think that is the case, privately ask the person if they meant to be rude. Perhaps the original response was from a *troll*[4] trying to stir up trouble. In that case, the best response is to ignore it.

Report inappropriate behavior: Occasionally someone will post a sexist or racist remark that is intended to hurt others. The best response is to send the details to a leader within the community. The leader will contact the person privately to see whether the remark was intentional and will remove that person from the community, if necessary.

---

[2] An example set of rules is at `www.freebsd.org/doc/en/articles/freebsd-questions/article.html#AEN92`

[3] `http://en.wikipedia.org/wiki/Flame_war`

[4] `http://en.wikipedia.org/wiki/Troll_%28Internet%29`

Keep these rules in mind whenever you participate in any online community.

Now that you know some netiquette, let's see what resources are available within the PC-BSD community.

PC-BSD Forums

Probably the best place for a new user to start is at the PC-BSD forums. The forums don't require you to install any additional software because they are accessed using your web browser. They make it easy to search for an answer, ask a question, and answer a question. Additionally, there are many forums to choose from, ranging from nontechnical and informal to very technical and informative.

The PC-BSD forums are located at `http://forums.pcbsd.org`, as seen in Figure 11-1.

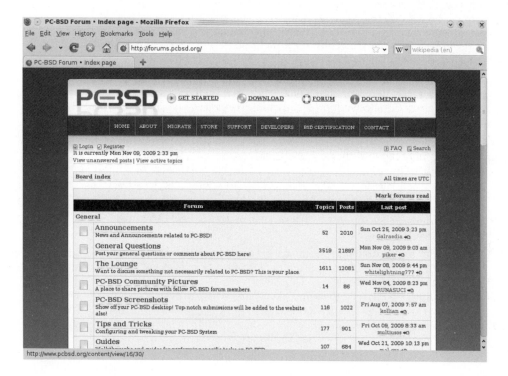

Figure 11-1. PC-BSD forums

The forums are categorized and described on the main forums page. If you are brand new to forums, take a moment to read the Frequently Asked Questions (FAQ) in the upper-right corner. If you have a specific question you need answered, use the Search hyperlink in the upper-right corner to see whether an answer is already available.

The forums are categorized as follows:

General: These forums are suited to anyone. They include nontechnical forums such as Announcements (in which new PC-BSD versions and promotions are announced), The Lounge (in which you can discuss just about anything), and forums in which you can share your PC-BSD–related pictures and screenshots. They also contain technical forums aimed at users, in which you can ask general questions, learn new tips and tricks, and read various how-to guides.

PC-BSD Software: These forums are for everything related to PBIs. If you'd like to see your favorite software turned into a PBI, add it to the Package Wishlist. There are also forums in which you can see which PBIs are ready for testing and which have been approved. If you have problems with a PBI, check out the Other PBI Discussion forum.

Support: This is the first place to look if you're having problems with your PC-BSD system. There are forums that deal with installation or problems with FreeBSD. Advanced users can post and review installation or general bug reports. If you find that something doesn't work like it should, take a look at the Usage Bug Reports forum.

Hardware Support: If you're having problems with your video card, sound, networking, removable media, or laptop, you'll find that each has its own forum. There is also a General Support forum for miscellaneous hardware issues.

Development: Chapter 12 will discuss in more detail how you can get involved in the development of PC-BSD. There are forums for those who want to assist in the creation of PBIs, Documentation, Translations, the PC-BSD Installer, Bluetooth Manager, or who are interested in general programming of the PC-BSD operating system. Any user can contribute their Feature Requests.

International: Contains forums in which you can discuss PC-BSD in Spanish, French, or German.

Think of a forum as a discussion area that contains a list of discussions (also known as topics). Anyone can read or search a discussion. If you register and log in, you can also add (or post) to an existing discussion or start a new discussion.

If you click a category, you will see the topics in that category with the most recent listed first, as seen in Figure 11-2.

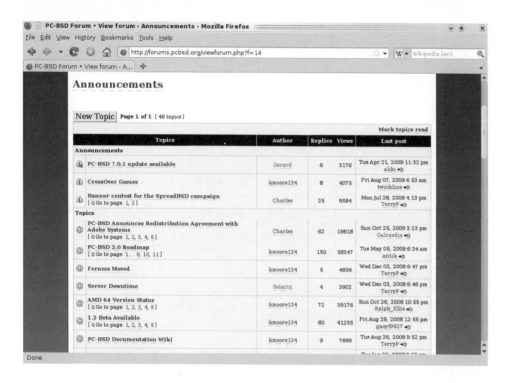

Figure 11-2. Most-recently-discussed topics in the PC-BSD Announcements forum

Each discussion has a topic title, the username of the person (author) who started the topic, the number of replies and views, the name of the user who last responded to the topic, and the date of the last response. Click the topic title to view the entire discussion, including all the replies.

Before replying to or starting a new topic, it is recommended that you spend some time reading the topics in the forums that interest you. This will give you a good idea of the tone used in each forum. You'll also get to see which types of questions get good answers and which get ignored—knowing this can help you to write better questions when asking for help.

Creating or Responding to a Post

Before posting a question, search the forums first. There is a very good chance that your question has already been answered. If you find that someone has already asked the question but did not get an answer, reply to the same post, indicating that you have the same problem, and if appropriate, add any additional information that will help others diagnose your problem. There are a few things to keep in mind before creating a post:

> **Choose a descriptive topic name:** A topic name such as "HELP ME!!!!" will not get a useful answer for several reasons. One, using all caps is known as shouting and is considered to be rude. Two, readers will assume that you if you haven't taken the time to come up with a good topic name, you also haven't bothered to research your problem. A topic name that lists the error message, such as "no

dump device defined", makes the topic easy to find for other users who are experiencing the same error message. If there's no particular error, use a descriptive topic name such as "will PC-BSD install on a Thinkpad T42 laptop?". Again, this will make it easier for other users who are wondering the same thing to find the topic.

Include the necessary information: This will show others that you have taken the time to do your homework before asking the question. It will also give them context so that they can understand your problem and offer an appropriate answer.

To create a new discussion (e.g., ask a question), look for the category that best matches the topic of your discussion. Click the category name and then the New Topic button. To reply to an existing discussion, click the Reply button within the discussion. You have to be logged in to perform these functions and will be prompted for your username and password if you are not. If you don't have a username yet, click the Register hyperlink to create one so you can log in. Figure 11-3 provides a screenshot of what you see if you click New Topic within the General Questions forum.

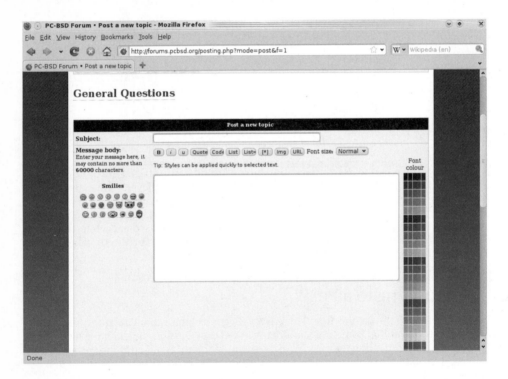

Figure 11-3. Posting a new topic to the General Questions forum

Type your descriptive topic name in the Subject area and the message itself into the Message body section. The controls around the Message body area allow you to select the font color, provide buttons for formatting text, and display the available emoticons[5] (smilies).

■ **Tip** Emoticons can be useful to let people know your intent if it is not obvious from the text; if you are making a joke, for example. However, they should be used sparingly, especially in a formal or very technical forum because they might detract from your text and irritate some users.

Several advanced options are also available for your post. They are described in detail in the phpBB User Guide;[6] phpBB is the software used by the PC-BSD forums. It is a good idea to preview your post to double-check for typos and ensure that it includes all the information other users need. If you need to save a draft of your post while you further research your question, click Save. The post won't actually be posted to the forum until you click Submit.

User Control Panel

Once logged in, extra hyperlinks will be added to the top of the forums page, as seen in Figure 11-4.

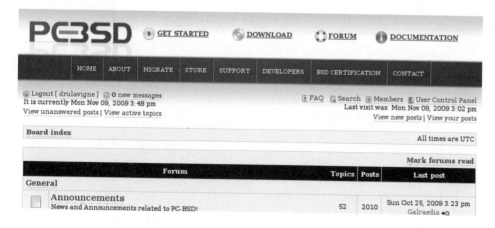

Figure 11-4. Extra settings for a logged-in user

---

[5] http://en.wikipedia.org/wiki/Emoticon

[6] www.phpbb.com/support/documentation/3.0/userguide/user_posting.php#posting_bbcodes

The User Control Panel, located in the upper-right corner, is seen in Figure 11-5.

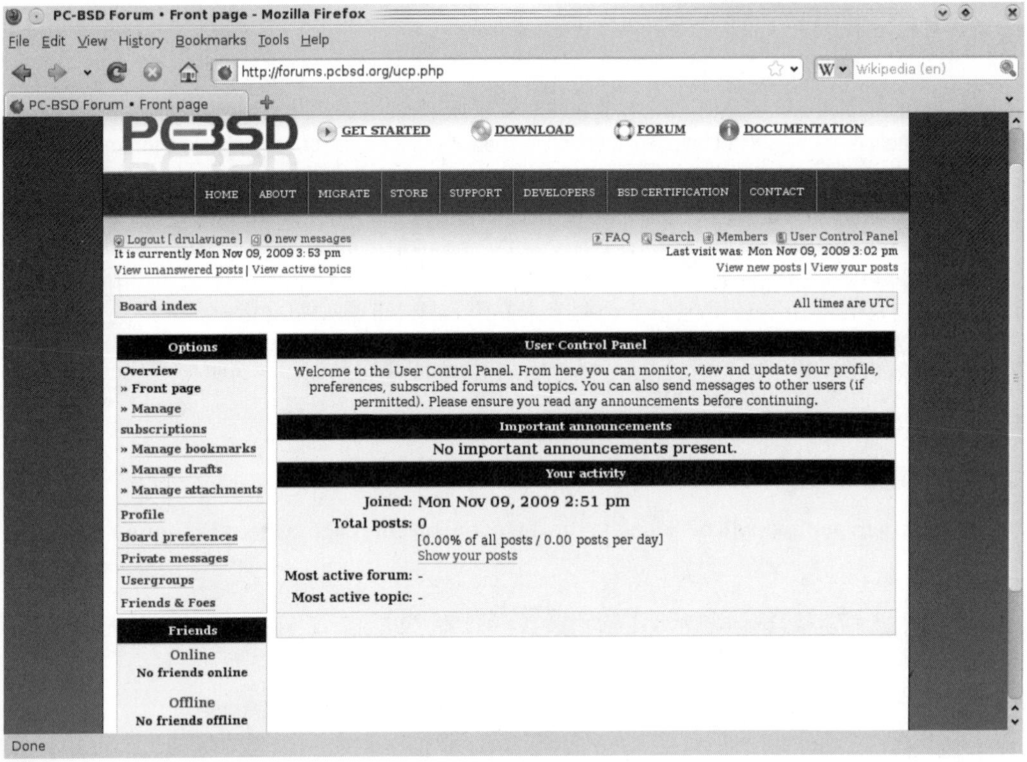

Figure 11-5. *User Control Panel at the PC-BSD forums*

You should review the Options panel on the left side; it allows you to configure and view the following:

> **Overview:** Allows you to view and remove your subscriptions and bookmarks. You will find links that allow you to subscribe to or bookmark a forum or topic near the New Topic button within the forum or topic. If you subscribe, you will be notified whenever there is an update to the forum or topic you have subscribed to. This can be very handy if you ask a question and are waiting for an answer. Bookmarks won't notify you when there is a change, but they are a handy way to quickly access topics that you find useful. If you have a message that you saved as a draft or if you have uploaded any files, you can also access them here.

Profile: Here you can control what other users see when they click your username. You can add your contact information, provide text (known as a signature) that will show at the bottom of all your posts, add your avatar (the image associated with your username), and change your e-mail address or password.

Board preferences: Here you can configure whether other users are allowed to contact you as well as how you want posts to be displayed in your browser.

Private messages: Provides an area in which you can e-mail other forum users.

Usergroups: Allows you to view which group(s) you belong to.

Friends & Foes: If you add another user to your friends list, you can quickly verify their online/offline status and send them a direct message from User Control Panel. If you add a foe, any of their forum posts will be hidden from you.

PC-BSD Wiki

The PC-BSD wiki is another source of information and is available at `http://wiki.pcbsd.org`. Figure 11-6 shows a snapshot of this site.

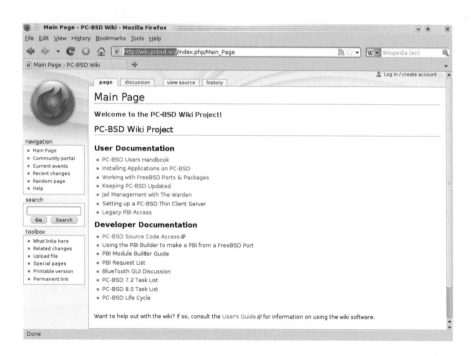

Figure 11-6. PC-BSD wiki

Consider the wiki as a read-only source of documentation that has been divided into general User Documentation and more advanced Developer Documentation. If you didn't find what you were looking for on the PC-BSD forums, the information might be located here. The listed topics do contain useful information and are well worth reading. You can also use the search box to search for specific keywords.

While it is possible to create a login account in order to modify the wiki contents, only members of the documentation team should do so. If you are interested in helping with PC-BSD documentation, Chapter 12 will show you how to introduce yourself and work with the documentation team.

■ **Caution** Don't make a change unless you are familiar with wiki formatting (described in the User's Guide link at the bottom of the page) and you have first discussed the edits with the PC-BSD documentation team.

PC-BSD IRC Channel

What do you do if you need an answer right away or want to talk to someone in "real time" instead of waiting for someone to respond to a forum post? You can try using the PC-BSD[7] Internet Relay Chat (IRC) channel. Just as forums are divided into categories, IRC provides areas in which it is appropriate to talk about a subject with other people who are interested in that subject. Similar to forums, some areas are very technical while others are more informal.

IRC Fundamentals

IRC uses several components:

- Servers, located somewhere on the Internet. PC-BSD uses the servers located at Freenode.net.

- A client application, installed on your system. Clients can be graphical or command-line–based. A list of PC-BSD IRC clients is available at `http://pbidir.com/bt/category/chat-im`. A list of FreeBSD IRC clients is available at `www.freshports.org/irc`.

- An IRC nick (username). This is the name that represents you on the IRC network, so it should create the impression you want to make, especially if you plan to participate in formal or highly technical channels. For example, "dlavigne" is probably a more useful nick than "xenawarriorprincess" or "iluvmypoodle".

---

[7] `http://en.wikipedia.org/wiki/Irc`

- An IRC channel. Think of a channel as a virtual room where users interested in that topic can chat with each other. The PC-BSD channel is called #pcbsd.

- IRC commands. These are listed at `http://en.wikipedia.org/wiki/List_of_Internet_Relay_Chat_commands`.

If you are new to IRC, consider starting with a graphical IRC client because it will allow you to use IRC right away without having to learn the syntax of the IRC commands first. The next section will demonstrate the use of the Pidgin client.

Configuring Pidgin for IRC

Pidgin[8] is an easy-to-use, graphical client that supports many chat protocols. It can be installed as a PBI, as described in Chapter 8. Figure 11-7 shows the screen you see the first time you start Pidgin and click the +Add button to add an IRC account.

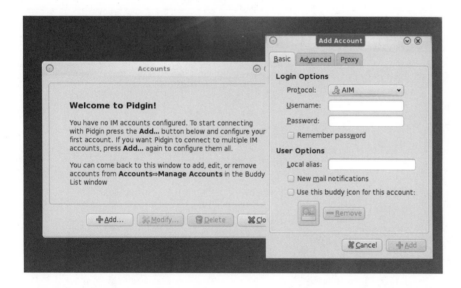

Figure 11-7. Pidgin welcome screen

Click AIM to access the drop-down Protocol menu. Select IRC and it will automatically fill in the correct server name of irc.freenode.net.

[8] `www.pidgin.im/`

■ **Tip** Pidgin supports many chat protocols such as Google Talk, MSN, and Yahoo Messenger. You can add the account information for each type of chat network in which you want to participate.

Type in the username and password that you want to use for your nick. If you check the Remember password box, you won't have to type your password every time you start Pidgin. Once you click +Add, Pidgin will connect to and log you into Freenode. A Buddy List window will open, indicating your status, an Accounts window will show your account information, and a Conversation window will open with a message from NickServ. These are seen in Figure 11-8.

■ **Tip** NickServ is the nickname service bot that IRC uses to register nicknames.

Figure 11-8. Buddy List, Accounts, and Conversation windows in Pidgin

In this example, the drulavigne account is connected to (Available) the Freenode network, but NickServ indicates that this is not a registered nick. It is a good idea to register your nick because some channels will not let you join the conversation with an unregistered nick. You also won't be able to chat directly with another user until you register your nick. To register your nick, reply to NickServ by typing the following command into the Conversation window: **/msg nickserv register password email**.

Replace **password** with the password you want to use and **email** with your e-mail address. NickServ will reply with a message indicating that instructions to activate your nick have been sent to that e-mail address and that you have a day to complete your registration before your temporary registration expires.

Participating in the Channel

Once you are connected, you will want to chat with someone other than NickServ. You do so by joining a channel. In the Buddy List window, click Buddies ➤ Join a Chat. To join the PC-BSD channel, type **#pcbsd** into the Channel bar and press Enter or click the Join button.

■ **Tip** The # is important. If you forget to put it at the beginning of the channel name, your command will fail and you will see a "No such channel" error message.

If you want the channel to show in your Buddy List window, use Buddies ➤ +Add Chat instead. This menu provides an extra option of autojoining the channel when you open Pidgin. If you don't select autojoin, you can join the chat at any time by clicking its name in your Buddy List. Both menus provide a Room List button which will list all available channels on Freenode. If one interests you, right-click it to either Join or Add it to your Buddy List.

Once you've joined a channel, a new tab with the channel name will appear in the Conversation window, as seen in Figure 11-9. You can join as many channels as you want, and each will appear in its own tab. To leave a channel, simply close the tab by clicking the *x* in the tab.

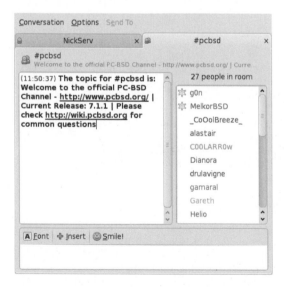

Figure 11-9. #pcbsd channel in the Pidgin Conversation window

Most channels have a welcome message that might indicate which topics are suitable as well as any resources that new channel users should be aware of. The PC-BSD welcome message reminds you that you should check the wiki first if you're looking for the answer to a commonly asked question.

The Conversation window is divided into several sections:

Left pane: Contains the conversation. By default, each comment in the conversation begins with the nick of the person who wrote it and the time it was posted. You can use the scroll bar to scroll through the conversation. Use Conversation ➤ Clear Scrollback if you want to erase the conversation so far.

Right pane: Displays the number of users in the channel and their nicknames. If your nick is registered, you can double-click another user's nick to start a private conversation (also known as a direct message [DM]) in a new tab. Right-click the name to send them a file, ignore them, get information about their nick, or add them to your Buddy List.

■ **Caution** It is considered rude to DM a person who does not know you. If you have a question and don't know anyone in the channel, introduce yourself and ask if anyone has a moment to help you.

Bottom pane: This is where you type your message. It won't appear in the conversation window until you press Enter.

■ **Tip** If you're pasting an error message, paste only a line or so at a time. If you paste too much information at once, the server will kick you out of the channel.

It's not a bad idea to lurk (watch the conversation without responding) in a new channel to get a feel for how chatty the channel is and the tone of most conversations. If the channel is quiet, introduce yourself. You might find that you already "know" some of the users from the PC-BSD forums; you might also make some new friends.

The Pidgin application is quite customizable. You can toggle logging, sounds, formatting toolbars, and timestamps off or on in the Options menu of the Conversation window. The Tools menu in the Buddy List contains Plugins and Preferences menus with many more options. The Pidgin User Guide[9] is a good reference for the settings that aren't intuitive to you. You can also ask Pidgin-specific questions that aren't answered in the Guide in the #pidgin IRC channel.

---

[9] http://developer.pidgin.im/wiki/Using%20Pidgin

PC-BSD Mailing Lists

Mailing lists provide another way to interact with other users. Some users are more comfortable using e-mail and prefer mailing lists to online forums. Other users prefer to have messages arrive in their inbox rather than having to search the forums. You'll often find that when you google a question, the answer is found on a mailing list. A *mailing list* is simply a list of users—when a user on the list sends an e-mail to the list, everyone gets a copy.

The PC-BSD community has several mailing lists at `www.pcbsd.org/content/view/22/29/`. Like the PC-BSD forums, each mailing list is designed for specific discussion topics:

> **Announcements:** A read-only list that informs you when new versions of PC-BSD become available.
>
> **General:** A general discussion list for topics that don't match any of the other mailing lists.
>
> **Support:** If you have a specific problem you need help with, this is the list to ask your question.
>
> **Translations:** The list translation team members use to discuss their translation work.
>
> **PBI Developers:** The list PBI developers use to discuss their PBI work.
>
> **Documentation Contributors:** The list documentation team members use to discuss documentation changes.
>
> **Developers:** The list PC-BSD developers use to discuss their work.
>
> **Beta Testers:** Anyone interested in testing beta[10] versions of PC-BSD should report the errors they come across here.

If you click a mailing list name, you will get more information about the list, as seen in Figure 11-10.

---

[10] See `http://en.wikipedia.org/wiki/Software_release_life_cycle#Beta` for a definition of a beta version.

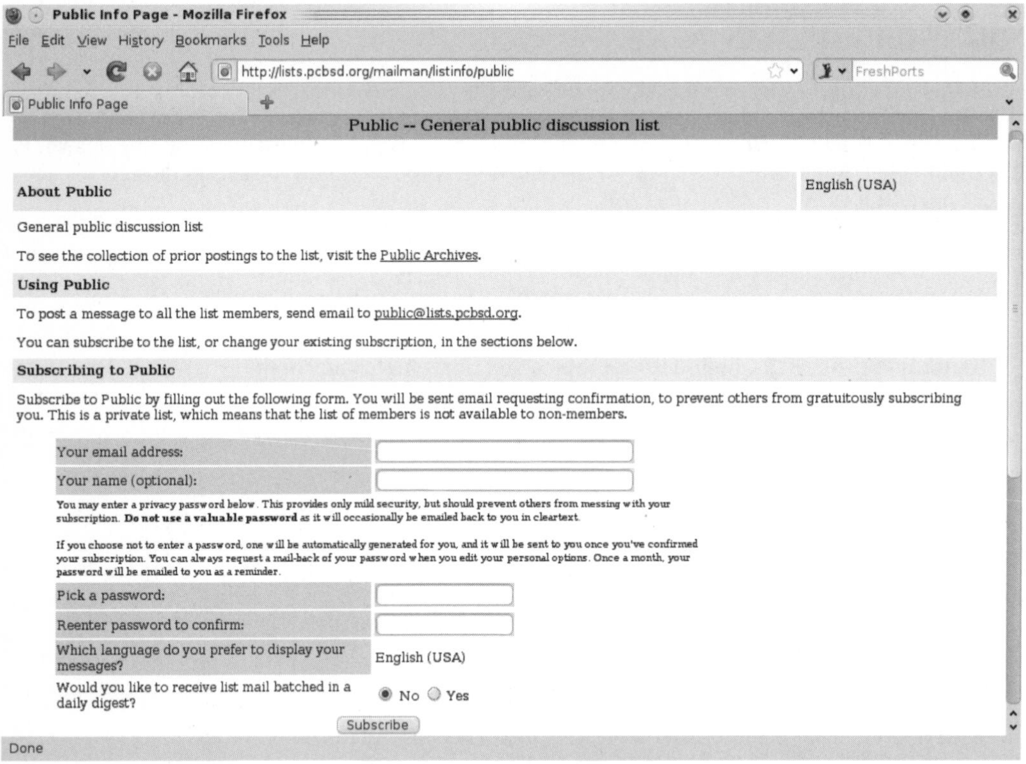

Figure 11-10. Information page for PC-BSD General mailing list

Each list's information page contains the following sections:

About: Provides a description of the topics that are suited to this mailing list. If you're unsure, take a look at the list's Archives to read its discussions—this will give you an idea of the appropriate tone and discussion topics for this list.

Using: Tells you what e-mail address to use when sending a question to the list.

Subscribing to: This is where you subscribe to the list. By default, you will receive a separate e-mail for every post to the list. If you prefer to have all the day's discussions sent in one e-mail, click the Yes button to receive the daily digest.

If you subscribe to the list, an automated e-mail will be sent to the e-mail address you indicated, asking you to confirm your subscription request. Once you confirm, another e-mail will be sent, indicating that you are now subscribed. This e-mail contains useful information about the list and instructions on how to send an e-mail to the list, change your subscription options, or unsubscribe.

When sending an e-mail to the list, remember to use a useful subject line and to include enough information in the message so that other users can help you. Mailing lists have their own netiquette that might vary from list to list, so you should read the list's archives first to get a good feel for what is considered acceptable. For example, some lists consider it rude if you write your reply at the beginning of the previous e-mail (this is called top posting[11]). When replying, you should leave enough of the original e-mail (this is called quoting) in place so other users know what you are replying to. However, it is considered rude to quote a very long e-mail only to add a few words at the bottom. When in doubt, watch how others reply to e-mail and make note of what someone else did wrong when another user complains about the way they replied to an e-mail.

Documentation

The previous sections described several methods of receiving help from the community by interacting with other users using the various PC-BSD communication methods. This section describes more-passive methods of finding the documentation you need.

PC-BSD FAQ and Knowledge Base

The Frequently Asked Questions (FAQ) document for any community is always a good document to read. As the name suggests, it contains answers to the questions that users ask most frequently. A *knowledge base* is a larger collection of FAQs and other useful information.

■ **Tip** FAQs are created to save repeat questions on communication channels. Don't expect a helpful (or even polite) reply if you ask a question that is already answered in the FAQ. Doing so is the equivalent of asking "where is the bathroom?" while standing next to a flashing neon sign pointing to the bathroom. It's embarrassing for you and irritating to others.

The PC-BSD FAQ and Knowledge Base is located at `http://faqs.pcbsd.org`. Figure 11-11 shows the results of clicking the Show all categories hyperlink in the left frame of this website.

---

[11] `http://en.wikipedia.org/wiki/Top_posting`

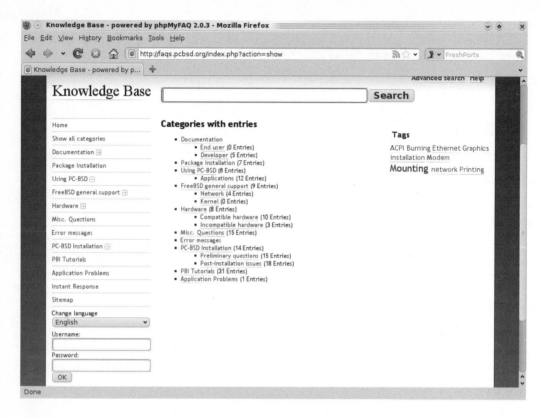

Figure 11-11. PC-BSD FAQ and Knowledge Base categories

If you're simply browsing for interesting information, read through the entries in the categories that interest you. If you're searching for the answer to a specific question, try using the Search bar. If you're considering asking a question on a forum or mailing list, double-check that it isn't answered here first.

PC-BSD Users Handbook

PC-BSD also provides a Users Handbook that shows you how to accomplish common tasks using PC-BSD. It is located on the Internet at `http://wiki.pcbsd.org/index.php/PC-BSD_Users_Handbook`. An icon was installed on the desktop so you can quickly access this website. Figure 11-12 shows a screenshot of the PC-BSD Users Handbook.

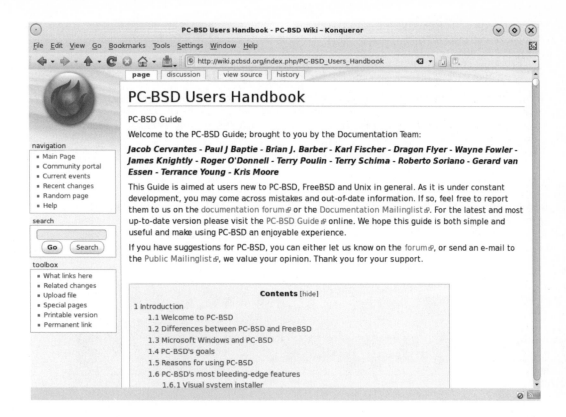

Figure 11-12. PC-BSD Users Handbook

Reading the Users Handbook is an excellent way to learn new skills. You can sit down and read through it like a book, or skip to the sections that interest you at the moment.

FreeBSD Resources

Since PC-BSD is FreeBSD under the hood, you can also tap into the wide range of resources that are available to FreeBSD users. The FreeBSD Handbook, available at `www.freebsd.org/handbook`, is the best place to start as it demonstrates how to do almost anything on FreeBSD.

You might also be interested in these other FreeBSD resources:

FreeBSD FAQ: The FAQ is available at `ww.freebsd.org/doc/en_US.IS08859-1/books/faq`.

FreeBSD mailing lists: These are listed at `www.freebsd.org/community/mailinglists.html`.

FreeBSD forums: These can be found at `http://forums.freebsd.org`.

FreeBSD IRC channels: Information about the channels can be found at `www.freebsd.org/community/irc.html`.

FreeBSD social networks: A variety of FreeBSD-related social networking sites are listed at `www.freebsd.org/community/social.html`.

Most of the information for FreeBSD also applies to PC-BSD systems. However, some things, such as the installer program, are different. If you are unsure whether you should try something you learned about from a FreeBSD resource on your PC-BSD system, ask on an appropriate PC-BSD forum, IRC channel, or mailing list.

KDE User Guide

Because KDE is the default desktop for PC-BSD, you might also find the KDE documentation found at `http://docs.kde.org/` to be useful. That page provides links to the KDE User Guide and FAQ and provides a search function for searching through KDE documentation. Figure 11-13 provides a screenshot of the documentation website.

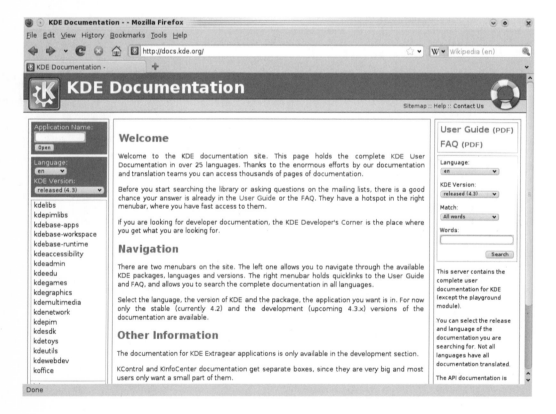

Figure 11-13. KDE documentation website

If you click a KDE software package in the left pane (e.g., kdeadmin), it will list all the utilities associated with that package. If you click the name of the utility, you can read its guide to learn how to get the most out of that KDE utility. KDE comes with a lot of utilities and functionality, so you can spend a lot of time here learning how to get the most out of your desktop! If you learn something useful that you haven't seen posted on the forums, consider adding a topic to share your discovery with other PC-BSD users.

Community Sites

If you speak German and want to interact with other users in your native language, check out the German-specific community at `www.pc-bsd.de`.

Commercial Support

While this chapter has focused on community, commercial support is still available for PC-BSD through iXsystems, `http://www.ixsystems.com`. Based in the heart of Silicon Valley, iXsystems is a BSD-friendly server and storage manufacturer that resulted from an employee buyout of the hardware assets of BSDi, the corporation that developed and distributed BSD/OS, the commercial variant of BSD Unix. iXsystems has been producing FreeBSD-certified servers and storage solutions in a state-of-the-art production facility since the early 1990s. In addition to being a huge proponent for the FreeBSD operating system, iXsystems is the corporate sponsor of the PC-BSD operating system, runs the FreeBSD Mall[12], and offers Professional Enterprise Support for FreeBSD and PC-BSD.

iXsystems provides incidental and packaged services, from installation support to system configuration to application support. The Support Team helps users set up secure home networks and provides assistance with the KDE Desktop Environment as well as with advanced system functions.

The iXsystems Professional Support Team can also help organizations run PC-BSD with the peace of mind of having a fully supported operating system at great savings over closed sourced alternatives. From setting up a thin client server to network administration to software development, the experienced professionals at iXsystems are available to meet all your organizational needs.

Summary

This chapter introduced you to the many resources available to you when you need help with your PC-BSD system. It also introduced you to the PC-BSD community of users.

The next chapter will demonstrate ways in which you can become more actively involved within the PC-BSD community.

---

[12] `www.freebsdmall.com`

CHAPTER 12

■ ■ ■

Getting Involved

Chapter 11 introduced you to the various sources of help within the PC-BSD community. New users often start out slowly by reading the various forums and occasionally posting a new topic when they have a question they can't find an answer to. Over time, as you become more familiar with the community and how to do things on your PC-BSD system, it is natural to find yourself getting more involved.

This chapter will introduce a variety of ways that anyone can use to give back to the PC-BSD community. While reading through this chapter, keep in mind the netiquette you learned in Chapter 11.

How You Can Help

It is a common misconception to think that you don't have anything to contribute, especially if you are still learning how to use PC-BSD yourself. You don't have to be a "guru" or know how to write source code to get involved and to help others within the PC-BSD community. Your life experience, what you know about PC-BSD so far, and your unique combination of skills and talents are useful to others. A community is made out of people, and every person has something to contribute. The more people that get involved, the more vibrant the community, and the more the software evolves to meet the needs of the people within that community.

This chapter suggests some of the more common ways to contribute back to the PC-BSD community. We suggest ways that are suited to both the novice and more experienced users. We haven't thought of everything, so if you have a good idea not listed here, be sure to bring it up on a FreeBSD forum, mailing list, or IRC channel. Better yet, just do it!

Submitting Feature Requests

Even if you don't consider yourself to be a technical user, you still have thoughts about what would be useful on your PC-BSD system. Maybe a specific application isn't available as a PBI, or you find that a specific feature is missing or could be improved upon.

When submitting an application or a feature request, keep in mind that implementing your request will require work on the part of another person. This should not deter you, but it should remind you to help make the other person's work as easy as possible. In other words, research your request first and give other users all the information they need to understand your request and possibly implement it.

Chapter 11 introduced you to the PC-BSD forums and how to post to a forum. Two of the forums are useful here: Feature Requests and Package Wishlist (discussed in the following sections).

Adding to the Package Wishlist

Before creating a new topic on the Package Wishlist forum, go through the following checklist for the software you want to see made available to PC-BSD users:

Search pbidir.com: Does a PBI already exist? If so, do you need a newer software version?

Search FreshPorts.org: Does a FreeBSD package/port already exist? If so, you want to ask if anyone can convert it to a PBI.

Search forums.pcbsd.org: Has anyone else made a request yet? If so, you should respond to that post after reading any of the previous responses.

If a topic doesn't already exist, make sure that your new topic includes the name of the software in the subject line so other users can find it easily. Your new forum message should include the following information:

Indicate if a PBI already exists: If so, include the reasons why you need a newer version. For example, does the new version introduce new functionality that you need, or does the old version have a serious security vulnerability?

If there is no PBI, indicate if a port/package already exists: It is easier for someone else to make the PBI from an existing port/package. Your message should also include the URL to the website for the application, a brief description of what the software does, and any reasons why you think a PBI would be useful to you and other PC-BSD users.

Requesting a Feature

If your feature request deals with the operating system, rather than a missing software application, you should create a new topic on the Feature Requests forum instead. Don't forget to search `forums.pcbsd.org` first to see whether someone else has already started a topic. If a topic already exists, reply to that topic. If there isn't a similar topic, create a new topic with a descriptive subject line so other users can find your request.

Some things to keep in mind if you make a feature request:

Don't take it personally if no one responds: It might just mean that no one else finds that feature useful at this time. Feature implementers might also be busy working on a new release of PC-BSD and don't have time to look at feature requests right now. If the feature is important to you, consider discussing it on the #pcbsd IRC channel.

It is okay if others disagree: What is a feature to one person might seem like a waste of time and resources to another. Keep the rules of netiquette in mind if someone disagrees with your request. And don't assume that this means that your feature won't be implemented. Sometimes having multiple points of view helps in the design of a feature that meets the needs of a wider group of users.

Don't assume a feature is too "small" to ask for: Useful features that are trivial to implement are often implemented quickly. The developer gets to feel a sense of accomplishment and other users end up benefitting from your original request.

Don't assume a feature is too "big" to ask for: Some features take a lot of design work and development time to implement correctly. However, they also offer great satisfaction to the developer who tackles the implementation. These types of requests often get a response of "great idea" with some sort of timeline of when it is realistic to expect the feature to be ready for testing. You can also help to test the feature and how to do so is discussed later in this chapter.

Not all features get implemented: Sometimes there are legal or technical restrictions that prevent the feature from being added. Sometimes the feature is a great idea, but no one has the time to develop the implementation at this time.

Some features do get implemented: What would be useful to you is often also useful to other PC-BSD users. Often developers think "that's a great idea, why didn't I think of that before?" and are happy to implement the new functionality. And you never know if you never ask.

Submitting Bug Reports

A software bug[1] occurs when an application acts in an unexpected or incorrect way. Examples include receiving an error message when you launch an application or having an application hang when you access one of its menu items.

Before submitting a bug report, use Google to research the problem first. Bugs are fixed by developers and they need a way to keep track of which bugs have already been reported, which are being worked on, and which have been fixed. Sometimes in order to fix some PC-BSD bugs, something needs to be fixed in the underlying FreeBSD operating system or in the KDE desktop. This means that information about your bug is probably located outside of the PC-BSD forums, and possibly even outside of the PC-BSD community.

In order for developers to fix a bug, they have to be able to re-create it so they can figure out what causes the bug and what exactly needs to be fixed. Occasionally a bug is not a bug at all, but a user error. Don't be embarrassed if this turns out to be the case—in reality, you have still uncovered a documentation or design bug. Obviously, if the interface is not intuitive enough to prevent errors, the design needs to be improved, or some form of documentation needs to be added to the FAQ or knowledge base. If you've managed to come across the error, chances are many other users have as well, and perhaps they did not have the time or know-how to report the error.

There are several ways to report a bug. Which method you choose will depend upon your technical level and the communication methods you are comfortable with. Regardless of the method you use, make sure your message about the bug includes information on how to re-create the bug. If your research shows that other users or developers have discussed the bug and its possible fixes, include those links in your message.

---

[1] See `http://en.wikipedia.org/wiki/Software bug` for a more detailed description.

Using the Forums

The PC-BSD forums contain three forums that deal with bugs: General Bug Reports, Startup/Installation Bug Reports, and Usage Bug Reports. It is a good idea to skim through these forums first to get a good idea of how others write bug reports and to see which topics belong in which bug forum. You'll note that each forum includes a topic reminding you to search the knowledge base first before posting. Other points to keep in mind:

> **Explain how to re-create the problem:** This should be at the beginning of your post because the first thing a developer will do is try to re-create the problem to figure out what is causing it.

> **If possible, determine if the problem is with PC-BSD, FreeBSD, or KDE:** Sometimes you can tell from your research; for example, if the bug is being discussed on a KDE mailing list, the problem is with KDE, not PC-BSD. Sometimes it might be difficult to figure out the underlying source of the bug. When in doubt, post on the PC-BSD forum first and be prepared to repost to a FreeBSD or KDE forum if a developer indicates that the bug report belongs there.

■ **Tip** The forum topic "If you see bugs that are KDE or FreeBSD-specific"[2] contains links for posting FreeBSD or KDE bug reports.

Using the Mailing Lists

If the bug is specific to a PBI, you can post your bug report on the PBI-bugs mailing list. Instructions for this list are at `http://lists.pcbsd.org/mailman/listinfo/pbi-bugs`.

Another mailing list, designed for developers who fix bugs, is Trac-bugs at `http://lists.pcbsd.org/mailman/listinfo/trac-bugs`. This is an automated mailing list that sends out an e-mail whenever a bug is reported using the trac[3] bug reporting system. Trac is discussed in more detail in the next section.

Using trac

Trac is software that allows software projects to track their software bugs. Users can submit bug reports that are automatically given a ticket number and added to the database of known bugs. Developers can report on their progress as they work on fixing the bug. Once the bug is fixed, the ticket is closed. Anyone can search the database to see which bugs have been reported and which have been fixed.

---

[2] `http://forums.pcbsd.org/viewtopic.php?f=7&t=3043&start=0`

[3] `http://trac.edgewall.org/`

The PC-BSD trac database is located at `http://trac.pcbsd.org`. Anyone can use the search feature in the upper-right corner to search for a bug or click View Tickets to browse all tickets. You will need to register for an account if you want to report a bug. Figure 12-1 shows the PC-BSD trac website with the dlavigne user logged in.

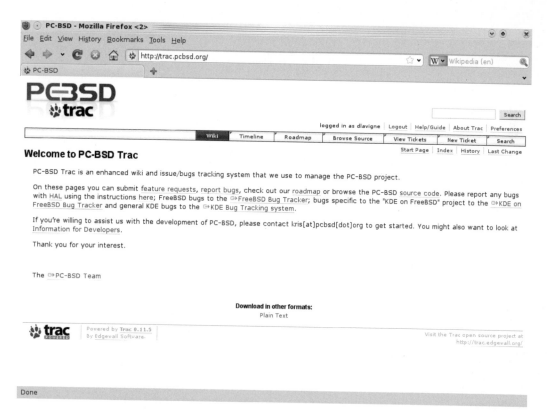

Figure 12-1. PC-BSD trac bug reporting database

To submit a feature request or bug report, click the feature requests or report bugs hyperlinks. You can also click New Ticket in the upper-right corner. Any of these options will open the Create New Ticket window, seen in Figure 12-2.

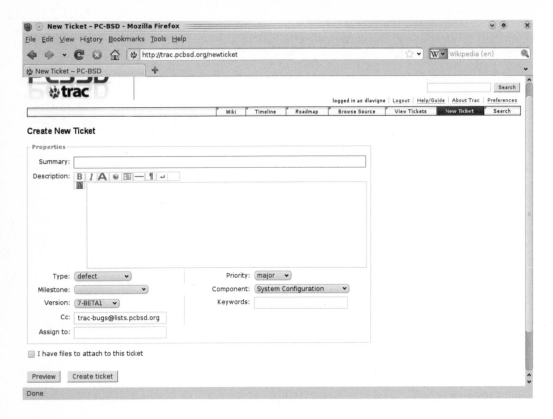

Figure 12-2. Creating a new ticket using the PC-BSD trac system

The ticket contains the following:

Summary: This is a descriptive subject to assist other users in finding the bug report.

Description: Include how to re-create the problem/feature here, as well as any other details needed to assist the developer in fixing the problem.

Type: Indicate whether the ticket is a bug report (defect) or feature request (enhancement).

Milestone: Select the version of PC-BSD you are using. Developers who are creating new features might pick a version that has not been released yet.

Version: Select the version of PC-BSD you are using.

Cc: Leave this as-is so a copy of the report is sent to the trac-bugs mailing list.

Assign to: Leave this empty because it will be filled in when a developer is assigned to fix the bug.

Priority: Indicate whether the bug/feature is of major or minor importance. Typically only developers tag a bug as critical.

Component: Read through the list of components and pick the one that most closely matches the part of the operating system that is affected by the bug/feature.

Keywords: These will be picked up by the search engine so include two or three words that you would find useful to search for and find your ticket.

Attached Files: If possible, include a screenshot or copy/paste of any error messages in a separate file. The description should be a short descriptive paragraph describing the bug/feature—all the necessary details should be in the attached file.

Before submitting the ticket, use the Preview button. Pretend you are someone else reading the ticket—does it contain all the information you would need to understand the problem? When finished your review, click Create Ticket to submit it to the database. It will now show under View Tickets.

The main page of the PC-BSD trac site also contains hyperlinks to the following:

Roadmap: You can view the tickets and their progress for the upcoming release of the operating system.

Source code: Source code for the operating system. Source code is discussed in more detail in Chapter 14.

The main page also contains links to submitting bug reports for HAL,[4] FreeBSD's version of KDE, KDE, and useful information for developers who want to assist the PC-BSD project.

Testing Prerelease Builds and PBIs

By the time an operating system is "released" (i.e., a new version becomes available), many developers and users have already tested all the new features to ensure they work as expected. This testing phase is called a beta[5] period. When the software is just created and hasn't been well tested, it is called an alpha period. Obviously, the more people who can test new features as they are created and who can retest bugs after they are fixed, the better the final release. You don't have to be a developer to participate in an alpha or beta period. You just have to be willing to spend some time trying out new features and writing up good reports that explain any errors you come across so they can be fixed by developers.

■ **Tip** If you are a developer, you can submit fixes using the PC-BSD trac system.

---

[4] http://en.wikipedia.org/wiki/HAL_%28software%29

[5] http://en.wikipedia.org/wiki/Software_beta

Information useful to PC-BSD beta testers is available in the testing mailing list at `http://lists.pcbsd.org/mailman/listinfo/testing`. Begin by looking at the most recent archives—this will tell you what version is currently being tested and where to download the International Organization for Standardization (ISO) image to the alpha or beta version.

■ **Tip** Beta ISOs tend to be large (at least 2GB), so it is best to have a fairly fast and reliable Internet connection.

Once you have the beta version, install it on a test system or virtual environment and then start to play with it. One approach is to try doing your regular tasks and see if you come across any problems. Another approach is to systematically start going through all the menus to see whether anything is missing or produces an error. As you find errors, post a message to the testing mailing list. Remember to research the error first (to see whether anyone else has already reported it), use a descriptive subject line, explain what you did that caused the error, and describe the error and/or cut and paste the error message.

If you prefer to test PBIs instead of the operating system, there is a "PBIs ready for test" forum at `forums.pcbsd.org`. You might want to subscribe to this forum to be notified whenever a new PBI is ready to be tested.

■ **Tip** PBIs do not get added to pbidir.com until after they have been tested by users. This helps to ensure that new users won't experience any problems when they install a PBI.

When a PBI developer finishes creating or updating a PBI, a new message is posted to this forum. The message will indicate where you can download a copy of the PBI to test. You can speed up the process of a PBI going from testing to final availability by volunteering to test the PBI. Install the PBI, try accessing all its menus, and perform some of its functions. If you come across any problems, reply to the original post. If the PBI works flawlessly for you, still reply to the post and indicate so in your message.

Join the Translation Team

If you speak and write a language other than English, consider joining the PC-BSD translation team. This team's efforts help to open up PC-BSD to a whole new group of users who otherwise would not be able to access the operating system because they understand a language other than English. The gateway containing links useful to PC-BSD translators is located at `http://translations.pcbsd.org`. Members of the translation team work on the following:

> **Localization:** The process of translating an operating system's menus and messages into another language.

> **Document translation:** Translation of existing documents, such as the PC-BSD User Guide, from English to another language.

These tasks are discussed in the following sections.

Localizing PC-BSD

The PC-BSD translation community uses the Pootle[6] application to manage translations. Pootle is short for PO-based Online Translation/Localization Engine because it uses translation PO files that end in the .po extension. The syntax for .po files can take some time to learn—fortunately, Pootle provides an easy-to-use, browser-based editor that allows you to concentrate on translating rather than spending time learning file syntax.

The PC-BSD Pootle installation, seen in Figure 12-3, is located at `http://Pootle2.pcbsd.org`.

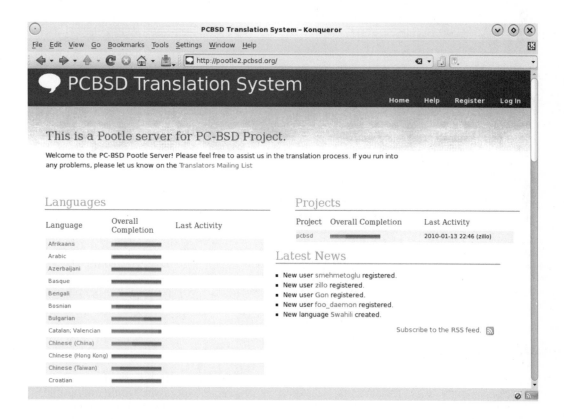

Figure 12-3. PC-BSD Pootle server

---

[6] `http://en.wikipedia.org/wiki/Pootle`

Each language that is being translated has its own hyperlink in the Languages section.

■ **Tip** If the language you want to translate is not listed, send an e-mail to the PC-BSD translations mailing list requesting that the language be added.

If you click a language, you will see the statistics for that language. Figure 12-4 shows the resulting screenshot for clicking the French language and then the pcbsd folder.

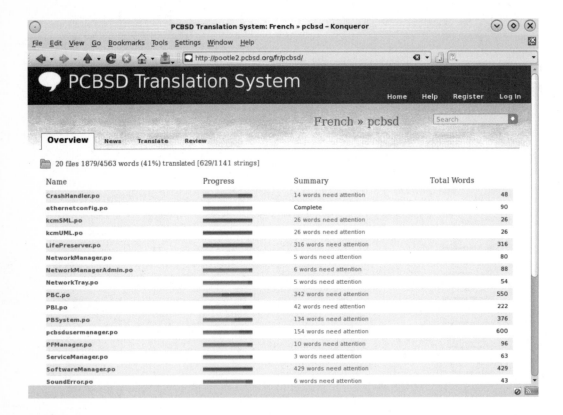

Figure 12-4. Viewing the translation statistics for the French PC-BSD team

The statistics contain the following for each translated menu:

Name: The name of the PC-BSD specific menu to be translated

■ **Tip** Menus that come with KDE are translated by the KDE translation team. See the KDE Translation HOWTO[7] for more information about joining this team.

Progress: Shows a bar graph representing the percentage of words that have been translated within a menu

Summary: Indicates which menus are complete and how many words need attention in incomplete menus

Total Words: Shows the number of translatable words within a menu

In order to translate a menu, you need to first register an account and then log in using the links at the top of the page. The first time you log in, you will be prompted to change options where you can set up your user interface language, the number of rows you want to see in translate and view modes, and the languages you want to translate. The language(s) you select will be added to your home page so you can quickly access your translation project(s).

Once you are logged in, you can begin to translate files. Figure 12-5 shows the interface seen by clicking the CrashHandler.po file in the French ➤ pcbsd folder.

---

[7] http://l10n.kde.org/docs/translation-howto/

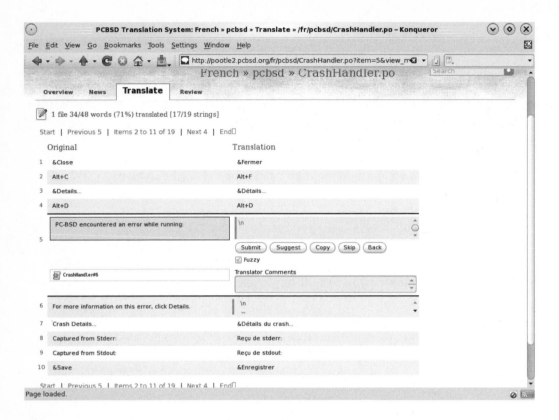

Figure 12-5. *Translating a block of text using PC-BSD Pootle*

Each possible block of words to be translated appears in Pootle's translation editor. If you click the number next to a block of text, an Edit link will appear. In this example, the number 5 has been clicked to open the editor for this block of menu text. The translator can now type in the translation and then press Submit to save the translated text.

■ **Note** The fuzzy checkbox indicates that another translator should still verify the accuracy of the translation. It is a good idea to keep this box checked when adding a translation.

Translating Documentation

While Pootle is used for localization of PC-BSD menus, translating existing documentation is discussed on the Translations forums at `forums.pcbsd.org`. Check this forum first to see which documents are currently being translated. If you want to start work on a document that isn't currently being translated, start a new topic on this forum.

Contributing Documentation

If English is your native language, you can also contribute new documentation. Here are some suggestions to get you started:

Add a new topic to the Tips & Tricks forum: Have you done something cool with your PC-BSD system that isn't listed in this forum? Or have you found a neat trick that other users might find useful? Start a new topic describing your tip or trick.

Add a new topic to the Guides forum: Have you discovered how to perform a task that isn't part of the PC-BSD Users Handbook? Clear instructions on how to perform the task would make a great new topic for this forum.

Join the docs mailing list: Have some good ideas about documentation? The people on this mailing list are also interested in documentation.

Start a blog about PC-BSD: Looking for a good blog idea? Consider blogging about your experience with PC-BSD and the things you learn along the way.

Already write for a column or magazine? If so, see if they are interested in publishing an article about PC-BSD or describing how to do something in PC-BSD.

■ **Tip** There is a magazine specific to BSD[8] which is always looking for writers.

Review the PC-BSD Knowledge Base and FAQs: Add documentation that you think is essential but missing.

Add to the PC-BSD wiki: Remember to discuss your edits first on the docs mailing list.

Contribute Artwork or Videos

PC-BSD provides several venues for contributing different types of media that other users might find cool or useful. You can do the following:

---

[8] See **www.bsdmag.org** for more information about BSD Magazine.

Submit pictures to the PC-BSD Community Pictures forum: Have pictures from a PC-BSD conference booth or of users using PC-BSD? Start a new topic and tell others where they can find the pictures.

Submit screenshots to the PC-BSD Screenshots forum: Let others see screenshots of your custom desktop or of PC-BSD running a cool application.

Upload videos: The PC-BSD users Ning group[9] has an area where you can upload videos of PC-BSD presentations, interviews, and how-tos. You have to sign up to join the community first.

If you have other art or design ideas, bring them up in a suitable forum. For example, you could offer to create PC-BSD brochures to hand out at conferences, create designs for stickers, or discuss T-shirt design ideas. The possibilities are endless! If it's cool to you, chances are it will be cool to other PC-BSD users as well.

Conferences

Until you've had an opportunity to attend a BSD or free software conference[10] (like a LinuxFest), you have no idea how valuable and personally satisfying it is to meet other users who are also interested in the PC-BSD operating system. Often you will have the chance to meet people that you have chatted with on IRC or whose forum posts you have read. You might also get to meet some of the people who develop PC-BSD, write its documentation, or work on a translation team. But don't just take our word for it—if you have a chance to attend a conference in your area or in a city you are able to travel to, attend the conference and see for yourself.

As an Attendee

If this is your first conference, don't worry if the scheduled talks sound too advanced. You will still get something interesting out of each talk, even if you don't understand everything the speaker is talking about. The real value of a conference is the "in between talks" time. This is where you get to chit chat with other attendees, find out what they are doing, and meet new friends. Here are some tips to keep in mind when attending a conference:

Bring your business cards and keep a pen handy: If you don't have any and can't afford to buy some, create your own cards containing your name and e-mail address using Open Office[11] and print them onto business card paper that is available from most office supply stores. Swapping business cards is a great way to have the contact details for the new people you will meet. When

---

[9] http://pcbsdusers.ning.com

[10] @bsdevents on Twitter posts the times and locations of upcoming conferences that will have BSD talks or booths.

[11] www.linuxjournal.com/node/1000428 has a nice how-to for creating business cards.

someone hands you a card, take a moment to write a note on the back so you remember who they are when you get back home.

Don't be shy: If it's your first conference, you probably don't know anyone— yet. That will change quickly once you start talking to people. If you have to, muster up the courage to introduce yourself to a few people. BSD users tend to be a friendly bunch, so it shouldn't take too many introductions to get the ball rolling. If you have a cool T-shirt or hardware device, bring it with you; people will come over and introduce themselves to you!

Don't dismiss the conference if you don't have the money to pay: While many conferences are free or have a minimal registration fee, others might be out of your price range or you might not have the money to travel to the conference location. See the next two sections if either applies to you.

As a Speaker

Being a speaker at a conference is a great way to attend a conference. You get to tell other people about the interesting things you are doing, and other attendees can benefit from your experience. Having a PC-BSD talk at a non-BSD conference is also a good way to spread the word about PC-BSD and to give users of other operating systems an opportunity to learn more about PC-BSD.

Every conference has a Call for Papers (CFP) where anyone is invited to submit an idea for a talk. Check the conference website a few months before the conference date to find out the guidelines and submission due date for the CFP. Read the guidelines and ask yourself if any of the suggested topics apply to what you are doing with PC-BSD. Depending upon the focus of the conference, many CFPs are looking for nondeveloper talks where those with other skills can discuss what they are doing and how others can get involved. Examples of possible talk ideas include the following:

Translations: What is it like to be a member of a translation team? How do you get started in translating documentation? How is Pootle used to assist a translation team?

Using PC-BSD: As an end user in a corporate environment, at a school or volunteer organization, useful tips and tricks, migrating from other operating systems, things that are different from Windows or Linux or Mac, and so on.

Running XYZ application on PC-BSD: Describe how you install and use an application such as a database, gaming system, server software, or Windows application on PC-BSD.

PC-BSD for FreeBSD, Windows, Linux, or Mac users: If you have experience with another operating system, explain how PC-BSD differs and any tricks you had to learn when you started using PC-BSD.

When submitting a talk proposal, double-check that your submission follows the submission guidelines. Most conferences will pay a speaker's registration fee but you should check to see if the conference also assists in travel costs or if speakers are responsible for their own travel.

If your talk gets accepted, spend some time creating and practicing your slides. Ask yourself: "If I were listening to this talk, what would I like to learn?" Find out how long the talk is expected to last; most talks last 40 minutes with 10 minutes afterward for questions. Practice your timing—if you have too many slides, you will be rushing at the end or won't have enough time left over for questions. If you don't have enough content or rush through your talk, you will be done in 15 minutes and will be left wondering what to do with the rest of the time. If possible, practice in front of friends or family members and have them tell you if you are talking too fast, mumbling, or are making distracting gestures or sounds.

Attendees will be interested in what you have to say and will want to know where to get a copy of your slides. If possible, upload your slides to your website, blog, or a slide sharing website such as SlideShare[12] before the conference. Include your contact e-mail address and the URL to your slides in the last slide and leave that slide up as you answer questions at the end of your talk.

As a Volunteer

If you are too shy to be a conference speaker, have trouble introducing yourself to people at conferences, or don't have the money to pay for the conference registration fee, an excellent idea is to volunteer to help out at the conference. Every conference needs volunteers to perform such activities as setting up the wireless network, helping at the registration desk, stuffing conference bags, acting as lunch monitor, and providing attendees with directions. Being a volunteer is a low-key, no-pressure way to meet other people because they will be coming to you for help.

Volunteering to organize and help out at a PC-BSD booth is another way to meet people while spreading the word about PC-BSD. This is especially useful at non-BSD conferences such as LinuxFests. Most Linux users have already heard of or have used BSD and are usually interested in talking about or trying out PC-BSD. If you are organizing a PC-BSD booth, contact @bsdevents on Twitter if you need help getting swag or other volunteers for the booth. @bsdevents will also help spread the word about your booth.

Summary

This chapter offered many practical ideas for becoming more involved within the PC-BSD community. I hope that you will try out the ideas that interest you and that you have fun doing so.

The next section of this book deals with ways advanced users can get the most out of their PC-BSD system.

---

[12] http://www.slideshare.net/

## PART 5

Going Beyond
the Basics

CHAPTER 13

■ ■ ■

Advanced Tasks

This chapter will introduce you to some of the more advanced tasks you can perform on your PC-BSD system. We'll discuss backups and snapshots, system upgrades and repairs, scripted and automated installations, virtualization using jails, creating a thin client network out of older hardware, and some of the command-line utilities unique to PC-BSD.

Backups

There are many ways to back up files and directories that are important to you. We offer some suggestions for what is available on your PC-BSD system. When deciding which backup solution to use, consider the following:

- How much data do you need to back up? Is it just a few files or directories, or gigabytes' worth of data?

- Where is the data? Is it all in one directory or scattered throughout your system?

- Where are you going to put the backup? On a USB drive, CD/DVD disk, another system?

- How often does your data change? Is it a big deal if you lose a change?

- Are you comfortable with command-line tools or do you prefer a GUI backup system?

If you are comfortable with using command-line tools, your PC-BSD system comes with many of the traditional Unix backup utilities: tar, cpio, pax, and dump.[1] After creating the backup archive, you could, for example, use sftp:// in Konqueror to drag and drop the backup to another system that is running an ssh server. Or, you could **scp** the backup to another host from within Konsole.

---

[1] `www.freebsd.org/doc/en_US.ISO8859-1/books/handbook/backup-basics.html` provides an introduction to these tools and the Internet has many how-tos if you are looking for examples.

If you need to back up only a few files on an as-needed basis, you might find it easiest to use Dolphin. For example, you could plug in a USB drive or thumb drive and use your mouse to drag and drop the files you want to back up onto the drive.

There are also PBIs available for backup solutions. Users already familiar with Bacula[2] can install the Bacula Bat PBI to interact with the Bacula Director daemon. Bacula is a feature-rich backup system that might be overkill on one computer but makes a comprehensive backup solution for a network of computers. If you're interested in learning more about Bacula, start with the Bacula Concepts and Overview Guide[3] to see if it is the right solution for you.

If Bacula seems too intimidating and you are looking for a graphical backup utility, consider installing and using the KBackup PBI. The next section will demonstrate creating a backup using KBackup.

KBackup

KBackup is designed to make it easy to back up files to a folder on a system, or to an external USB thumb drive or hard drive. Figure 13-1 shows a screenshot of KBackup's main screen.

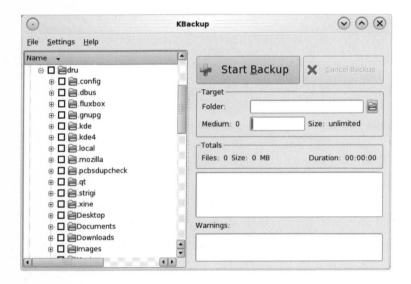

Figure 13-1. KBackup utility

---

[2] www.bacula.org/en/

[3] www.bacula.org/3.0.x-manuals/en/concepts/concepts/index.html

Simply check the box next to each file or directory that you want to back up. If you check a directory, it will automatically check the box for each of its subdirectories and files. You can uncheck any files or subdirectories that you don't want to include in the backup. After making your selections, use the browse folder icon to specify the folder in which to save the backup. If you have a USB drive plugged into the system, you can select that drive as the backup location. Be sure to double-check first (e.g., within Dolphin) that the backup directory or drive has sufficient space to hold the backup.

■ **Caution** Don't save the backup in a folder that you are backing up! You also need write permission to the backup folder.

After selecting what to back up and which folder to back up to, click the Start Backup button. You can watch the backup progress because the file names will appear in the window as they are backed up. If you see any messages in the Warnings box, you probably do not have permission to back up the specified file or directory.

KBackup will give you a message when the backup is complete. Your backup will have a name that begins with **backup_** followed by the date and time, and ending with a .tar extension.

■ **Note** At the time of this writing, KBackup did not provide a restore button, though this functionality might be included in the PBI you installed. If it is not, please refer to the backup resource mentioned in footnote 1 for instructions on how to restore a .tar file.

Life Preserver

Starting with version 8, PC-BSD provides the Life Preserver utility for backing up your entire system using rsync and ssh. While it is common to use rsync and ssh for backups, it usually takes some time to install and configure all the software needed for this type of backup solution. Fortunately, PC-BSD has already done all the work for you—you only need to have enough disk space to hold your backups.

■ **Note** rsync and ssh need to be running on the computer that will hold the backups. Because PC-BSD already sets this up for you, we recommend using another PC-BSD system as the computer to back up to. If you plan to back up to a computer running another operating system, you will need to research how to install and set up rsync and ssh on that system.

Life Preserver is found in Kickoff ➤ Applications ➤ System ➤ Life Preserver. Because this utility will back up all the data on your computer, it will ask you for the administrative password when you start this program.

When you first run this utility, it will present you with an empty Life Preserver screen. Click File ➤ New Preserver to launch the wizard shown in Figure 13-2.

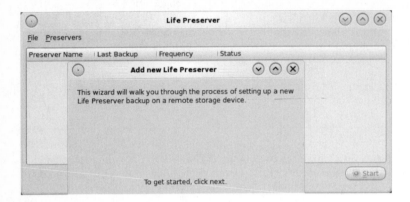

Figure 13-2. Creating a backup profile (Life Preserver) using the Life Preserver Wizard

If you click Next, you will see the screen seen in Figure 13-3.

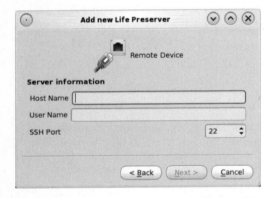

Figure 13-3. Configuring the host to send the backup to

Simply type in the IP address of the system to hold the backups, and the username and TCP port used to ssh to that system. Click Next to configure the scheduling of the backups. That screen is seen in Figure 13-4.

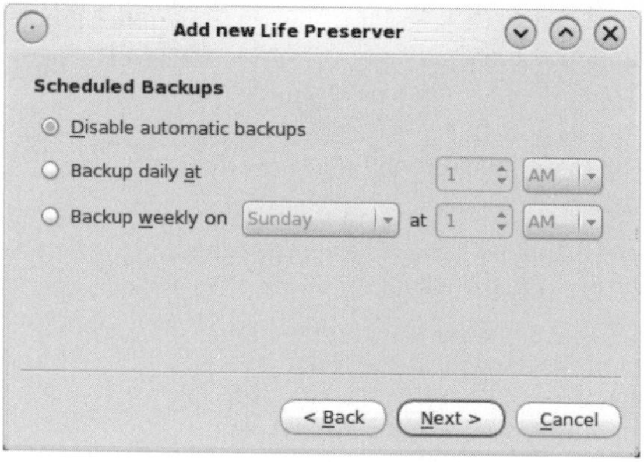

Figure 13-4. Configuring the backup schedule in Life Preserver

After selecting your schedule, click Next and then click Finish. Life Preserver will test the connection to the specified host, and if successful, your new "preserver" will now show as an entry in the main menu. You can change your preserver's settings by right-clicking its entry and selecting Edit, as seen in Figure 13-5.

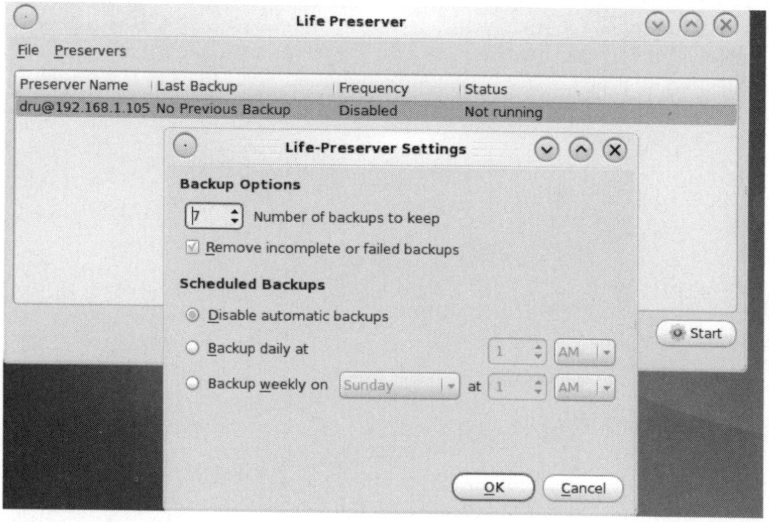

Figure 13-5. Editing a preserver's backup schedule

You can manually create a backup any time by clicking the Start button. We recommend that you manually run the first backup, verify the amount of disk space needed to complete that backup (as discussed in the next paragraph), and then schedule subsequent backups for a time when the host system is not that busy. The Last Backup column will show you the date and time of the last backup and indicate whether or not it was successful.

Because Life Preserver backs up the entire system, backups can take a long time and require a lot of disk space. It is well worth your while to take a closer look at the contents of /PCBSD/lifePreserver, which include the following:

conf/rsync-excludes: The full pathnames to any directories that do not need to be included in your backups should be added to this file; this will significantly reduce backup time and the size of the backups.

preservers/$/last-result: Where $ represents the name of a preserver you have created; this file contains the status and time of the last backup.

preservers/$/logs: Contains the backup logs that are named according to the time and date; if a backup fails, check the error messages at the end of the associated log file. You might want to watch the log of your first backup with "**tail -f**" to ensure that you aren't backing up unnecessary data; if you are, add the unneeded pathnames to rsync-excludes.

scripts: Directory containing the scripts used by Life Preserver; advanced users can read these to see how Life Preserver works or include them in their own scripts.

On the system hosting the backups, completed backups will be found in the life-preserver/subdirectory of the home directory of the user you configured in Figure 13-3. There will be a directory for each backup, up to the amount you specified in Figure 13-5. The latest backup will be copied to the current directory that will contain all the directories and files that were backed up—that is, they won't be in an archive format, making it easy to review and access the backed-up files. If you need a file, you can simply copy it from the backup server or you can use Life Preserver's restore utility.

In Figure 13-6, the user has right-clicked a successful backup and selected Restore from the right-click menu. In this example, there is only one backup stored on the host server; if there were multiple backups, the user could select which backup to restore.

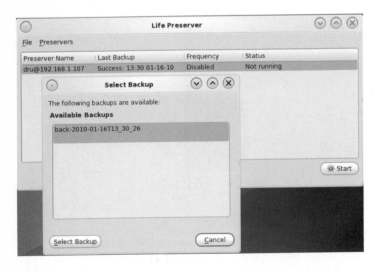

Figure 13-6. Selecting a backup to restore in Life Preserver

Highlight the backup you want to restore and click the Select Backup button to see the screen in Figure 13-7. Indicate the name of the files or directories you want to restore and browse to the directory you want to restore to.

Figure 13-7. Selecting the location to restore to in Life Preserver

System Snapshots

If you're interested in backing up an entire file system, consider taking a file system snapshot.

■ **Tip** Need more information about file systems or the differences between UFS and ZFS? Check out www.freebsd.org/doc/en_US.ISO8859-1/books/handbook/file systems.html.

A file system snapshot is an exact replica of a file system at the time the snapshot is taken. Depending upon its size, the resulting snapshot file can be saved to backup media such as DVDs, magnetic tapes, or USB drives. It can also be treated as a file system image, allowing you to mount and explore the contents of the snapshot. Think of a snapshot as a picture of the entire file system at a given point in time.

The command you use to take the snapshot depends upon whether the partition is using the UFS or the ZFS file system. You can find more information about UFS file system snapshots at www.freebsd.org/doc/en_US.ISO8859-1/books/handbook/snapshots.html. You can find more information about ZFS file system snapshots at http://wiki.freebsd.org/ZFSQuickStartGuide.

Figure 13-8 demonstrates creating a UFS snapshot on a PC-BSD system.

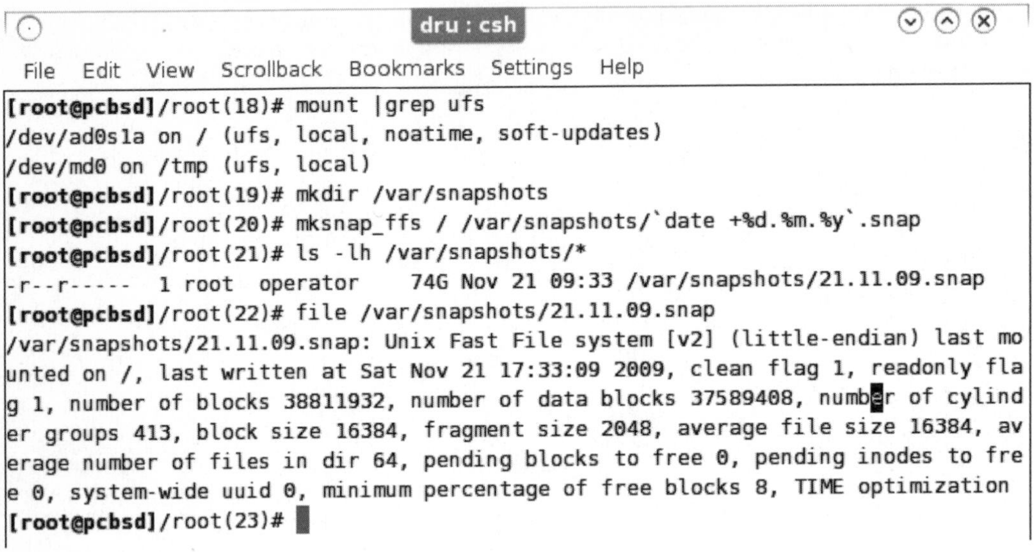

```
┌─────────────────────────────────────────────────────────────────────────┐
│  ◉              ⎡ dru : csh ⎤                            ⊘  ⊙  ⊗         │
│                                                                           │
│  File   Edit   View   Scrollback   Bookmarks   Settings   Help           │
├───────────────────────────────────────────────────────────────────────── │
│ [root@pcbsd]/root(18)# mount |grep ufs                                    │
│ /dev/ad0s1a on / (ufs, local, noatime, soft-updates)                      │
│ /dev/md0 on /tmp (ufs, local)                                             │
│ [root@pcbsd]/root(19)# mkdir /var/snapshots                               │
│ [root@pcbsd]/root(20)# mksnap_ffs / /var/snapshots/`date +%d.%m.%y`.snap  │
│ [root@pcbsd]/root(21)# ls -lh /var/snapshots/*                            │
│ -r--r-----  1 root  operator    74G Nov 21 09:33 /var/snapshots/21.11.09.snap │
│ [root@pcbsd]/root(22)# file /var/snapshots/21.11.09.snap                  │
│ /var/snapshots/21.11.09.snap: Unix Fast File system [v2] (little-endian) last mo │
│ unted on /, last written at Sat Nov 21 17:33:09 2009, clean flag 1, readonly fla │
│ g 1, number of blocks 38811932, number of data blocks 37589408, number of cylind │
│ er groups 413, block size 16384, fragment size 2048, average file size 16384, av │
│ erage number of files in dir 64, pending blocks to free 0, pending inodes to fre │
│ e 0, system-wide uuid 0, minimum percentage of free blocks 8, TIME optimization  │
│ [root@pcbsd]/root(23)# ▉                                                   │
└─────────────────────────────────────────────────────────────────────────┘
```

Figure 13-8. Creating a UFS file system snapshot

In this example, the **mount** command was used to determine which UFS file systems were currently mounted. On this system, /dev/ad0s1a is mounted on / and a memory disk (/dev/md0) is mounted on /tmp. A snapshots directory was created in /var to hold the snapshot. The **mksnap_ffs** command was used to take a snapshot of the / file system. The **date** command was used to generate a snapshot name containing the current day, month, and year. Note that the backtick is used on both sides of the **date** command. The resulting snapshot size is quite large and will always be the size of the file system, regardless of how much data it holds. In other words, a 74 GB file system containing 1 GB of data will have a snapshot size of 74 GB.

■ **Caution** If you decide to script the creation of file system snapshots on a regular basis, make sure that you have enough disk space to store the snapshots. UFS supports only 20 snapshots per file system, so your script will also need to remove older snapshots to stay under that maximum limit.

In order to **mount** the snapshot, you need to create a block device first, using the **mdconfig**[4] command. Figure 13-9 provides an example in which **mdconfig** is used to attach the snapshot to a memory disk. Because the previous **mount** command indicated that md0 was already in use, /dev/md2 was selected (-u 2) as the memory device to use.

---

[4] See **man mdconfig** for more information about this command and its switches.

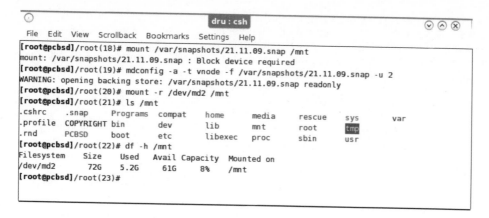

Figure 13-9. Mounting a UFS file system snapshot

The output of the **mdconfig** command indicates that the snapshot is read only. Once mounted, the contents and size of the snapshot were displayed using the **ls** and **df** commands.

■ **Tip** If you ever receive a "Device busy" error when using **mdconfig**, specify a different number because the requested memory device is already in use.

Even though the snapshot is read only, you can still copy its contents, making it a possible backup solution. It can also be handy if you ever need to see the "state" of a file system at a given point in time (for example, if you want to track the history of file changes from day to day or you are investigating suspicious file system activity).

Upgrading PC-BSD

The PC-BSD installer provides an option to upgrade to a newer version of PC-BSD. If you want to upgrade, download or purchase the latest DVD from the Download page of **pcbsd.org**.

■ **Caution** Before performing an upgrade, back up the data that is important to you to another hard drive or computer. Important data usually includes your home directory and any customized configuration files that you have created outside of your home directory.

When a newer version of PC-BSD is released, consider whether you want to upgrade to the newer version or install the new version from scratch. An upgrade will not reformat your PC-BSD partition(s) and it retains some of the operating system's original configuration files. The advantage of an upgrade is that all your data and most of your customizations should be retained for you—though it is an excellent idea to back up your data anyway, just in case. Some people prefer to start from scratch by installing the new version, which reformats the PC-BSD partition(s). This starts you off with a clean operating system and assumes that you will restore your data from a backup onto the new operating system.

■ **Tip** The /PCBSD/pc-sysinstall/conf/exclude-from-upgrade file contains a list of the files and directories that remain intact during an upgrade. See the "Custom Installation" section later on in this chapter for more information about this file.

If you decide to upgrade, insert the DVD for the new version into the DVD drive and boot the computer to start the installation program, as described in Chapter 2. In the screen shown in Figure 13-10, choose the Upgrade button.

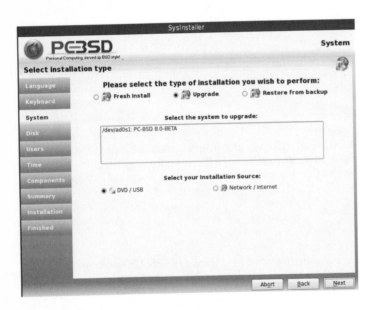

Figure 13-10. Using the installer to perform an upgrade or restore

As seen in Figure 13-10, the installer will find your existing installation. Highlight the installation and press Next to continue. The installation will skip to the Optional Components screen (refer to Figure 2-18) so you can select which applications to install with the upgraded version of the operating system. You can then continue through the remaining installation screens, as described in Chapter 2.

Restoring PC-BSD

PC-BSD's installer provides an option to restore your PC-BSD system from an existing Life Preserver backup. To restore the system, start the installation using the DVD for your current version of PC-BSD. This time, select the Restore button, as seen in Figure 13-11.

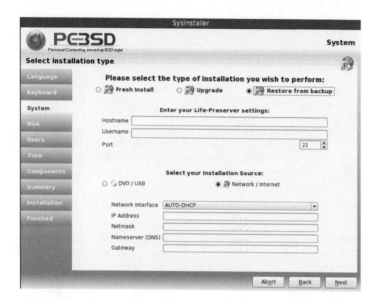

Figure 13-11. Performing a restore from the PC-BSD installer

Input the same IP address and username you used when creating your preserver; then press Next. The installer will connect to the backup server and a pop-up menu will allow you to select the backup you want to restore from. Highlight the desired backup and press the Select button. You can then proceed through the rest of the installation screens as described in Chapter 2.

■ **Tip** You will need a full system backup to perform a system restore. If you choose to customize what gets backed up with Life Preserver (as described earlier in this chapter), perform at least one full backup and store it in area where it will not get erased by Life Preserver.

Single User Mode

If you have messed up a file that is preventing your system from booting properly, you can use single user mode to repair that file. Single user mode is a partial boot of the system. It will not load the network or any graphical utilities. However, it does provide complete access to the files on the system without needing to know the superuser password (real handy if you ever forget the superuser password and need to reset it).

To access single user mode, boot the system and watch the startup messages. When you see the Welcome to PC-BSD! screen, press 4 to select the "Boot PC-BSD in single user mode" option.

■ **Tip** If this screen goes by too fast for you to make your selection, reboot and press the spacebar to pause the selection timer.

After selecting single user mode, the system will continue to boot. When finished, you will see a message saying "Enter full pathname of shell or RETURN for /bin/sh:" After pressing Enter, you will be in the Bourne shell.

By default, single user mode will mount all your filesystems as read only, meaning that you can't edit the file you want to fix. Once you have a shell, type **/sbin/mount -a -o rw** to remount all the filesystems as read-write. You can now use the **vi** or **ee** editor to fix the typo in the file. After saving your changes, type **Exit** to leave single user mode and continue booting the system.

Using /rescue

Your PC-BSD system provides a /rescue directory, which contains the applications considered necessary for repairing the operating system. Consider these tools as a last resort if the commands in /bin and /sbin fail to work in single user mode. This situation is very rare, but it is possible that a command you need to use (such as **mount** or **vi**) has become corrupt or was accidentally deleted. Read through **man rescue** before using any of the commands in /rescue as it explains all the things that you need to be aware of.

If your system really is that mucked up, you should probably consider doing a restore or re-install of the operating system using PC-BSD's installer. If you have important data that has not been backed up yet, back it up first because it will be lost during the restore or re-install.

■ **Tip** If you can't boot the system, perform the backup in single user mode. While you won't be able to back up to the network in single user mode, you can still store the backup on a mounted USB drive.

Custom Installation

Starting with version 8, PC-BSD provides a series of scripts and configuration files that allow you to create your own custom installation. Even if you don't decide to use the scripts or change the configuration files, reading through them will give you a better understanding of how the PC-BSD installer works and what it is capable of doing. Everything you need can be found in the /PCBSD/pc-sysinstall directory.

The `/PCBSD/pc-sysinstall/` directory contains the following directories and files:

> **backend:** Directory containing Bourne shell scripts, one for each function in the installation program, as well as the `startautoinstall.sh` script, which is used to start an automated installation.

> **backend-query:** Directory containing Bourne shell scripts for probing hardware, software components, and available languages.

> **components:** Directory containing a subdirectory for each available software component. Each subdirectory contains a `component.cfg` configuration file and installation script for that software.

> **conf:** Directory containing a list of available languages (`avail-langs`), files to exclude from an upgrade (`exclude-from-upgrade`), a directory of license texts, and configuration options for `pc-sysinstall` (`pc-sysinstall.conf`).

> **doc:** Contains files controlling the text seen when you type **pc-sysinstall help**.

> **examples:** Contains pcinstall.cfg.* configuration examples for the following types of installs: gmirror, network install, restore, rsync, upgrade, and zfs. It also contains the pc-autoinstall.conf file, which contains the configuration for an automated install.

> **pc-sysinstall:** The script that provides the backend for performing system installations. It is read by both the GUI installation program and any custom installs that you create.

Custom Configuration with pcinstall.cfg

The pcinstall.cfg file is read by the installer. If you want to create a customized installation, copy an appropriate sample configuration file from the examples directory to `/PCBSD/pc-sysinstall/pcinstall.cfg`, and review it to see if you want to edit any of its variables. Table 13-1 contains a description of the variables that can be used in this configuration file. Note that the table is in the order that the variables appear, rather than alphabetical order.

Table 13-1. pcinstall.cfg variables

Variable	Description
installMode=	Choices are fresh (new install) or upgrade.
installInteractive=	Choices are yes (require user input) or no (fully automated install[5]).
hostname=	Set the system's hostname. This should be unique for each host in the network.
disk0=	The name of the disk to install onto. Run **pc-sysinstall disk-list**[6] to get the list of supported disks.
partition=	The name of the partition to install into. Specify either a slice number or the keyword **all**.
bootManager=	Choices are none or bsd.
commitDiskPart	Leave as-is for the installation to set the disk parameters.
disk0-part=	Sets the size (in MB) and file system types for each partition. Supported types are UFS, UFS+S (plus soft updates[7]), UFS+J (plus journaling[8]), ZFS, and SWAP. Add a line for each partition you want to create during the install.
commitDiskLabel	Leave as-is for the installation to set up the disk label.
netDev=	Choices are AUTO-DHCP or the name of a network interface to use during the install. Run **pc-sysinstall detect-nics** to get a list of supported interfaces.
netIP=	Set the IP address to use for the install.
netMask=	Set the subnet mask to use for the install.
netNameServer=.	Set the address of the primary DNS server to use for the install

---

[5] If you select a fully automated install, make sure that everything you want to set up during the install is specified in pcinstall.cfg because the installer will not prompt for any user input.

[6] Of course, this and other detection commands only make sense on the hardware you want to install onto.

[7] http://en.wikipedia.org/wiki/Soft_updates

[8] http://en.wikipedia.org/wiki/Journaling_file_system

Variable	Description
netDefaultRouter=	Set the address of the default gateway to use for the install.
netSaveDev=	Choices are AUTO-DHCP or the name of a network interface to set up after the install.
netSaveIP=	Use to manually set IP address of specified network interface.
netSaveMask=	Use to manually set the subnet mask of specified network interface.
netSaveNameServer=	Use to manually set the address of the primary DNS server.
netSaveDefaultRouter=	Use to manually set the address of the default gateway.
installType=	Choices are PCBSD or FreeBSD.
installMedium=	Choices are dvd, ftp, usb, or rsync[9].
ftpPath=	Set the path to the FTP server if installMedium is set to ftp.
rsyncPath=	Set the path to an rsync server.
rsyncUser=	The username that connects to the rsync server.
rsyncHost=	The IP address of the rsync server.
rsyncPort=	The TCP port used to connect to the rsync server.
packageType=	Choices are uzip (for PC-BSD), tar (for FreeBSD), or rsync.
commitInstall	Leave as-is for the installation to perform the install.
installComponents=	Choices are amarok, filezilla, firefox, gimp, k3b, openoffice, opera, pidgin, ports, src, thunderbird, and vlc. Separate the list of components to install with a comma and no spaces. Note that install.cfg currently supports only PBIs, not FreeBSD packages.
autoLoginUser=	Name of the user account that is allowed to automatically log in.
rootPass=root	Set the root password.

[9] http://rsync.samba.org/

Variable	Description
userName=	Name of the primary user account.
userComment=	Comment for the primary user account.
userPass=	Password for the primary user account.
userShell=	Default shell for the primary user account.
userHome=	Home directory for the primary user account.
userGroups=	The primary group(s) for the primary user account. Include the wheel group if this user should have superuser permission.
commitUser	Keep this as-is if you want the install to create a primary user account.
localizeLang=	Select the default language (two-letter code) from the list in pc-sysinstall/conf/avail-langs or from the output of **pc-sysinstall query-langs**.
localizeKeyLayout=	Select the default keyboard layout (two-letter code). Run **pc-sysinstall xkeyboard-layouts** to see the possible layouts.
localizeKeyModel=	Select the default key model. Run **pc-sysinstall xkeyboard-models** to see the list of models.
LocalizeKeyVariant=	Run **pc-sysinstall xkeyboard-variants** to see the list of variants.
runCommand=	Specify a command to run after the install is complete.
runScript=	Specify a custom script to run after the install is complete.
runExtCommand=	Run a command on the live file system.

Before customizing pcinstall.cfg, it is highly recommended that you first read /PCBSD/pc-sysinstall/examples/README. This file contains a more complete description of how and when to use each variable. If you make any changes to the pcinstall.cfg file, double-check your changes for typos. While the installer will do a basic sanity check, it won't notice if you mistype a hostname or IP address.

Starting a Custom Install

Once you have a customized configuration file, the **pc-sysinstall** script can be used to start a custom installation. This script controls the backend of the PC-BSD installation program. The beginning of this script contains some user-editable configuration variables in which you can set an alternate path to **pc-sysinstall** and its components. You should leave the rest of the file as-is. Feel free to read through it to get a better understanding of the installation process.

If you run **pc-sysinstall** with no arguments, it will provide a description of the command's arguments. Some of these arguments (such as **pc-sysinstall xkeyboard-models**) were listed in Table 13-1. Table 13-2 contains a description of other useful arguments.

Table 13-2. arguments to pc-sysinstall program

Command	Description
pc-sysinstall disk-info	Shows information about the specified disk (e.g., ad0). Use **pc-sysinstall disk-list** to get the disk names for the system.
pc-sysinstall detect-laptop	Probes to see whether the system is a laptop or not.
pc-sysinstall detect-vmware	Probes to see whether the system is running in a VMware[10] session.
pc-sysinstall test-netup	Probes to see whether the connection to the ftp server needs passive mode.[11]

Figure 13-12 demonstrates the commands to start a custom install.

```
%cp /root/mycustom_pcinstall.cfg /tmp/pc-sysinstall.cfg
%/PCBSD/pc-sysinstall/pc-sysinstall start-autoinstall /tmp/pc-sysinstall.cfg
cat: /PCBSDVERSION: No such file or directory
Type in 'install' to begin automated installation. Warning: Data on target disks
 may be destroyed!
```

Figure 13-12. Starting a customized PC-BSD installation

---

[10] http://en.wikipedia.org/wiki/Vmware

[11] http://en.wikipedia.org/wiki/File_Transfer_Protocol#Connection_methods

In this example, the customized `mycustom_pcinstall.cfg` file was moved to the name expected by the installer: `/tmp/pc-sysinstall.cfg`. The **pc-sysinstall** utility was then run with the **start-autoinstall** option. Once the word **install** is typed in, the installer will parse the custom configuration file and install the system according to that file's variables.

Rolling Your Own ISO

If you want, you can also create your own installation DVD that contains your customized configuration file. If this interests you, read through `/PCBSD/pc-sysinstall/examples/pc-autoinstall.conf` first because a customized version of that file will need to be added to the `/boot/` directory of the DVD.

Follow these steps to create your custom installation DVD:

1. Insert a PC-BSD DVD and wait for it to become available in Dolphin.

2. Create a new folder.

3. Drag the DVD to your new folder to copy its contents into the folder.

4. Copy `/PCBSD/pc-sysinstall/examples/pc-autoinstall.conf` to the `boot/` directory in your new folder.

5. Edit `boot/pc-autoinstall.conf` to meet your requirements.

6. Copy your customized `pcinstall.cfg` to the new folder.

You are now ready to see whether your custom DVD works. The following command will burn the DVD on the fly, meaning that it will not save a copy of an .iso file to your hard disk: **growisofs -Z /dev/cd0 -J -R -no-emul-boot -b boot/cdboot -iso-level 3**. Run the command from within your new folder.

To instead create an ISO that you can then burn at your leisure, use this command: **mkisofs -V mycustomPCBSD -J -R -b boot/cdboot -no-emul-boot -o custompcbsd.iso**.

Once you have a DVD, boot it on a test system to see whether the installation proceeds according to your customizations.

■ **Tip** Using a rewritable DVD media is useful when testing a customized DVD.

Jail Management with The Warden

FreeBSD provides a mechanism, known as a jail,[12] which allows one physical computer to act as multiple virtual computers. Each jail contains a copy of the operating system, its own user accounts, and whatever applications you want to install in the jail. The system that created the jail is known as the host, and you can install as many jails on that host as you have disk space to support.

Creating jails can be useful if you need to provide services to multiple clients. For example, a company that provides web hosting can give each customer a jail containing their own web and mail server. Rather than having to buy a separate computer for each customer, one machine can host multiple jails. The reason why it is called a *jail* is because an application installed into a jail is not allowed to "break out" and affect the other jails or the operating system running on the host machine. So, if an application within a jail is exploited, it will affect only that one jail.

There are many reasons to create a jail. Some examples include the following:

- A classroom in which each student gets their own jail to practice their exercises.

- A test environment when you are learning how to build kernels, set up databases, configure web or mail servers, or practice firewall rules.

- You want to install different versions of the same application within different jails.

- You want to study software viruses without negatively affecting your main operating system.

On FreeBSD, jail creation and management is command-line based. While the commands are well documented,[13] it can take a bit of time to prepare the host system for the jails and to create the jails. PC-BSD provides a graphical environment that prepares the jail environment for you and makes it easier to create, stop, and start jails. It is called **TheWarden** and is available as a PBI. There is a PC-BSD mailing list for TheWarden[14] as well as a wiki page.[15]

■ **Note** If you did not install TheWarden during installation, you can still do so using a PC-BSD DVD. Use Dolphin to navigate the contents of the inserted DVD; you'll find the PBI in extras ➤ PBI.

---

[12] http://en.wikipedia.org/wiki/FreeBSD_jail

[13] See the man jail at www.freebsd.org/cgi/man.cgi?query=jail&format=html.

[14] http://lists.pcbsd.org/mailman/listinfo/pcbsd-warden

[15] http://wiki.pcbsd.org/index.php/Using_the_Warden

Once installed, you can start TheWarden from Kickoff ➤ Applications ➤ System ➤ TheWarden. After entering the administrative password, the main menu of TheWarden will open. Figure 13-13 shows the Create new jail menu, which can be accessed from File ➤ New Jail.

Figure 13-13. Creating a new jail in TheWarden

Input an IP address that isn't currently being used by your operating system or another jail. You can either accept the default hostname or input a unique hostname. If you plan to build kernels inside the jail, check the Include system source box. If you plan to compile ports within the jail, check the Include ports tree box. If you don't check the box for Start jail at system boot, you will have to start the jail manually from TheWarden after the system boots.

■ **Tip** If you check to include the source or the ports tree within the jail, make sure that they are installed on the host system. You can install on the host system from the System Tasks – Advanced Users Only section of Kickoff ➤ System Settings ➤ System Manager ➤ Tasks.

Once you click Create, the Setup Users menu will open and prompt you to create an administrative password for the jail, and the username and password for the primary user of the jail. Remember, the jail is considered to be a virtual computer with its own superuser and user accounts. After inputting the password information and pressing Save, a Creating Jail menu will open showing the progress of building the jail. Creating the jail will take a few minutes, especially if you have selected the source or ports check boxes, because the world, source, and ports
will be installed into the new jail. Once the jail-creation process is finished, you'll receive a Success! message and can close the menu. Your new jail will now show in TheWarden's main menu as seen in Figure 13-14.

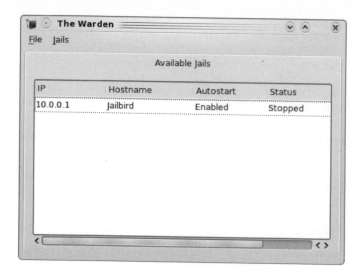

Figure 13-14. List of current jails in TheWarden

The Autostart column indicates that this jail will automatically start at system bootup. However, the jail still needs to be manually started in order to access its contents. You can do so by right-clicking the jail and selecting Start this jail from the menu, which will change the jail's Status to Running.

To access the jail, **ssh** to its IP address.

Once you have logged in to the jail, you can do anything (at the command line) that you would normally do on a FreeBSD system. For example, you can install software using packages or ports, configure services, or compile a new kernel[16].

The jail's right-click menu contains these entries:

> **Start/Stop this Jail:** Changes the jail's current status to running or stopped. A jail's contents are not available while it is stopped.

> **Toggle Autostart:** Determines whether the jail will start automatically when the computer starts. Disabled means it will not.

---

[16] See www.freebsd.org/doc/en_US.IS08859-1/books/handbook/kernelconfig.html for instructions on how to compile a kernel.

Install Inmate into jail: An inmate is a server environment that has been preconfigured for you and saved as a .wit file. Search for the term inmate in Software Manager to find which inmate PBIs are available. Examples of inmates include an Apache, MySQL, and PHP (AMP)[17] and a Joomla[18] environment. Once you have installed the PBI for an inmate, browse to the location of its .wit file to install it into the specified jail. Once the inmate is installed into the jail, run **pkg_info** inside the jail to see what software was installed.

View installed packages: Shows the output of **pkg_info** so you can quickly view what software is installed within the jail. It will also indicate if any inmates are installed.

Export jail to .wdn file: Creates a full, compressed copy of the jail. This file can be imported, using the File menu, allowing you to migrate the jail to another system. It can also be imported on the same system, in order to clone (create an identical copy of) an existing jail with a new IP address. Creating the .wdn might take some time, especially if you have source, ports, or a lot of data in the jail.

Delete jail: Removes the jail and all its contents from the host system. If any data in the jail is important, back up that data or export the jail first.

The Jails menu contains a Configuration option in which you can modify the network interface, directory that holds the jails, and temporary directory used by TheWarden. A screenshot of this menu is seen in Figure 13-15.

Figure 13-15. Configuration menu for jails in TheWarden

---

[17] This inmate saves you from installing these manually from the FreeBSD ports collection.

[18] http://en.wikipedia.org/wiki/Joomla

The operation of TheWarden is controlled by a Bourne shell script named /Programs/TheWarden/bin/warden. If you run this script with no arguments, you will receive its list of arguments. Figure 13-16 shows a screenshot of running **warden menu**, which allows you to create and manage jails using a menu while at the command line.

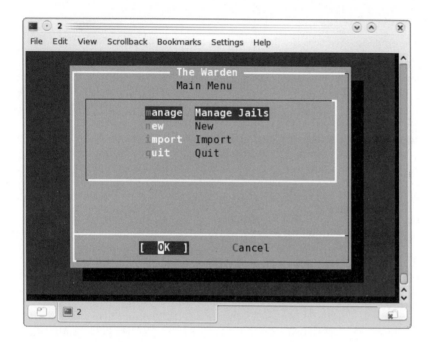

Figure 13-16. Jail management using The Warden's command-line menu.

The **Warden** script contains many useful command-line arguments. For example, you can create your own inmates using **warden mkinmate**. If you're interested in getting the most out of jail management on your PC-BSD system or want a better understanding of how TheWarden works, take some time to read through The **Warden** script; it is well commented and contains several useful examples.

Thin Client Server

PC-BSD allows you to set up a network of thin clients[19] with a PC-BSD system acting as the thin client server. In a thin client network, all the work is done on the server—the rest of the machines connect to the server in order to access data and to run applications. This allows you to make the most out of older

---

[19] http://en.wikipedia.org/wiki/Thin_client

hardware because the client machines themselves can have a small (or no) hard drive, a minimum amount of memory, and an older CPU. The server machine should have sufficient hard drive space, memory, and CPU in order to support the clients that will connect to it.

A thin client server needs the following components:

> **DHCP server:** As a thin client boots up, it will receive an IP address from the Dynamic Host Configuration Protocol (DHCP) server.

> **NFS server:** Stores the data that is accessible to the thin clients.

> **TFTP server:** Contains an operating system environment for the thin client to use. This allows computers with no hard drives to still access the thin client server.

The thin client does not require any software, but it does need a network card that understands PXE[20] (most network cards made in the past 10 years do). You can check by accessing the BIOS utility[21] on the thin client computer. The BIOS menu will include an option that controls startup. Access that menu; if it contains any entries for a network or a list of network cards to boot from, that computer is capable of acting as a thin client. You should change the boot priority order on the thin client computer so that the network card is listed first.

PC-BSD provides a thin client server PBI and a wiki entry[22] to get you started. The PBI sets up the DHCP, NFS, and TFTP servers for you—meaning that your thin client network should "just work." During the installation of the PBI, a pxeboot user will be created with a default password. You should immediately change this password using the command **passwd pxeboot**. If the computer has multiple network cards, it will ask you which card you want to use. Select the card that is used to connect to the thin client computers in your network. After the PBI is finished installing, it will prompt you to reboot the computer so all the changes can take effect.

To test your setup, make sure that the thin client computer's BIOS is set to boot from the network. Boot the client and watch its startup messages. You should see messages indicating the name of the computer's PXE boot software and that it is trying to initialize and establish the link. If the link fails, double-check that you have selected the correct network interface and that its network cable is plugged in correctly. If the connection is successful, you'll see messages as the client receives an IP address and the operating system loads. After a few minutes, you should be presented with a login screen. After logging in, you should see your usual desktop environment.

■ **Tip** Create a unique user account for each thin client user on the thin client server.

---

[20] http://en.wikipedia.org/wiki/Preboot_Execution_Environment

[21] How to do so varies with the computer hardware. See http://michaelstevenstech.com/bios_manufacturer.htm for a list of the most common keys used to access a computer's BIOS.

[22] http://wiki.pcbsd.org/index.php/ThinClientServer

From the users' perspective, everything should look the same. In reality, everything users see is happening on the server. If users create or edit any files, they are doing so on the server system because the hard drive is not being used at all on the thin client system. The hardware requirements on the server will depend upon the number of thin clients that connect at the same time. It should be noted that should the thin client server or the thin client network become unavailable, none of the thin clients will be able to access data until the server and the network are back up.

PC-BSD–Specific Scripts and Programs

An excellent way to get a better understanding of how your operating system works is to read the scripts that come with the operating system. This gives you behind-the-scenes insight into which commands are run when the operating system starts, is shut down, as well as how some of the commands that came with the operating system work. Most scripts contain comments (which start with #) to explain what the script itself or a certain command within the script does. You might find some of the scripts useful enough to include within your own scripts. Most will work at the command line even if you have **ssh**'d into a PC-BSD system or are using a minimal desktop on your PC-BSD system. To run a script, give the full path to the script; if you are in the same directory as the script, put a **./** in front of the script's name.

■ **Caution** Make sure that you understand what a script does before running it manually. If you are unsure, consider running it on a test system first.

Table 13-3 provides a description of the subdirectories and scripts contained in **/PCBSD/Scripts/**. Many of these scripts are used by the Software Manager and System Manager programs. Others set up your PC-BSD system when it boots or clean it up when it is shut down.

Table 13-3. PC-BSD scripts found in /PCBSD/Scripts

Command	Description
Context/	The scripts in this directory are used by the PBI system. There are scripts to check a PBI's md5 checksum, extract the PBI, remove an installed PBI, and compress or uncompress the PBI.
Helper/audiocd.sh	Used by the Amarok CD player to launch an audio CD.
Helper/getlang.sh	Used by KDE programs to determine which language to use.
System/GenDiagSheet.sh	Used by System Manager when you press the Generate button to generate a diagnostic sheet.
System/InstallKernel.sh	Used by System Manager when you select to boot from an alternate kernel.
System/changes.sh	Used by System Manager when you fetch ports.

Command	Description
System/fastest_cvsup	Used by System Manager when you fetch source or ports to determine which server to fetch from. You might also want to refer to this script when you create your own notification script, as described in Chapter 10.
System/portsnap.sh	Used by System Manager when you fetch ports.
UpdateHints.sh	Updates the hints file used by kernel modules.
adduser.sh	Used to add a user account to the system.
checkXloader.sh	Checks whether user selected Run the Display Setup Wizard from the boot menu.
cleanpbilog.sh	Removes any existing PBI log files when the system shuts down.
installPatch.sh	Used by Update Manager when installing a system update.
registerPatch.sh	Used by Update Manager when installing a system update.
reset-firewall	Used by System Settings ➤ Firewall when you click the Reset default configuration button.
runpbi.sh	Used to start the PBI Installer.
swapmonitor.sh	Used to monitor swap space and increase its size as needed.
system-start.sh	Runs at system startup.
system-stop.sh	Runs when the system is shut down.

Table 13-4 describes scripts that are used by the System Updater. They can be found in the /PCBSD/SystemUpdater/ directory.

Table 13-4. Scripts used by PC-BSD's System Updater application

Script	Description
bin/checkStartup.sh	Checks to see if System Updater is set to run automatically.
bin/downloadSysUpdates.sh	Downloads any available updates.
bin/installSysUpdates.sh	Installs the available updates.
bin/readSysUpdates.sh	Reads the system updates to determine which need to be installed.
bin/readSysUpdatesUser.sh	Same as readSysUpdates.sh, but can be run as a regular user.

Information about the updates can be found in **/PCBSD/SystemUpdater/systemupdates/installed/$VER/**, where $VER represents the version of PC-BSD that is installed on the computer. Figure 13-17 shows an example of a file listing of this directory from a system running PC-BSD version 7.1.

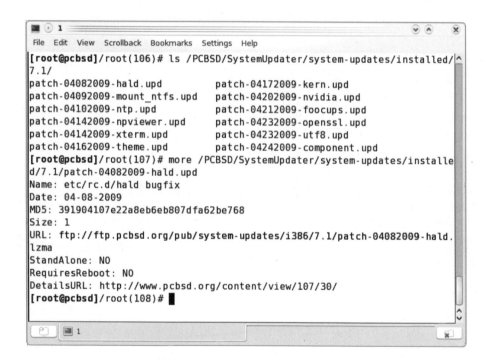

Figure 13-17. Updates installed on a PC-BSD 7.1 system

The file name for each update indicates the date (in day/month/year format) the update became available as well as a name describing what the update addresses. Each update ends in an .upd extension. The files contain information about the update, including the URL to the patch and the URL containing the details of what the patch does.

PC-BSD also contains commands unique to the PC-BSD operating system. Because these are binary applications instead of than scripts, you can't just read their contents. However, if you type **strings command-name|more**, you might still be able to find some comments that provide a bit more insight into the inner workings of the command.

Table 13-5 summarizes the command-line utilities and remaining scripts that are unique to PC-BSD.

Table 13-5. PC-BSD command-line utilities and scripts

Command	Description
/PCBSD/bin/CrashHandler-bin	Tells PC-BSD how to handle an application crash.
/PCBSD/bin/PBIdelete	Removes a PBI.
/PCBSD/bin/PBReg	Allows you to interact with PC-BSD's registry. (This is discussed in more detail in the next section.)
/PCBSD/bin/SoundError	Tells PC-BSD what to do when it cannot get sound working.
/PCBSD/bin/pdm	Script that controls the graphical login manager.
/PCBSD/bin/rerunXsetup.sh	Script that reruns the Display Setup Wizard.

Mini-Registry

PC-BSD provides a command-line registry.[23] Similar to the registry on a Windows system, the PC-BSD registry is used to store keys and their values. Because it is command-line–based, it can be used by shell scripts. Because it uses QT libraries, any QT (e.g., KDE) application can also access the information stored in the registry. The registry itself is located in the text file **/root/config/PCBSD.conf**; a quick skim through this file shows that it is used by Software Manager and some PBIs. If you run **pbreg** without any arguments, it will print its usage instructions (see Figure 13-18).

---

[23] http://faqs.pcbsd.org/index.php?action=artikel&cat=18&id=318&artlang=en

```
%
%pbreg
pbreg Version 1.0
--------
pbreg <command> <key> <value>

Commands:
  get - Gets a variable from the registry
  set - Sets a variable specified by <value> in the registry
  rem - Removes a variable from the registry

Examples:

 # pbreg get /PC-BSD/Version
 # pbreg set /PC-BSD/Version 1.0
 # pbreg rem /PC-BSD/Version
%
```

Figure 13-18. Running pbreg with no arguments

The **get**, **set**, and **rem** commands can be used to refer to variables within the registry. As a simple example, consider a portion of a script that toggles between GUI and command modes. It could be written this way:

```
# Check if the GUI is enabled
if [ "`pbreg get /MyApp/enableGui`" = "true" ]
then
    # disable the GUI
    pbreg set /MyApp/enableGui false
fi
```

Uses for the registry are limited only by the script writer's imagination. Because real-world usage examples are currently in short supply, consider adding a how-to to the PC-BSD forums, explaining how you use **pbreg** in a script. Your experience will be invaluable to others.

Summary

This chapter allowed you to take a closer look at some of the inner workings of your PC-BSD system. It has also given you a better appreciation that there are many ways to perform a task, such as a backup or an installation. The deeper you dig into the programs and configurations that came with your system, the more you will find ways to perform tasks in ways that better meet your needs. There is always something new to be discovered and improved upon!

The next chapter will build upon these explorations even further and introduce you to ways in which you can contribute your own improvements and discoveries.

## CHAPTER 14

Becoming a Developer

Chapter 12 introduced you to some of the areas any PC-BSD user can explore to contribute to the PC-BSD community. This chapter covers more advanced forms of contribution that typically require programming skills. If you are a programmer, taking programming in school and looking for opportunities to practice your skills, or if you are interested in learning more about how the PC-BSD operating system and push button installer applications (PBIs) are developed, this chapter is for you.

We begin by describing the PC-BSD release engineering process and the resources available to developers to give you an idea of what to expect. If you have limited programming knowledge, you can still successfully complete the tasks found in the section on "Converting a FreeBSD Port Using PBI Builder."

PC-BSD Release Engineering Process

Any large software project needs a set of guiding principles and processes. Ideally, a project's processes are documented so new developers know what to expect. Processes are meant to address how the software project manages its code development, answering questions such as:

- Where is the source code located? Is it browsable? Is it downloadable?"

- Who is allowed to make (commit) changes to the source code? Are changes monitored or checked by other developers?

- Can a committer make a change anywhere in the code base or are committers given write permission to only certain sections of the code?

- How often are new changes tested against the entire code base? If a commit breaks something, who is alerted and who fixes the problem?

- Are commits made against the current released version of the software or to a testing version that has not been released yet?

- Who determines what features should go into the next software release?

- Are there any rules governing what style of code developers are expected to use?

- How often are new versions of the software released?

- How long are older versions of the software maintained for security patches?

The rest of this section provides an overview of how PC-BSD manages its development process.

■ **Tip** It is useful to remember that PC-BSD is based on FreeBSD and closely follows FreeBSD's set of processes that are documented in the FreeBSD Release Engineering[1] document.

The code base for PC-BSD is kept in a subversion server, and trac provides browse and search mechanisms for the code base. Chapter 12 introduced you to the PC-BSD trac system. PC-BSD's code base is divided into branches, with each branch representing a different version of the software. Figure 14-1 shows the branches for the "**pcbsd**" code base from versions 1.4 to 7.1.1.

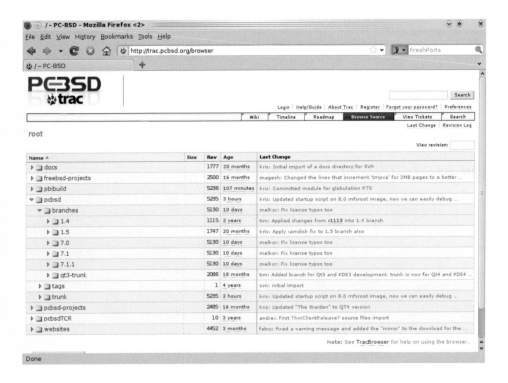

Figure 14-1. PC-BSD branches

---

[1] http://www.freebsd.org/doc/en_US.ISO8859-1/articles/releng/article.html

New commits are made against trunk, which represents the current version that hasn't been released yet. Figure 14-1 was taken before the release of PC-BSD 8, meaning that version 8 was the trunk version at that time.

After a version is released, it is moved from trunk to a new version number in branches, and a new trunk is created for the next expected version. It is rare for a commit to be made against a released version because it is considered to be released (or finalized).

trunk and each branch version are divided into modules, which allow developers to follow and commit to the modules that interest them. Most modules contain the source files and configurations for a PC-BSD utility. The modules for trunk (version 8.0 before it was released) are seen in Figure 14-2 and briefly described in Table 14-1.

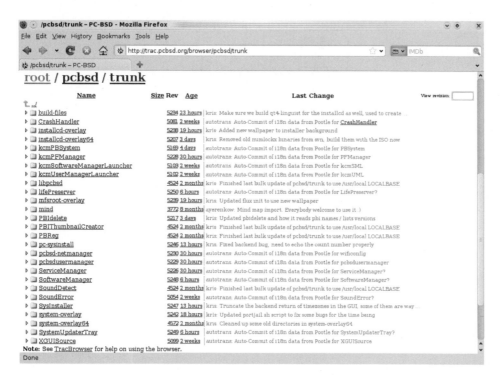

Figure 14-2. PC-BSD development modules

Table 14-1. Overview of PC-BSD Software Modules

Module	Description
build-files	Configuration files and patches used to build PC-BSD
CrashHandler	Program that is executed when a PBI's executable exits with an error condition
installcd-overlay	Filesystem on the 32-bit version of the installation CD/DVD
installcd-overlay64	64-bit version of files that differ from the 32-bit version found in installcd-overlay
kcmPBSystem	Files needed for System Manager to work in KDE
kcmPFManager	Files needed for Firewall Manager to work in KDE
kcmSoftwareManagerLauncher	Files needed for Software Manager to work in KDE
kcmUserManagerLauncher	Files needed for User Manager to work in KDE
libpcbsd	Libraries specific to PC-BSD
lifePreserver	Life Preserver backup utility
mfsroot-overlay	The list of files copied to the memory filesystem during installation
mind	Mind map template for XMind[2]
PBIdelete	PBI uninstaller
PBIThumbnailCreator	PBI thumbnail creator
PBReg	PC-BSD registry tool
pc-sysinstall	PC-BSD installer backend

---

[2] `http://www.xmind.net/` is a popular one source mind mapping application.

Module	Description
pcbsd-netmanager	PC-BSD networking utilities
pcbsdusermanager	User manager
ServiceManager	Service Manager
SoftwareManager	Software Manager
SoundDetect	Utility to detect installed sound cards
SoundError	Utility that creates a diagnostic sheet when no sound card is detected
SysInstaller	PC-BSD installer program
system-overlay	Filesystem for 32-bit version of PC-BSD
system-overlay64	64-bit version of files that differ from the 32-bit version found in system-overlay
SystemUpdaterTray	System Updater
XGUISource	Display setup program

Security patches are not stored on the trac server because they are usually based on the FreeBSD security advisory system.[3] Every PC-BSD security patch installed by Update Manager contains the URL to the associated security advisory.

■ **Tip** You can also view each available, ignored, and installed system patch for your system in /PCBSD/SystemUpdater/system-updates/.

As changes are committed to the PC-BSD code base, an email containing the details of the change is automatically sent to the Commits mailing list.[4] Browsing through that list's archives gives you a good idea of the changes made to the PC-BSD code base.

---

[3] See **http://security.freebsd.org/** for more details.

[4] **http://lists.pcbsd.org/mailman/listinfo/commits**

As the trunk version of PC-BSD gets closer to being released, installable versions of the operating system are periodically released to the Testing mailing list.[5] As described in Chapter 12, everyone is encouraged to install and try the testing version and to report any bugs so that developers can fix them. This helps to ensure that when the new version is released, it has been tested on many different types of hardware and is as bug-free as possible.

System Developer Resources

In addition to the resources mentioned in the previous section, the following resources are available to programmers interested in contributing to the development of the PC-BSD operating system.

- *Dev[6] mailing list:* For general development discussion. This is where features are planned and discussed.

- *Development team:[7]* In addition to the contact information for each team member, this page lists which development tasks are needed for system development and translation, quality assurance, PBI development, PBI quality assurance, documentation, web development, and system administration. It also lists who to contact if you are interested in helping in one of these areas.

- *Development Guidelines:[8]* Discusses naming conventions, indentation, internationalization support, documentation, and licensing.

If you are interested in PC-BSD system development, you should also take the time to familiarize yourself with the following documentation because PC-BSD is based on FreeBSD and KDE.

- FreeBSD Developer's Handbook[9]

- KDE API Reference[10]

- Qt Reference Documentation[11]

---

[5] http://lists.pcbsd.org/mailman/listinfo/testing

[6] http://lists.pcbsd.org/mailman/listinfo/dev

[7] http://www.pcbsd.org/content/view/23/30/

[8] http://trac.pcbsd.org/wiki/DevelopmentGuidelines

[9] http://www.freebsd.org/doc/en_US.ISO8859-1/books/developers-handbook/index.html

[10] http://api.kde.org/

[11] http://doc.trolltech.com/

Getting System Source

Anyone can browse and download any portion of the PC-BSD code base. If you are interested only in a few files, you can use your browser to download them from the trac server. If you would like to follow the changes being made in an entire branch while keeping the files you have downloaded "in sync" with the changes on the subversion server, you should use the svn utility to "check out" (download) the files you need.

Your PC-BSD system comes with the svn utility installed, and the Getting Source guide[12] contains instructions for downloading all the branches, **trunk** only, or a specified branch. svn comes with a lot of options; following are the ones developers use most often.

- **svn co**: Checks out the specified directory. It creates a directory of the same name in your current working directory. For example, if you check out the repository using the command "svn co svn://svn.pcbsd.org/pcbsd," a directory named "pcbsd" is created that contains everything you see under "pcbsd" on the trac server. You should see a list of files as they are copied. If you receive a message similar to "Checked out revision 5487," your copy is identical to the one on the trac server.

- **svn up**: Updates your already downloaded copy so that it contains all the files on the trac server. Always run this command in the directory name that matches the directory you would like to sync with.

- **svn help**: Lists all the possible commands. If you add help to a command, it shows its usage (for example, **svn help co**).

Only PC-BSD committers are able to make changes to the code on the trac server. If you have created code patches, submit them using the methods described in Chapter 12. Over time, the community gets to know you and your development style. If you submit many useful patches, don't be surprised if you are asked whether you would like to have a commit bit, the term used to signify that you now have the necessary permissions to upload your changes directly to the code base.

PC-BSD committers are also able to use the following svn commands.

- **svn add**: Adds the specified file to the code base

- **svn rm**: Removes the specified file from the code base

- **svn ci**: Checks in (uploads) your changed files to the code base

Overview of PBI Development Process

The previous sections describe the development process for the PC-BSD operating system. This section concentrates on the development process for PBIs.

---

[12] http://trac.pcbsd.org/wiki/GettingSource

PBIs are stored on the PC-BSD Project's official PBI build servers (`http://pbibuild.pcbsd.org` and `http://pbibuild64.pcbsd.org`). Every Monday through Friday night, each server checks and builds the PBIs that meet any of these criteria:

- The PBI is newly added.

- The PBI's underlying FreeBSD port has been updated.

- The PBI committer sets a configuration value indicating that the PBI should be rebuilt.

If the build of a PBI fails, an email is automatically sent to the Pbibuild mailing list.[13] The email contains the last 50 lines of the build log, which should include the error message. The full build log can be downloaded from the PBI build server. Figure 14-3 shows a screenshot from the build server, which indicates that the astro/googleearth build has failed.

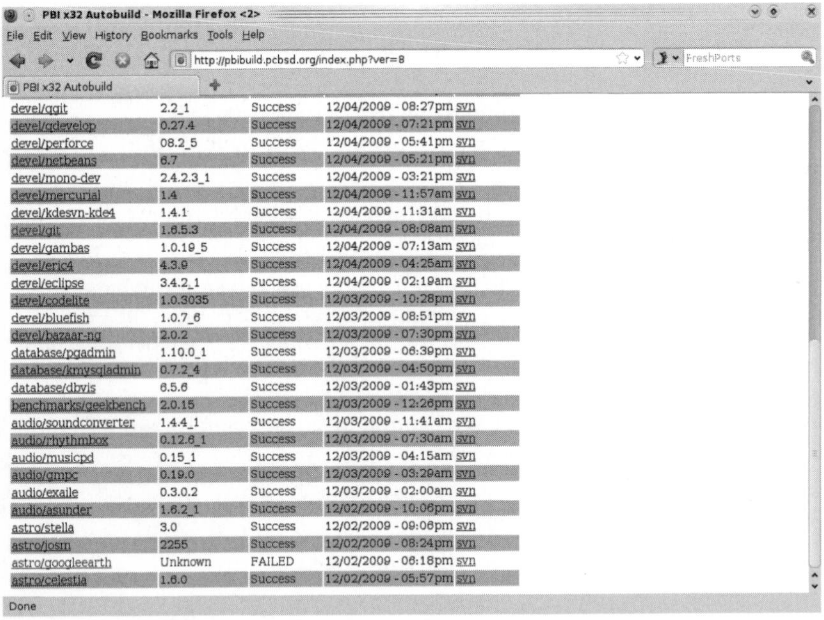

Figure 14-3. Build failure for astro/googleearth on the PBI build server

To access the build log, click the hyperlink for the failed PBI, in this case astro/googleearth. The build log has a .bz extension, which indicates that it has been compressed. You can uncompress the file using the **bunzip2** command that came with your PC-BSD system.

---

[13] `http://lists.pcbsd.org/mailman/listinfo/pbibuild`

The configuration information used for building a PBI is known as a module. PBI modules are created by the PBI maintainer. The next section demonstrates how to create a PBI module. You can browse through all the modules at **http://trac.pcbsd.org/browser/pbibuild/modules**. Browsing through the modules can be helpful if you are stuck building a PBI or aren't sure how to modify a PBI's configuration files and want to see how other PBI developers handled their module's configuration. Two tools are available for creating a PBI. The recommended method is to use PBI Builder[14] when a FreeBSD port already exists. If a FreeBSD port does not exist, PBI Creator[15] can be used to create the PBI. PBI Builder is recommended for several reasons, including:

- Most of the development work has already been done for you by the person who ported the software to FreeBSD.

- PBI Builder is fairly straight-forward to use, meaning anyone with a bit of time and patience should be able to create a PBI.

- PBI Builder creates a sandbox environment for building the PBI. This means that you don't have to create an environment on a separate build computer, it won't harm your computer, and the resulting PBI has everything it needs to work on a PC-BSD system.

- PBI Builder enables you to create the module files understood by the PBI build server. After it is on the PBI build server, your PBI automatically updates whenever the underlying FreeBSD port changes.

- The PBI build server sends out an automatic email message and generates a build log if your PBI ever fails to build.

In contrast, PBI Creator isn't recommended for several reasons, including:

- It requires you to create your own clean build system, which means you want to use a separate computer (or virtual environment) that needs to be returned to a default PC-BSD install for every PBI that is built.

- It requires you to manually populate your build environment with the application source and dependencies (PBI Builder automatically does this for you).

- There are more than 21,000 FreeBSD ports, which means there is already plenty of software waiting to be built using PBI Builder.

---

[14] Available for download from **http://www.pcbsd.org/content/view/45/30/**

[15] Available for download from **http://www.pbidir.com**. Information for using this utility is available at **http://www.pcbsd.org/content/view/39/30/**.

- If you are using PBI Creator because no FreeBSD port exists, you get to do all the porting work. Depending upon the size of the application, the number of its dependencies and what assumptions were coded into the software (for example, expected paths, libraries, devices, and so on), this work can range from trivial to really hard and time consuming to far exceeds your coding knowledge. We recommend that if you do all of the work required to port the software, you should submit the port to the FreeBSD ports collection and then use PBI Builder to convert the port to a PBI. This enables the ported software to be used by both FreeBSD and PC-BSD users and enables the resulting PBI to take advantage of the benefits provided by the PBI build server.

For these reasons, this chapter demonstrates only how to use PBI Builder. If you would like to tackle porting software to a FreeBSD port, work your way through the FreeBSD Porter's Handbook.[16]

After a PBI is created, it needs to be tested by others before it is added to the PBI build server and made available for download at pbidir.com. This helps to ensure the quality of the software available to PC-BSD users and provides a check that the developer didn't miss anything when creating the PBI.

Anyone can test a PBI. Feedback regarding a PBI should be sent to the Pbi-dev mailing list. This list should also be used if you ever find a bug in a PBI that is already available at pbidir.com so the developer can fix the bug.

PBI Developer Resources

In addition to the resources mentioned in the previous section, several resources are available to PBI developers, including:

Using the PBI Builder:[17] General usage instructions for PBI Builder

PBI Module Builder Guide:[18] The definitive reference for creating PBI modules

Creating PC-BSD Packages forum:[19] Contains useful information and some how-tos

PBI FAQs:[20] Answers to frequently asked questions about building PBIs

---

[16] http://www.freebsd.org/doc/en/books/porters-handbook/

[17] http://wiki.pcbsd.org/index.php/Using_the_PBI_Builder

[18] http://wiki.pcbsd.org/index.php/PBI_Module_Builder_Guide

[19] http://forums.pcbsd.org/viewforum.php?f=4

[20] http://faqs.pcbsd.org/index.php?action=show&cat=19

Converting a FreeBSD Port Using PBI Builder

Chapters 9 and 10 introduced you to FreeBSD ports and packages and gave some insight into the work port maintainers go through so that the package and port "just work." PBI Builder simplifies the process of converting an existing FreeBSD port into a PBI, which means anyone can create a PBI without needing much (if any) previous development experience. If you have a bit of time to spare, like to learn new things, and are interested in seeing as much software as possible available to the PC-BSD community, try your hand at creating a PBI with PBI Builder. The more PBIs that are available, the better it is for everyone because it ensures that even brand new PC-BSD users can safely install the software they need and keep it up to date.

Information about and the download for PBI Builder can be found at `http://www.pcbsd.org/content/view/45/30/`. PBI Builder is a command-line utility that requires you to edit a few configuration variables that are used when the PBI is built. PBI Builder automates the entire build process: the creation of the build sandbox, fetching the source for the port and all its dependencies, building everything that is needed, and converting the results into the PBI.

PBI Builder uses a large archive that contains the system source and world environment used by PC-BSD. It provides all the libraries needed to ensure that the resulting PBI works on the version of PC-BSD that matches the version of PBI Builder.

■ **Tip** The file /pbi-build/docs/HOWTO-MODULES is well worth reading because it fully explains all the files contained in the archive and the PBI creation process. If you're curious about what commands are executed when building a PBI, read through the scripts in /pbi-build/scripts/. You can also find some examples in /pbi-build/docs/module-examples.

Building Your First PBI

Before building your PBI

1. Check that a PBI for that software doesn't currently exist at pbidir.com or pbibuild.pcbsd.com.

2. Check that the Pbi-dev mailing list isn't currently testing a PBI for that software.

3. Check to see if a module already exists at `http://trac.pcbsd.org/browser/pbibuild/modules`.

4. Search for the software at freshports.org. Some of the FreshPorts details for that software come in handy when you configure your PBI module.

5. Download and untar the PBI Builder archive according to the instructions in the "Using the PBI Builder"[21] document.

Now that your system is ready for building PBIs, download the PBI module template.

```
# cd /pbi-build/modules
# fetch http://www.pcbsd.org/files/templates/module-template.tgz
# tar xvzf module-template.tgz
```

Create a directory structure for your module that represents the port's category and name. Copy the contents of the template directory to your new directory. We use the example of creating a module named /pbi-build/modules/irc/conspire.

```
# mkdir -p irc/conspire
# cp -R template/* irc/conspire/
# ls -F irc/conspire
build.sh        kmenu-dir/      overlay-dir/     preportmake.sh
copy-files      mime-dir/       pbi.conf
```

Most PBIs can be successfully built after modifying a few lines in pbi.conf and kmenu-dir/0mymenu. This section shows you how to make those changes, and the next section demonstrates more advanced configurations.

To successfully configure your module, you *must* modify the following variables in the pbi.conf file.

- **PROGNAME**: The name of the PBI. This should be the same name as the FreeBSD port. Don't include the version number unless there is already another PBI for a different version.

- **PROGWEB**: The Main Web Site URL for the port as listed at Freshports.

- **PROGAUTHOR**: Most software is maintained by a project rather than an individual. Examples of suitable values are The Mozilla Foundation (for firefox) or the BitchX team (for bitchx).

- **PROGICON**: At Freshports, check the **pkg-plist** in the CVSWeb for the port to find the path to the **png** file representing the icon for the application. If there is more than one, look for the **png** with the same name as the port. If there is no **png** for the software, check the software's website to see if it has an icon image. If there is an image available, download the image, convert it to **png** if it is in another format, save the **png** to the module's overlay-dir directory, and provide only the name of the **png**.

- **PBIPORT**: The full path to the port to be built.

---

[21] http://wiki.pcbsd.org/index.php/Using_the_PBI_Builder

Here is an example of the changes made to **/pbi-build/modules/irc/conspire/pbi.conf**:

```
# Program Name
PROGNAME="conspire"

# Program Website
PROGWEB="http://confluence.atheme.org/display/CON/Home"

# Program Author
PROGAUTHOR="Conspire Team"

# Default Icon (Relative to overlay-dir)
# Please only use PNG files for the program icon
PROGICON="share/pixmaps/conspire.png"

# FreeBSD Port we want to build
PBIPORT="/usr/ports/irc/conspire"
```

Next, you *must* modify the first three variables in **kmenu-dir/Omymenu**.

- **ExePath**: The path to the executable that should start when the application is launched. You can find the correct path name at Freshports. Click the CVSWeb link for the port, and then click the **pkg-plist**. The binary has "bin" somewhere in the path. If there are multiple binary paths, select the binary that seems the most reasonable name for the application.

- **ExeIcon**: The same path you used in **PROGICON= in pbi.conf**. This allows the icon to show in the KDE menu.

- **ExeDescr**: A short (2–3 words) description that shows up in the KDE menu.

The example for **/pbi-build/modules/irc/conspire/kmenu-dir/Omymenu** looks like this:

```
ExePath: bin/conspire
ExeIcon: share/pixmaps/conspire.png
ExeDescr: IRC Client
```

When you finish making your changes, ensure that the system is connected to the Internet because you require connectivity to build the underlying port.

You're now ready to **cd** into the **/pbi-build** directory and start the **pbibuld.sh** script. Include the name of the module you wish to build. If you don't provide any arguments, the script builds every module that exists in the modules directory. The script provides some messages as the build progresses, as seen in the following example:

```
# cd /pbi-build
# ./pbibuild.sh irc/conspire
Running portsnap to update ports tree
Starting module traversal...
Copying /pbi-build/buildworld to /pbi-build/pbisandbox
Copying /pbi-build/ports to /pbi-build/pbisandbox/usr/ports
Starting build of irc/conspire
Rebuilding module irc/conspire...
```

```
Found preportmake.sh, running it...
Running port build...
SUCCESS! Build finished for irc/conspire
#
```

If you want to watch the details of the build process, you can monitor the build log using "`tail -f /pbi-build/outgoing/irc/conspire/build.log`" and substitute the pathname for your PBI.

Although the PBI build process is completely automated and should just work, it does take time. The amount of time depends upon the size of the application, the number of dependencies, and the speed of your build system.

When the build is finished, you receive your prompt back and the PBI is placed in a subdirectory of `/pbi-build/outgoing/` with the same name as the module you built. In this example, the PBI is found in `/pbi-build/outgoing/irc/conspire/conspire4.0.35-PVO.pbi`.

Advanced Module Configuration

Most PBIs can be built by simply modifying the variables mentioned in the previous section. This section provides an overview of the more advanced configurations that are possible through modifying the other variables and files that come with the modules template.

- **build.sh**: This script is run after all the files have been copied to the PBI's directory and can contain any commands you wish to run at that time. The PBI Module Builder Guide[22] provides an example that modifies the version number.

- **copy-files**: It is rare to need this file, but you can use it to modify where certain files get populated to.

- **kmenu-dir/0mymenu**: The variables in this file control how the application appears in the KDE menu. Table 14-2 provides a description of each variable.

- **mime-dir/00mymime**: Some applications require their MIME types to be listed to work correctly. See the PBI Module Builder Guide for usage examples and gotchas.

- **overlay-dir/**: PBI builder automatically populates all the files needed by the PBI, according to the underlying port's instructions. If you have an additional file you would like to include (for example a README for the PBI) or a customized graphic, include it here. You can also customize the PBI scripts that came with this directory but should only do so if you have a good reason to make the change.

- **pbi.conf**: Table 14-3 summarizes the remaining variables in this file.

- **preportmake.sh**: Allows you to execute commands needed for the port to build properly. See the PBI Module Builder Guide for an example.

---

[22] http://wiki.pcbsd.org/index.php/PBI_Module_Builder_Guide

Table 14-2. Variables that Control a PBI's Appearance in the KDE Menu

Variable	Description
ExePath	The path to the application's executable as listed at Freshports.
ExeIcon	The path to the application's icon as listed at Freshports or the name of the custom icon you have created in overlay-dir/.
ExeDescr	A brief description of the application.
ExeNoDesktop	Set to 0 if you want a desktop icon and to 1 if you don't.
ExeNoMenu	Set to 0 if you want an icon in the KDE menu and 1 if you don't.
ExeRunRoot	Some applications require superuser access to run correctly. Set this to 1 to require the user to enter the administrative password when the application launches.
ExeRunShell	Set to 0 if the application should run in a GUI and set to 1 if the application is command-line based and should be executed in a Konsole session.
ExeNotify	Set to 0 to disable the bouncy application loading icon and set to 1 to enable it (the preferred setting).
ExeLink	Set to 1 to open the **ExePath** value in Konqueror, and set to 0 to launch the **ExePath** value as an executable.
ExeWebLink	If the ExePath value is an URL, set to 1 to open the URL in Konqueror; otherwise, leave it set as 0.
ExeTaskbar	Places application in system tray; this feature is currently unimplemented.
ExeOwndir	0 places the application name in top level directory of KDE menu, 1 places the application name in its own directory under the category indicated by **ExeKdeCat**, and 2 places the application name in the category indicated by **ExeKdeCat**.
ExeKdeCat	Set to one of the category names listed in Kickoff ➤ Applications.

If you right-click Kickoff and select Menu Editor, you can see the settings that come with every application in the KDE menu. Comparing the General and Advanced tab of an application should give you a better understanding of the effect that the variables in Table 14-3 have on the KDE menu. Figure 14-4 shows a screenshot for the installed conspire PBI.

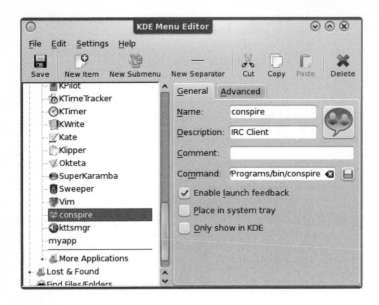

Figure 14-4. KDE menu settings for the conspire PBI

Table 14-3 briefly describes the remaining variables that can be set in **pbi.conf**.

Table 14-3. Remaining Variables for pbi.conf

Variable	Description
PBIVERSION=	Enables you to override the PBI version if the build fails to automatically detect it.
PROGLIBS=	Leave at **AUTO**; otherwise, you have to manually populate the PBI's directory. If you need to override a file that is populated, use **copy-files** instead.
PBIUPDATE=	Leave as-is as needed by the PBI build server.
OTHERPORT=	If you want to include another port in your PBI (besides the dependencies listed in the port's **Makefile**), add its category and portname; this is useful for applications that have additional plugins or skins that are available as separate ports.
MAKEOPTS=	Enables you to pass make targets that are used when the PBI is built; Chapter 10 discusses targets.
BUILDKEY=	Committers can temporarily change this number to force the build server to rebuild the PBI.

Variable	Description
PBIDISABLEFONTLINK=	Use this if you want to use the application's internal fonts instead of the system fonts.
PBIKEEPGL=	Use this to use the applications internal libGL libraries instead of the system libraries.
PBIPRUNE*	Several prune variables allow you to keep include directories, python files, perl files, or doc files that were created during the PBI build.
BUILDINMATE=	Uncomment this line if you are building an inmate file instead of a PBI.
INMATEVER=	Uncomment and set a version number for the inmate; increment the number for each later version.

Troubleshooting

As long as there isn't a problem with the underlying FreeBSD port and assuming you have followed all of the steps in the section on "Building your First PBI," PBI Builder should just work. If the build fails, double-check Freshports to confirm that the port isn't broken, forbidden, or restricted.

If the port looks fine, check the error message that appeared when you received your prompt back. It contains the number of the script that failed. The 2.1 in the following example indicates that /pbi-build/scripts/2.1.startmake.sh failed. Any script with a lower number is successful, and any script with a higher number has not run yet.

```
ERROR: 2.1 Build failed of irc/conspire!!!
```

When PBI Builder exits, it compresses the log of the PBI build process, so you need to uncompress it with the bunzip2 command. Take the time to go through the build log, starting at the end, because this is where the error occurred. Usually, the problem is obvious from the error. If it is not, work your way backwards to see what happened successfully before the error occurred. If the error indicates that the port build was unable to fetch a required file, double-check your Internet connectivity.

After you resolve the error, remove the .lock file and rerun buildpbi.sh. The build starts over again to ensure that your sandbox environment is clean.

If you are stuck, send an email to the Pbi-dev mailing list that includes the error and enough contextual information to enable other developers to help you figure out what went wrong.

Testing and Submitting Your PBI

After you have a PBI, you want to test it yourself before making it available for others to test. From Dolphin, navigate to your PBI, right-click it, and select Open with PBI Launcher. The PNG for your PBI should show in the PBI's icon within Dolphin. As the PBI installs, check the initial installation screen to ensure that the Vendor (PROGAUTHOR variable) and URL (PROGURL variable) are displayed correctly. After the PBI is finished installing, start the application to make sure that the correct binary starts. After the application launches, try out all the screens in the program to make sure that nothing is missing and none of the menus causes the application to crash. Finally, find your PBI in Menu Editor, and make sure that all the desired features show for the KDE menu.

If you find a typo or need to fix a configuration file in your module, you don't have to rebuild the underlying port. Simply run **/pbi-build/scripts/3.makepbi.sh** after making your configuration change. This rerolls the PBI so you can test your changes.

■ **Tip** pbibuild.sh creates a clean environment every time it runs. This means that it removes everything that was previously built and starts over again. If your build successfully finished, you don't have to rebuild to reroll the PBI with your new configurations. You can save *a lot* of time by running the 3.makepbi.sh script.

When you are satisfied that your PBI works correctly, create a compressed archive of its directory. The following example creates a compressed archive named **/conspire.tar.bz2**.

```
# cd /pbi-build/modules/irc
# tar cvf /conspire.tar
# bzip2 /conspire.tar
```

Upload the archive to a publicly available server. If you don't have a server of your own, contact the leader of the PBI development team[23] for credentials to the PBI ftp server. After the PBI is uploaded, send an email to the Pbi-dev mailing list.[24] Your email should include a subject line of "submit module category/portname" (for example, submit module irc/conspire). The body of the email should contain the location where testers can download the archive for the module to build and test it.

Summary

This chapter discussed the most advanced tasks you can perform on your PC-BSD system, including those that enable you to contribute software back to the PC-BSD community so other users can benefit from it.

We cover a lot of ground in this book. It is our hope that you enjoyed learning more about the PC-BSD operating system and that this book is a handy guide you refer to often. We also hope that you have as much fun reading and using it as we had writing it!

---

[23] http://www.pcbsd.org/content/view/23/30/#pbi-dev

[24] http://lists.pcbsd.org/mailman/listinfo/pbi-dev

APPENDIX

■ ■ ■

Reference Tables

The tables in this appendix provide a handy reference.

Table A-1 describes the contents of each folder that is installed on the root of the PC-BSD filesystem. You will see these folders if you click the Root folder in Dolphin. Most of these folders are system folders, and should be left as-is where indicated in the table. If you want to create files on your PC-BSD computer, create them in your Home folder. Never delete or modify a file in a system folder unless you know what you are doing.

Table A-1. *Description of PC-BSD default directories*

Folder	Description
bin	Stores user programs that came with the operating system. You should leave this directory as-is.
boot	Stores the files the operating system needs to load. You should leave this directory as-is.
compat	Provides the files that Linux programs need to run. You should leave this directory as-is.
dev	Contains information your operating system needs to access hardware devices. Note that you rarely, if ever, have to install drivers on PC-BSD; if you do, they will not go here. You should leave this directory as-is.
etc	Contains configuration information needed by the operating system. You should leave this directory as-is.
home	Contains home directories, one for each user on the system. Users should store their own files somewhere in their home directory.
lib	Contains libraries needed by the programs that came with the operating system. You should leave this directory as-is.
libexec	Contains libraries needed by the programs that came with the operating system. You should leave this directory as-is.

Folder	Description
media	Used by programs to provide access to data on a removable media such as a thumb drive or DVD.
mnt	Used by some programs to provide access to data on other filesystems.
PCBSD	Contains the programs, scripts, and configuration files that are unique to PC-BSD.
proc	Contains information about running processes. Each subdirectory is a number that represents the ID of a running process.
Programs	Used by installed PBIs. Each installed PBI has its own subdirectory containing all the information it needs to run. The associated subdirectory will be removed for you when you uninstall the PBI. Chapter 8 discusses PBIs in detail.
rescue	Contains the programs needed to rescue a system. Chapter 13 will show you how to repair a PC-BSD system.
root	The home directory for the super (administrative) user.
sbin	Contains programs installed with the operating system that only the super (administrative) user can run.
tmp	Contains temporary files used by the operating system and programs.
usr	Contains the user applications, as well as their libraries and configuration files, which aren't considered essential to the operating system.
var	Contains files which vary (change often) such as system logs and print jobs.

Table A-2 describes which KDE applications are available to perform common tasks. The tasks have been sorted in alphabetical order to make them easier to find. For each task, the name of the application is given. If you type the name of the application into the search bar at http://docs.kde.org, you can read the Guide for that application. Additionally, if you press F1 while in the application, it should also open up its Guide. You will find all the locations in the Table in Kickoff ➤ Applications.

In addition to the applications mentioned here, you will find dozens more in the Development, Education, and Games categories of Kickoff ➤ Applications.

Table A-2. Built-in KDE applications for common tasks

Task	Application	Location in Applications
Add network folder	KnetAttach	Internet ➤ Network Folder Wizard
Address book	KAddressBook	Office ➤ Address Manager
Alarm	KAlarm	Utilities ➤ Personal Alarm Scheduler
BitTorrent	KTorrent	Internet ➤ BitTorrent Client
Browse the Internet	Konqueror	Internet ➤ Web Browser
Calculator	KCalc	Utilities ➤ Scientific Calculator
Capture screenshots	KSnapshot	Graphics ➤ Screen Capture Program
Clear private data	Sweeper	Utilities ➤ System Cleaner
Clipboard	Klipper	Utilities ➤ Clipboard Tool
Control audio settings	KMix	Multimedia ➤ Sound Mixer
Draw and edit images	KolourPaint	Graphics ➤ Paint Program
E-mail	KMail	Internet ➤ Mail Client
Format floppies	KFloppy	Utilities ➤ Floppy Formatter
HotSync	KPilot	Utilities ➤ PalmPilot Tool
Instant messaging	Kopete	Internet ➤ Instant Messenger
Manage compressed files	Ark	Utilities ➤ Archiving Tool
Manage encryption	KGpg	Utilities ➤ Encryption Tool
Manage notes	KJots	Utilities ➤ Note Taker
Manage notes	KNotes	Utilities ➤ Popup Notes

Task	Application	Location in Applications
Manage photos	digiKam	Graphics ➤ Photo Management Program
NNTP news reader	KNode	Internet ➤ News Reader
Open a command prompt	Konsole	System ➤ Terminal
Personal Information Management	Kontact	Office ➤ Personal Info Manager
Play most audio and video formats	KMPlayer	Multimedia ➤ Media Player
Play music CDs	KsCD	Multimedia ➤ CD Player
Play DVDs	Dragon Player	Multimedia ➤ Video Player
Play music (e.g., mp3s)	JuK	Multimedia ➤ Music Player
Resume/manage downloads	KGet	Internet ➤ Download Manager
RSS feeder	Akregator	Internet ➤ Feed Reader
Search and replace files	KFileReplace	Utilities ➤ Search & Replace Tool
Share your Desktop	Krfb	Internet ➤ Desktop Sharing
Shared calendar	KOrganizer	Office ➤ Personal Organizer
Text editor	KWrite	Utilities ➤ Text Editor
Text editor	Vim	Utilities ➤ Vim Editor
Track time	KTimeTracker	Office ➤ Personal Time Tracker
Use a scanner	Skanlite	Graphics ➤ Image Scanning
Use Remote Desktop Protocol	KRDC	Internet ➤ Remote Desktop
View disk usage	KDiskFree	System ➤ View Disk Usage
View and edit photos	showFoto	Graphics ➤ Photo Viewer/Editor

Task	Application	Location in Applications
View and tag images	Gwenview	Graphics ➤ Image Viewer
View hardware information	KInfoCenter	System ➤ Info Center
View images, PDFs, and PS files	Okular	Graphics ➤ Document Viewer
View system logs	KSystemLog	System ➤ System Logs Viewer

Table A-3 lists some popular open source applications that are available as PBIs. They are again organized by alphabetical task. The website for each application is listed if you want to research the program's capabilities before installing the PBI.

If you want to install any of the applications listed in Table A-3, be sure to install them using the Software Manager utility described in Chapter 8. Not only is this the easiest way to install the application but it also guarantees that the program has been pretested to work on PC-BSD. It provides the added benefit that PC-BSD will let you know whenever a newer version of the application becomes available.

Table A-3. *Popular software available from the PC-BSD PBI system*

Task	Application	Website
3D modeling	Blender	www.blender.org
3D modeling	OpenCascade	www.opencascade.org
Accounting	Eqonomize	http://eqonomize.sourceforge.net
Accounting	KmyMoney	http://kmymoney2.sourceforge.net
Antivirus	KlamAV	http://klamav.sourceforge.net
Audio editor	Audacity	http://audacity.sourceforge.net
Audio editor	Avidemux	http://fixounet.free.fr/avidemux
Audio editor	Kdenlive	www.kdenlive.org
Audio editor	Kino	www.kinodv.org
Backup	Bacula	www.bacula.org
CD/DVD burner	K3b	http://k3b.plainblack.com

Task	Application	Website
Database administration	dbVisualizer	www.dbvis.com/
Database administration	pgAdmin	www.pgadmin.org/
Database administration	Kmysqladmin	http://alwins-world.de/programs/kmysqladmin
Desktop recorder	recordMyDesktop	http://recordmydesktop.sourceforge.net
Development IDE	Codelite	http://codelite.org/
Development IDE	Eclipse	www.eclipse.org
Development IDE	NetBeans	http://netbeans.org/
Diagram creator	Dia	http://projects.gnome.org/dia
E-mail	Evolution	http://projects.gnome.org/evolution
E-mail	Sylpheed	http://sylphee
E-mail	Thunderbird	www.mozillamessaging.com
File manager	emelFM2	http://emelfm2.net
File manager	muCommander	www.mucommander.com
File manager	TotalCommander	www.ghisler.com
FTP client	FileZilla	http://filezilla-project.org
FTP client	gFTP	http://gftp.seul.org
FTP client	Kasablanca	http://kasablanca.berlios.de
FTP client	wxDownload Fast	http://dfast.sourceforge.net
Geospatial	Google Earth	http://earth.google.com/
HTML editor	Bluefish	http://bluefish.openoffice.nl/
HTML editor	KompoZer	www.kompozer.net/

Task	Application	Website
Image editor	Gimp	www.gimp.org
Image editor	Inkscape	www.inkscape.org
Instant messaging	Pidgin	www.pidgin.im
IRC	Konversation	http://konversation.kde.org
IRC	Kvirc	www.kvirc.net
IRC	Xchat	www.xchat.org
iTunes	aTunes	www.atunes.org
iTunes	gtkpod	www.gtkpod.org
MSN	aMSN	www.amsn-project.net
Multimedia player	VLC	www.videolan.org/vlc
Multimedia player	Xine	www.xine-project.org
Music creator	Schism Tracker	http://rigelseven.com/schism/
Music player	Amarok	http://amarok.kde.org
Music player	Audacious	http://audacious-media-player.org
Music player	gxmms2	http://wejp.k.vu/projects/xmms2/gxmms2
Office suite	OpenOffice	www.openoffice.org
PDF editor	PDFedit	http://pdfedit.petricek.net
Photo manager	Google Picasa	http://picasa.google.com
Project management	Taskjuggler	www.taskjuggler.org/
Publishing	Scribus	www.scribus.net
Run Windows applications	Bordeaux	http://bordeauxgroup.com

Task	Application	Website
Run Windows applications	Crossover Games	www.codeweavers.com
Run Windows applications	Wine	www.winehq.org
Shared editor	Gobby	http://gobby.0x539.de
System administration	Webmin	www.webmin.com
Telephone over Internet	Skype	www.skype.com
Version control	Bazaar	http://bazaar.canonical.com
Version control	Git	http://git-scm.com/
Version control	KDESvn	http://kdesvn.alwins-world.de/
Version control	Mercurial	http://mercurial.selenic.com/
Version control	Perforce	www.perforce.com/
Video player	Miro	www.getmiro.com
Virtualization	Virtual Box	www.virtualbox.org
Web browser	Firefox	www.mozilla.com/firefox
Web browser	Opera	www.opera.com
Web server/proxy	Abyss	www.aprelium.com/
Web server/proxy	Apache	http://httpd.apache.org/
Web server/proxy	Squid	www.squid-cache.org/
Word processing	Abiword	www.abisource.com

Table A-4 provides some equivalents for popular Windows software applications. The equivalents are either already installed on your PC-BSD system or are available as a PBI.

***Table A-4.** PC-BSD and Windows software equivalents*

Windows Software	Equivalent PBI or Built-in Application
3D Studio Max	Blender
ACDSee	Graphics ➤ Image Viewer
Adobe Acrobat Reader	Graphics ➤ Document Viewer
Adobe Audition	Audacity
Adobe Illustrator	Inkscape
Adobe PageMaker	Scribus
Adobe PhotoAlbum	Digikam
Adobe Photoshop	Gimp
Adobe Premiere	Kino
Dreamweaver	Bluefish
Microsoft Internet Explorer	Firefox
Microsoft Money	KMyMoney
Microsoft Office	OpenOffice
MSN Messenger	aMSN
Nero	K3b
Notepad	Utilities ➤ Text Editor
Outlook	Evolution
Paint	Graphics ➤ Paint Program
Winamp	xmms2
Windows Media Player	Multimedia ➤ Media Player
Windows Movie Maker	Kdenlive

Index

■F

■G

■H

Configure Window Behavior menu, 68
configuring, 65
configuring window actions, 71
configuring window titles, 70
moving, 71
Special Window Settings, 68
supported desktop effects, 69
title bar, 65
video cards and, 70
Windows (Microsoft) and PC-BSD
software equivalents, 350

■X, Y
Xine backend engine, 160

Z
ZFS filesystem, 10, 29, 301

You Need the Companion eBook

Your purchase of this book entitles you to buy the companion PDF-version eBook for only $10. Take the weightless companion with you anywhere.

We believe this Apress title will prove so indispensable that you'll want to carry it with you everywhere, which is why we are offering the companion eBook (in PDF format) for $10 to customers who purchase this book now. Convenient and fully searchable, the PDF version of any content-rich, page-heavy Apress book makes a valuable addition to your programming library. You can easily find and copy code—or perform examples by quickly toggling between instructions and the application. Even simultaneously tackling a donut, diet soda, and complex code becomes simplified with hands-free eBooks!

Once you purchase your book, getting the $10 companion eBook is simple:

❶ Visit **www.apress.com/promo/tendollars/**.

❷ Complete a basic registration form to receive a randomly generated question about this title.

❸ Answer the question correctly in 60 seconds, and you will receive a promotional code to redeem for the $10.00 eBook.

233 Spring Street, New York, NY 10013

All Apress eBooks subject to copyright protection. No part may be reproduced or transmitted in any form or by any means, electronic or mechanical, including photocopying, recording, or by any information storage or retrieval system, without the prior written permission of the copyright owner and the publisher. The purchaser may print the work in full or in part for their own noncommercial use. The purchaser may place the eBook title on any of their personal computers for their own personal reading and reference.

Offer valid through 8/10.